AF493150

MOTHERSELF: an Artist's Memoir

Motherself
AN ARTIST'S MEMOIR

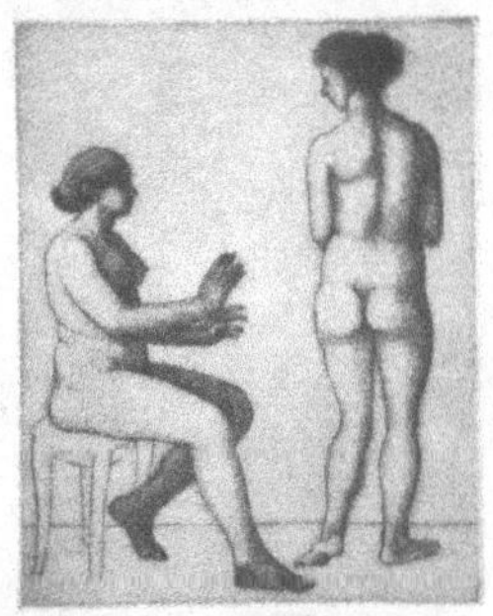

ALAN FELTUS

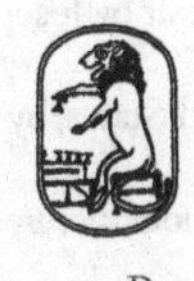

VICARIOUS PICTURES

a Vɪᴄᴀʀɪᴏᴜs Pɪᴄᴛᴜʀᴇs publication

Copyright © Alan Feltus 2024

All rights reserved. No part of this publication may be reproduced or transmitted in any form or by any means, electronic or mechanical, including photocopy, photographic or video recording, or any other information storage and retrieval system, without prior permission in writing from the publisher.

Library of Congress Control Number: 2024915054

ISBN Hardback (linen bound): 979-8-9911242-0-1
Hardback (case laminate): 979-8-9911242-3-2
Paperback: 979-8-9911242-2-5
eBook: 979-8-9911242-1-8

Design & layout by Joseph Feltus

Published in Arizona, United States, by Vicarious Pictures, Inc.

www.VicariousPictures.com

to Anne

PUBLISHER'S NOTE

This book is printed entirely in black and white. To the reader who is not acquainted with the work of Alan Feltus, please note that all reproductions of paintings and collages have been converted from color to black and white, and that color versions of the same reproductions are available online, at www.AlanFeltus.com.

Moreover, a decision was made to not include reproductions of any of the works by other artists referenced in the text. These are mostly easily found through an Internet search, or in books.

CONTENTS

PROLOGUE. 1
1. ICARUS. 3
2. BEGINNINGS 9
3. MEXICO 21
4. BACK IN THE CITY 23
5. SHERWOOD STUDIOS. 39
6. STOCKBRIDGE 55
7. EUROPE AT AGE SEVENTEEN. 71
8. TYLER & COOPER UNION 85
9. PROVINCETOWN. 97
10. MARILYN 107
11. GORKY'S MOTHER 109
12. NINETEEN SIXTY-EIGHT. 123
13. DAYTON. 129
14. SUSANNA. 137
15. CHAGALL'S KISS. 153
16. ITALIE 171
17. ANNE IN THE 1970s 183
18. MARYLAND. 195
19. GIVING UP TEACHING. 211
20. ASSISI 1987. 215
21. INDIA 227
22. WHILE THE MUSIC PLAYED 237
23. MOTHERSELF. 243
24. EARTHQUAKE 253
25. LIFE IN THE STUDIO 259
26. LOOKING BACK. 273
POSTSCRIPT. 289

PLATES 293
ACKNOWLEDGEMENTS. 333
ARTWORKS. 334
PHOTOGRAPHS. 336
ABOUT THE AUTHOR 339

PROLOGUE

One hot summer day in New York my mother took me and my brother
to a carnival. Maybe it was Coney Island, maybe an itinerant carnival
momentarily set up somewhere in the city. It was the late 1940s, I was just
a boy, and this could be my clearest early memory. We were funneled into
an enclosed space and made to walk in front of seated men on raised rows
of benches. There was a clown gesturing to the men while saying things to
my mother, who seemed suddenly uncomfortable and was trying to avoid
him, pressing her hands to her body, holding down her skirt. Her two boys
with no idea what was going on. The atmosphere of disappointment among
waiting men shifted to anticipation as the clown started poking a wand
at my mother. Then his wand shocked her hands just as a blast of air from
below blew her skirt up almost over her head. In a second what ought to
remain private was made public. A triumph for the miserable little clown
working his ignoble job. My mother's exposure and her embarrassment
was what the men there were hoping to see, better than when Marilyn
Monroe's skirt was blown up by air from a subway vent in *The Seven Year Itch*.
My mother was very beautiful, and this was real.

My mother used to wear very full pleated skirts because they didn't show
that her hips were wider than she liked, more full than her delicate torso
would have indicated. And I hadn't known before that moment that on very
hot city days she didn't wear panties.

Somehow the boy I sometimes still see myself as is no longer. Sometimes friends send snapshots of me after a visit, not intended to scare me because to them this is how I look, still they can scare me. A ghoulish old person is what I see. So what happened to me? Life happened, and now as I start to write seventy one years have happened. So it is.

1

ICARUS

I started writing this book when I was off my feet with a virus or flu of some sort in August 2014, and I had started to read Cormac McCarthy's *Suttree* again. Cormac McCarthy has been my favorite writer, and reading *Suttree* I started to think maybe I should try writing something of my own. Cormac does that to me. It is the richness of his language more than his stories that interests me. And I thought if I am to start writing a book, the only thing I know anything about is myself. So I thought to start writing an autobiography/memoir and include in it how I understand art, and the ways I taught drawing and painting.

I am not a writer. I am a painter. An artist and teacher by profession. A husband and a father. I decided to start writing with what I could remember and see where it went, see if something worthy of a book might emerge. I could dig up bits and pieces of journals once kept and long abandoned, study old family photographs to bring back the atmosphere of times I knew once as the present. I have lots of letters from when letters were still sent by post. I could reread those. I could find memories to revisit, if they would cooperate. I could start at a beginning that predates anything I might know from childhood memories, and then let the writing wander, with the hope that what I came up with would provide some plausible context within which to tell a story that might be interesting.

I brought several of our books into my son Tobias' bedroom, where I had been sleeping while sick, and read bits of each of them to give myself a better sense of how a memoir is written. I began writing notes and passages in pencil in notebooks. Then I was over my virus and still spending my days in Tobias' room writing, at that point transcribing into the computer what I had written by hand in the notebooks.

On September 6th, 2014 I woke up at about six, as I most often do, and washed and dressed and sat at the computer. And while I was sitting there, re-reading some hand-written notes from a few days earlier, I experienced a moment of extreme dizziness that was very scary. I saw the room rotating from left to right in a big circular motion. I had never felt anything like that before in my life. I shut my eyes for what might have been a minute, and when I reopened them the rotating had stopped but the room was tipped at a forty-five degree angle and I felt a force trying to pull me down to the floor. It was very strange and frightening. I shut my eyes again and turned so I could reach the end of the bed behind me with a hand and pulled myself to a position stretched out on the bed so I wouldn't fall to the floor and opened my eyes again. The room was no longer spinning and it wasn't tipped at that crazy angle anymore. But I was completely wet with sweat and my face felt cold. I thought no more than a minute or two had passed but I didn't think I could have become wet and cold like that in so short a time.

Whatever had happened to me was a portent of something more threatening than anything I could remember. I described it to Lani and she phoned our doctor who said Lani should take me to the *Pronto Soccorso* immediately. They admitted me right away at the hospital in Branca, near Gubbio, and started a series of tests that included two MRIs, electrocardiograms and various other kinds of tests over five days while I stayed in the *Ictus Ricovero* ward. I had had a stroke. Extensive tests and consultations revealed that I have a congenital anomaly whereby one of the arteries on the back of my neck that takes blood to the brain is narrower than it should be, and a small clot must have blocked the movement of blood there. I hadn't known the word ictus, the Italian for stroke. Ictus sounded like Icarus, and I saw myself as the boy whose wings melted when he flew too close to the sun and fell into the sea.

I stayed in the *Ictus Ricovero* ward for five days. I liked being expected only to rest, and being attended to by doctors and nurses while I watched the theater of the situation I was in the middle of. There was a television on the table at the foot of the two beds. Often it was turned on with the sound too low to hear. There were game shows and news programs and stories about beached whales somewhere in the world. And there was an old Italian TV series my roommate's sons would leave on after a visit. It was a drama taking place somewhere near the sea, with extraordinarily beautiful female stars with long perfect dark hair gently tossing with the sea breeze, beauties alike as only sisters could be, or women of a different breed, more perfect in their beauty than one might see in a lifetime. Or was it for my precarious state of health that I was seeing such perfection in those women I thought I might never again be able to see?

Other times the TV was turned off and in the slightly curved gray of the screen I saw the image of our room reflected in gentle distortion. The large window on the left wall transforming a hospital room into a Vermeer painting, with the doctors attending to my roommate on his bed, or his wife and sons standing and sitting next to him barely shifting in their positions, like a slow moving film.

The two youngest nurses were very beautiful. They both brought back feelings of when I was a boy being attracted to girls in school, wanting to know them better. The youngest reminded me of someone I had known fairly well, but I couldn't place who that was. And then, I saw it. I realized that she looked like photographs of myself when I was a little boy. My mother's friend Ylla Koffler had taken many photographs of me and my brother playing naked on a quiet pebble beach. Ylla was a famous animal photographer; Hungarian, born in Vienna.

I find it amazing that all my life I accepted the whole issue of balance without questioning it. I believed it to be a simple and natural and unconscious part of how I lived every day, without being aware of it other than when we totter on one foot while pulling on a sock, or something like that. But this Ictus experience was something else entirely. I saw it as having a gyroscope, like the one I had when I was a kid, inside my head. Pull the string and the gyroscope would spin, and the spinning kept it balanced perfectly upright until the spinning lost momentum and it started to tip and wobble and then fall over. My inner gyroscope had stopped spinning. If a tiny blood clot is somewhere it shouldn't be, the mechanisms of internal organs that are so incredibly perfect will malfunction. I now understand better how we, and all animals who don't live under water where gravity works in wholly different ways, live with a gyroscope in our heads.

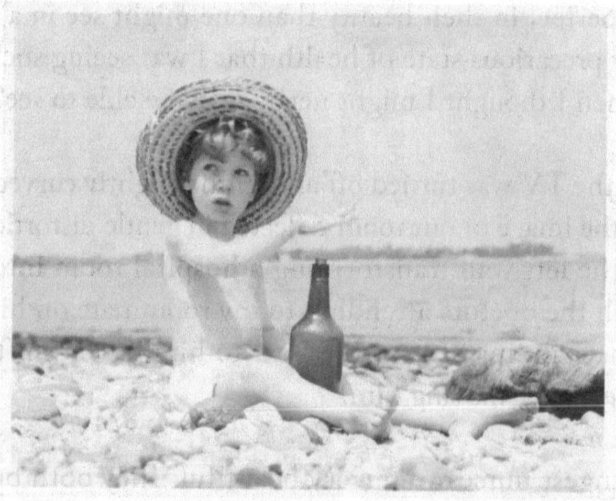

Oyster Bay, 1945. Photograph by Ylla (Camilla Koffler)

My Ictus hospitalization wasn't so displeasurable, though surely it was a wake-up call, a warning saying that at my age I can't expect things not to go wrong. I can see it as an event that could be intertwined with the writing of this book in the sense that this is the time to look back over my life, to revisit old memories before they are gone, and to slow down, to be less concerned with accomplishing a lot in the studio in these months. It was what the memento mori theme was about in art for centuries. Their images have things like a skull or bones or a flower dropping its petals. These subjects, once much more common than they are in the art of today, served to remind us of our mortality. Additional medications would have to be taken regularly, and maybe there would be some physical jobs around our property I should not try to do myself. I now sometimes feel as though I am living on borrowed time.

2

BEGINNINGS

My mother was born in Bridgeport, Connecticut on April 28, 1917. Her name was Anna Eva Victor. Her mother, my grandmother, was Rassya Kessner, from Kiev. My grandmother's name changed to Ruth Victor when she married Jacob Awigderovich, whose American name was Jacob Victor. My grandmother's father was Frank Kessner, whose name had been changed from the Russian name Fibish Kushnirsky. They were Russian Jews and they were atheists. My grandmother and her family arrived in the US just before the 1917 Russian Revolution, entering through Canada. Jacob Victor was then already in America. That's how my notes taken from what my uncle George told me have it. According to my uncle's notes, their father Jacob had been an anarchist in Russia who attended political anarchist meetings in tea houses and slept with a gun under his pillow. His parents took him to live in the US in 1910 or 1912 for fear that he would be killed. In New York he became a taxi driver but continued to attend anarchist and political meetings.

According to George, Jacob's first anarchist assignment was to kill John D. Rockefeller, Jr., the chief owner of the Colorado Fuel and Iron Company, said to have been responsible for the Ludlow Massacre that killed coal miners and their family members in their tent dwellings during the Colorado Coal Strike in 1914. Jacob was at the Rockefeller estate, ready to fulfill what he saw as his duty for the good of society, when the strike was settled and the assassination was called off. I don't believe he ever carried out any such assignment or we would have known about it. This account of my mother's father I believed to be true because my uncle George was not like my mother, who was known to invent colorful stories to make her persona more intriguing. There are some issues with timing in what George told me, but it could be my uncle was as bad in math as I have always been, and the logic or lack of logic about dates could have eluded him altogether. I was never very interested in ancestry. The only grandparent I ever knew, or had even seen, or can remember having seen even in a photograph, was my grandmother, Ruth Victor, whom I loved.

My mother changed her name to Anne Winter when she left home at seventeen because she hated her father and had little respect for her mother. For most of my life she told a romantic story in which her real father was an Englishman named Julian Lucien Winter, who met her mother in Russia, where he participated in the Archangel Expedition that, according to my mother's story, was to secure an open sea route from England to St. Petersburg.

The final version of this Russian fable Anne told me when she was in early stages of Alzheimer's, her facts and memories slipping away and lost, but while she could still read and speak with some comprehension. In that last variant of her story my grandmother, Ruth Victor, was not Anne's actual mother at all but was the nursemaid who took care of Anne when Anne's Russian mother and English father returned to Russia from Connecticut when Anne was 3 years old. Julian Lucien Winter and his wife died of typhus in Russia. Supposedly. But I don't accept that story. I now have Anne's birth certificate that names her parents as Jacob Victor and Ruth Kessner. Anne was still rewriting her family history, recreating her own identity to be more fanciful and more romantic, which was entirely in keeping with her character. The fact is that my mother was complex and not easy to know in any real sense. And if our relationship had not been so difficult, I might say she was quite a wonderful mother to have had.

In that last rewrite of her origins, Czar Nicholas II was under house arrest hidden in Siberia and wanted to flee with his son to America to live quietly. In anticipation of his own escape he sent a carrier ahead of his planned trip to New York with documents and money. This carrier, Anne told me, was her grandfather, and while he himself was not a Jew, he was responsible for this group of Russian Jews, who emigrated to America as a cover to avoid suspicion and conceal the importing of the Czar's money and documents.

In a 1994 letter to me from my mother's brother, George Victor, there is this:

> I don't mind any more Anne not remembering me, and I can explain her story. Partly it's grandiosity to counter humble self-image/ origins. She had a brilliant mind, went to the NY High School of Performing Arts, and was a beauty. I imagine much was expected of her, and her failure to accomplish contributed to low self-esteem. If I remember right, in an earlier version, the Englishman was of nobility. Her first story of noble origins was that our mother had an ancestor who was raped by a Mongol prince - giving offspring noble blood. The Czar connection is new to me.
>
> You will recall that after moving out of our parents' home when 17, Anne gave up the name Victor. Formerly Ann (I think), she took the name Anne Winter as a stage name. That was her explanation then of Winter. She refused further contact with our father angrily. The facts behind that are clear to me. He had been nasty to her - really abusive verbally - for at least three years. My earliest memory (have I told you?) is of a family stroll when I was 3, Anne 14. She stopped in a drug store and bought a chap-stick - colorless. On seeing it he went into a rage: it was a lipstick; she was a whore. Over the next three years he was often in a rage over her staying out later than she 'should' and her 'wild' friends - all of which meant she was misbehaving sexually. That's why Anne left home.
>
> When I became a psychologist I learned that such fatherly behavior is a negative reaction in fathers who are strongly attracted to daughters and cannot tolerate the attraction. I remember Anne at 16 as extraordinarily beautiful and sexy. She used to take me - then 5 - out to the zoo and other places, and men would whistle

and proposition or flirt. To put them off, she would pretend to be my mother (she looked mature). Attractiveness in a daughter is unnecessary for fathers to develop the nasty possessiveness our father did, but it helps. The same for sexiness.

These are facts - now my interpretation. Daughters are, of course, also attracted to fathers, especially to fathers who are attracted to them. I infer that Anne was attracted to our father and also found the attraction intolerable, especially because of his being attracted and persecuting her as sexually degenerate. I infer this led to her first distortion - that he was not her father, while Ruth and I were her mother and brother. You may recall that until you were older Anne fully recognized Ruth and me as blood relatives. (In pictures of Anne and me as young children we did look alike, before age and her plastic surgery - making her nose much smaller - made us look different. Your nose - in my eyes, is more like the young Anne's and mine and Ruth's and Jacob's than like the mature Anne's and Randy's. Also Peter's is more like my family's - maybe).

I hope this helps. Nothing new here.

With love,

George

PS. In writing this, I realized I wanted you to accept my version as the true one. The wish comes from quarrels long ago in our family between Ruth and Jacob. Both were given to deception as well as spontaneous distortion, and both were stubborn, contributing to my craziness. Probably the deception, distortion, stubbornness, and grudge-holding of Ruth and Jacob contributed also to Anne's craziness, which did not emerge until her break-up with Randy.

Rereading his letter now, as I am starting to write and to make sense of my life, what George had written seems relevant. My life, like any other, has been complicated and whole periods are lost from conscious memory, never told to anyone, not even to myself by myself. Some experiences once lived were allowed to slide off into nothingness because there seemed no reason to have had them to begin with, or to save them to revisit later. I would not have thought there would ever be a purpose to them, or I would just not have thought anything about them. I had a sense that memory space is limited, and not a lot that passes through our consciousness is worth keeping. That may have been true, but who was I to make those judgements?

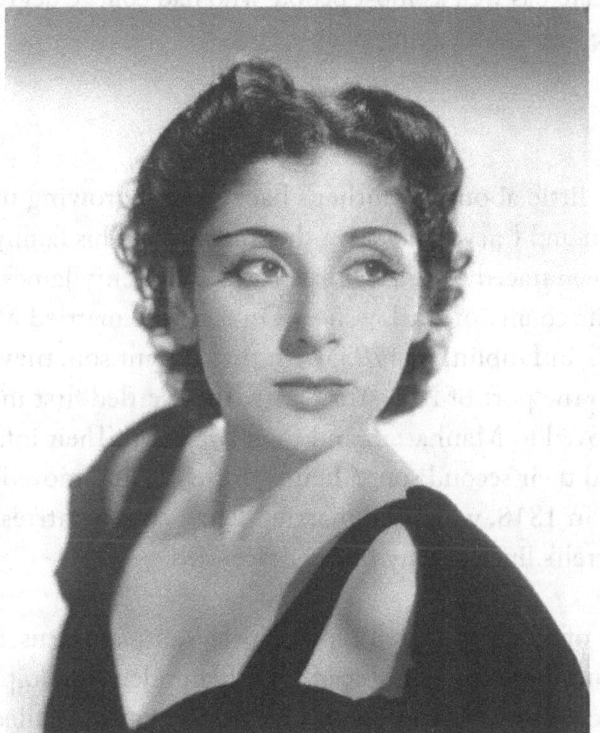

My mother Anne Winter, circa 1937,
in a photograph used by the press around the time of her accident, in
which she was referred to as Eve Winter.

The life of my mother was not an easy one, partly due to events beyond her control and partly for what she chose. She dropped out of high school, and she never went to college. After living in New York City for a few years she went to Los Angeles to start an acting career in Hollywood. Soon after arriving there, she was in a car crash on Christmas day of 1937. The driver of the car was film writer/director/producer Henry Lehrman. I have two newspaper clippings about this accident, and photographs of my mother with her face half covered in bandages. This is all factual. The rear view mirror shattered in my mother's face destroying her right eye, and any hopes she had of becoming a movie star were dashed. She was twenty years old. After the accident my mother was in Mexico where she met my father. Though Anne dropped out of school early on, as a self-taught person she seemed educated as well as most people who had college degrees. She read a lot and she knew interesting people.

* * *

I knew very little about my father's background growing up, as he was mostly absent and I never met any other members of his family. Our Feltus family has been traced back as far as a Reverend Henry James Feltus, born in 1775 in the county of Carlow, near Dublin, who married Martha Ryan, born in 1777 in Dublin. In 1795, with their infant son, they sailed from Liverpool to the port of New York City. They settled first in New Jersey and then moved to Manhattan and then Brooklyn. Their infant son died that year, and their second son, Abram Morrell Feltus, moved to Natchez, Mississippi in 1818, where he married Eliza Ann Ventrress. It is from Abram Morrell's line that my father descended.

In 1861 one of Abram Morrell's sons, Lovic Ventress Feltus, married Ella Eugenia Randolph, the daughter of John Hampden Randolph, who built the 7,000-acre sugar plantation and its grand mansion called Nottoway, in White Castle, Louisiana near New Orleans.

Not having been properly raised by my father, and not knowing much at all about his family, I have preferred to distance myself from his side of the family because of its past associations with slave owning, for which I feel a deep sense of sadness and shame.

In *The Feltus Family Book* (printed privately in 1917 and available on the Internet in its entirety) I found that Eliza Ann Ventress, the wife of Abram Morrell Feltus and my great-great grandmother, has a rather distinguished Scottish lineage starting with Robert the Bruce (King of Scots from 1306 to 1329) and the royal Stewart family of Scotland[1].

During the war my father worked in Washington DC as an Assistant to the Secretary of the Treasury, and other similar positions. My mother wouldn't permit Randy, as he was called, to fight in the war. That was how she put it.

* * *

My brother, Peter John Hampden Randolph Feltus (named after our father, John Hampden Randolph Feltus), was born January first, 1942, in New Orleans, our father's family hometown. I was born in Washington DC on May 1st, 1943, and was given first and middle names Alan Evan from my mother's Anna Eva. Soon after my birth, Anne and Randy relocated to midtown Manhattan, where I spent my childhood. Randy continued to work in Washington for a while and then in New York. But my father wasn't around very much in my childhood even before he and Anne separated when I was six.

I loved my grandmother, Ruth. Peter and I used to visit her on our own, taking a bus uptown on the West side to where she had a small apartment. Our uncle George kept a room there but he had already been on his own for years. In my mother's childhood Yiddish was spoken at home. Though they were an atheist family of Russian Jews, Anne raised me and Peter without any of the Russian or Jewish holidays and rituals she might have known from her own childhood. We were raised American, melting pot bland, in the belief that we would have an easier time in schools and after. Though she may have been right, I was sorry about that.

---

1   in Appendix A, page 57 of *The Feltus Family Book*, by Feltus George Haws (Rev. M.A.), privately printed, Elmhurst, New York City, 1917.

Before our parents separated we lived in a rented brownstone house on 56th Street between Park and Lexington. Peter and I slept and played on the top floor with a nice couple who took care of us while our parents lived downstairs. Lilly and Wilbur, the elderly black couple, were probably more tender and caring to us than Anne and Randy had been, at least on a day-to-day basis. But those memories are very few and vague. I suppose it could be said that Peter and I visited Mommy and Papa rather than that we shared a life with them. Anne seemed more absorbed in other things than in her children. She was at times loving, it is true, but more often she was distant.

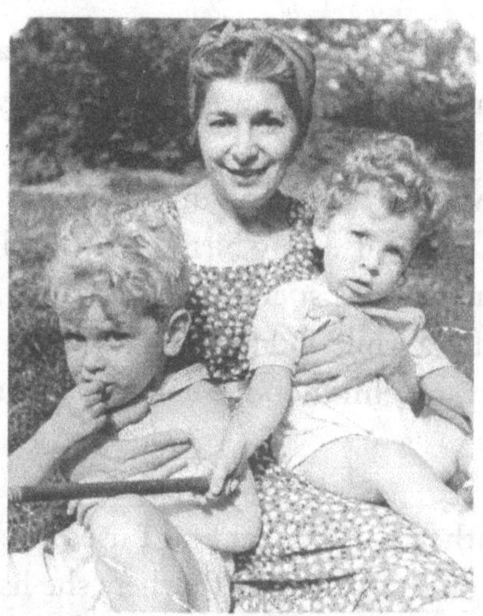

Peter (left) and myself with our grandmother, Ruth Victor

The street floor of the brownstone was an office Randy shared with a partner in a public relations business, one of those professions a child didn't know anything about because there was nothing made that could be seen. As a small child, I could only know that my father did something he carried in a briefcase.

I have few memories of that period. I remember there were ice delivery trucks for the ice boxes people had. Icemen using giant tongs carrying heavy blocks of ice up front steps, rubber capes to keep their backs dry. I remember icepicks. I remember that milk came in heavy glass bottles with cream at the top and was delivered to houses. And then it came in tall square boxes of wax covered paper that I liked to scrape with a fingernail. There was chocolate milk back then too. Grownups smoked cigarettes. Men wore hats. Women wore gloves that matched their shoes and their handbags. Most of the rest remains vague in my memory. Sidewalks and people, of course. I remember the sound that cars made shifting gears as they moved out from a red light. I liked that sound. There was a kindergarten room that had partition dividers between cots we took naps on. Little chairs and little desks. School desks in my childhood had a round hole in the top for ink bottles and a groove to keep pencils and pens from rolling off. There was a Third Avenue El train then, and a double decker bus on Fifth Avenue. Big yellow taxicabs with jump seats that folded down for when more than three passengers rode. Black and white checkered bands along the sides. They stayed in circulation for many years. There were orangeade drinks in conical wax paper containers and animal crackers in circus train car boxes still made. Tootsie rolls and little candy drops stuck to long strips of paper. There were black wax mustaches and red wax lips for children. We held them onto our faces by biting the part that didn't show from the front; they were a funny version of a mask and could be chewed. Small flat sheets of bubblegum were sold with baseball cards in flat packages. Kids collected the cards and we used to trade them and we used to flip them in such a way that they would turn a few times before landing on the sidewalk face-up or backside-up, and face-up would win the other. And I remember chocolate cigarettes in packs resembling real cigarette packs.

Peter and I had wooden spinning tops we wound a string around and threw in a particular way at the sidewalk. It took practice to have them stay upright while spinning. When we were littler we had the metal tops with printed pictures on them and wood handle atop a twisted rod we pushed down on to start them spinning on their bases. Yo-yos that would turn at an angle and foul up. And slinky toys that tangled. And erector sets for building towers.

There was a framed reproduction of Picasso's *Three Musicians* (1921) over the mantelpiece on 56th Street, the only painting in that house that I can bring back in memory, which seems odd to me. But I would have been only five or six when I last saw the house and what was in it. There was a large Turkoman rug in the living room but my memory of that doesn't go back to 56th Street. The rug was in storage with a few pieces of furniture for years, and then my mother had it in her various apartments after she got some things back from the storage when they auctioned some of her belongings to cover unpaid bills in the 1960s. On 89th Street, Anne had the rug across the floor and up one wall to the picture molding just below the ceiling because there was no floor space in the apartment large enough for it to lie flat. I remember that well. It was in my first years as a Cooper Union student.

What I remember best is the way the city was then and how I, a quiet shy boy, somehow grew up right there in the middle of everything, unnoticed and at the same time accepted as belonging. Before experiencing how reading could transport a boy's thoughts to other places, perhaps more purposeful places, I had become a silent observer of the life around me. I was within it, absorbing it, being a part of it and knowing it for what it was. The city was fascinating in its immense variety and how it could be crowded with people who mostly didn't know each other at all and didn't have a problem not interacting, unlike how people behave in small towns. If the word community has a meaning when thinking of New York City, it would be in reference to ethnic neighborhoods where immigrant families settled and had their various separate languages and customs, just beyond where the tall office buildings are, where people walk fast going wherever it is they go to work. When I was a little older, I used to try to pass the fastest walker on a block, coming up from behind and overtaking them the way cars overtake other cars on roads. That was a game I played to amuse myself, a real challenge in so frenetic a city where so many people are walking fast. I would look at them as I came close, seeing if I could read anything about them from their faces and how they were dressed. Then they would be behind me and I would do it with the next person.

I remember the summer my mother and Mercedes Matter shared a house on Georgica Pond near East Hampton. I remember throwing a chicken leg tied to a string out into the water and very slowly bringing it in to where I could scoop up a blue crab with a net on the end of a long stick. Jackson Pollock was living nearby. Randy would come from the city some weekends and he and Pollock would get drunk together. For that summer Anne bought an old Ford Model A that someone had cut the back off of with a blowtorch and made into a small pickup truck and we children would ride in the open back. Mercedes' son, Pundy, and Peter and me. I would have been five at the time. Small dirt roads with dune grass growing down the middle stay in my mind close enough to the surface that every time I see that kind of dirt road with weeds growing between the two bare tire paths I sense there is something meaningful to me in that road without knowing why that is, and then realize it has to be a memory from my boyhood summer at Georgica Pond riding that old Ford on the sand dunes. My happiest early childhood memories are from that summer.

Another summer, Peter and I were on a beach with our mother and her friend Wifredo Lam. I have a photograph of the two of us, small boys, with Wifredo's pen drawings on our skinny chests. I would love to remember that day other than from a single photograph. Wifredo was a Cuban artist, who lived in Havana and Madrid and Barcelona and Paris and knew Picasso well. He was a surrealist painter whose work had influences from Cuban and African origins.

Peter and I were allowed to smoke one cigarette a month, with our parents. It was a family tradition they started that lasted only a couple of years, I think. We puffed the cigarette, squinting from the little trail of smoke it made, not inhaling. I never smoked in my life other than those few cigarettes way back then, except for a little of my time in graduate school when I smoked a pipe. I liked the sweet fruity smell of pipe tobacco. I liked holding a warm pipe in my hand walking in the cold air. I didn't inhale the smoke. I disliked the very bitter moisture that would come back through the pipestem into my mouth. Smoking one cigarette a month in front of our parents is a memory from when we lived on 56th Street.

Sadly, what I remember of my father when I was little amounts to a few tricks. We were two little boys looking up to our occasionally present father. Papa we called him. The memories were sweet enough to engender in me a longing for the father I wished I had had. Randy taught us a completely useless thing. He showed us that we could take a Parliament cigarette, because of the kind of filter Parliaments had, and roll it between our fingers, filter end up, until all the tobacco dropped out leaving a weightless empty paper tube attached to the filter. Then, after carefully, gently wetting the edge of the filter as our front teeth softened it, we could throw it up to the ceiling in one smooth movement, and it would stick there, hanging down. That was the finest of the tricks he taught us. Another was, starting with a closed fist, to make a rubber band jump from the two fingers it bound to the two it didn't hold when we opened our hand. That trick was nice enough that I have taught children how to do it over the years. And there was the one we have all seen, of the thumb that seems to be separated from the hand as we moved it out and then back to where it started. I have no problem with being taught little tricks, but I don't like that my father is reduced in childhood memory to three little tricks he showed us.

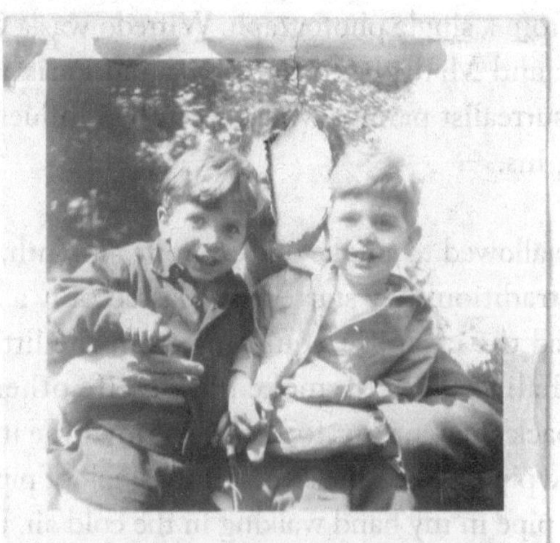

With my father and Peter (right), circa 1945.
Anne defaced most of the pictures of Randy.

3

MEXICO

In April of 1949, Anne took me and Peter to Mexico for nine months. Our parents had separated. We were in a sort of camp or school for a little while but otherwise with our mother. Two skinny little boys and their beautiful 32 year old mother. Anne wore a glass eye back then. A bit later she started wearing a black eyepatch because the glass eye didn't track with her left eye very well and was uncomfortable. She replaced the wide flat ribbon of her eyepatches with a narrow velvet ribbon that made a thin dark line across her forehead. Anne wore an eyepatch as though it were a piece of jewelry. It didn't diminish her beauty so much as it drew attention to herself, which she was perfectly comfortable with. She tended to be regarded as exotic, and mysterious. Peter and I liked that our mother was unique among mothers, wearing her eyepatch that matched the pure black of her hair that she dyed with something she told us was the same thing Mexican bullfighters used. She really was striking looking.

In Mexico Anne hadn't concerned herself with our schooling, apart from what might have been two or three weeks at the camp. There I remember we played games together sitting in a circle on the grass, singing in Spanish. I remember a black scorpion on the whitewashed wall in the dining room, and there were a few goats. Mostly we three were together, and Anne did what she could to distract us from thoughts about the instability of our situation. We went to see pre-Columbian ruins and spent some time on beaches. One night we went on a little trek to near the top of a live volcano called Parícutin.

Peter and I were on one donkey wrapped together in a blanket. I remember molten lava glowing red in the blackness.

I liked Mexico and our adventures there. I liked the foreignness of it all, with a new language and things we were told never to do, like to buy an ice cream from a street vendor because it would make us sick. I did that one time, and I did get a stomach ache, but the temptation when it was really hot was too hard to resist. Thinking back on that day, I can still remember the heat and the dust and something so good about that ice cream. I liked the smell of coconut oil my mother used on her skin when we went to the beaches. She wore a bikini that she made from the red and white paisley printed Mexican bandannas, folded to make triangles that she sewed together at their corners and tied at her hips and her bosoms. It was a nicely simple and beautiful design she created. There was a particular smell of straw baskets and hats in the street markets on hot days that I liked. There were Mexican boys firing little pieces of orange peel at me and Peter, hitting our bare legs; their slingshots nothing more than a rubber band held between a forefinger and thumb. I remember being in a house talking to a boy and there was a Nazi flag hanging on the wall. The boy said we should pledge allegiance to the flag. I didn't know what that was, the flag or to pledge allegiance. It meant nothing to me. I thought it was boy's play and nothing more. In retrospect, I assumed that boy's father was German and had fled to Mexico at the end of the war five years earlier.

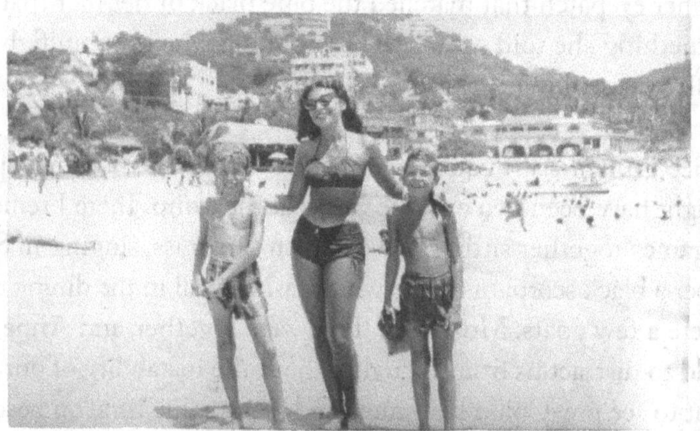

Peter (left), Anne and myself, Acapulco, 1949

4

BACK IN THE CITY

When we returned to New York, we arrived in the middle of a great blizzard on Thanksgiving weekend. The worst storm of the century, they said. And after that there was no more home, and no more father. There was just the city we had left nine months earlier and our little family of three.

After Mexico, Peter and I were in public schools. I was way behind in learning to read because I missed the grade when other children were taught to read. In school I felt stupid because I couldn't read. I did learn to, of course, but I have never been able to read faster than the spoken word, and my concentration and comprehension were never what they should have been. My mind wanders easily. All through my younger years I had to work harder at schoolwork than my classmates to keep up.

Classrooms in public schools back then have all but disappeared from my memory. I did learn about pledging allegiance to a flag, something we did daily in school, with our right hand on our hearts, and I remember the air raid drills when we all got under our desks. I wondered how school children would be able to carry on in the world if we were the only survivors because we knew to get under our school desks.

There was white chalk that made fast tapping sounds and screeched terribly when the teacher wrote on the blackboard. There were arcing smears left by blackboard erasers made of stitched together layers of thick gray felt. Teachers rewarded good behavior by letting some kid clap two blackboard erasers together, creating a white cloud of chalk dust nobody should have to breathe. I used to sit at the back of the classroom those public school years, looking out the window, daydreaming, and hoping I wouldn't be asked to answer a question. Teachers didn't like calling on the kids who held a hand raised all the time, their other hand supporting the elbow of the raised arm, squirming in their seats because they knew the answer. I was one of those who wanted to be saved by the bell. But I could draw better than other kids. I think that might have been the only thing I could do at all well. I have no memories about what was being taught.

There are very few books I can remember at all from early childhood. One I do remember, because I loved the illustrations, was called *The Funny Thing*, by Wanda Gag. If there were others, I can't remember them, nor can I remember ever having been read to, except when Peter read *Charlotte's Web* to me. I don't remember my mother reading to me, or to us, at all, ever. Peter being sixteen months older had learned to read before I did.

Later I had *The Little Prince*, by Antoine de Saint-Exupéry. It was a sweet story about a boy's loneliness, and for that I liked it. At Christine Magriel's apartment, where we house-sat a few times, there were *Babar* books. Babar the Elephant. I loved those books and their illustrations. Christine had the only TV Peter and I saw in our childhood. Anne had no books in the period of our living out of suitcases, and not many when we finally had the studio apartment on 57th Street and Sixth Avenue. Anne used to read the Sunday NY Times and liked to do the crossword puzzles.

I remember ball point pens that had a funny smell and ball point pens that leaked a sticky ink. I had a fountain pen that I refilled from a bottle of ink. It had a little lever that pulled out and then when the nib was in the ink bottle, I'd slowly release it and the ink would be drawn up inside the pen. I liked that pen. Blue ink stained fingers. Men's shirt pockets sometimes had blue spots that didn't wash out. I remember when we all used little bottles of mucilage with a slanted pink rubber top that when pushed against a piece of paper would let out a drop of glue and would also spread the glue. And typewriter erasers were round pink discs of hard gritty rubber with a green plastic brush attached, and typewriter ribbons were divided horizontally, half red, half black, with two open spools that fit on the typewriter and advanced with the typing. I liked how the ribbon would shift up and down behind the letters on their type bars when a finger pushed down on a key. Typewriters fascinated me for how they worked. I remember black carbon paper and thin onionskin typing paper. They were my mother's typewriter and paper. I didn't know how to type at all until I was grown up.

Peter and I might have had no more than one pair of sneakers and one or two pairs of blue jeans each to wear in the period after the separation of our parents. All through childhood our blue jeans were bought too big and were rolled up at the bottom two or three turns so there would be room to grow into them. Jeans in those days would shrink a size or two but my mother accounted for that and still bought them large and they didn't fit. And that made no difference to me. I remember T-shirts with colored horizontal stripes before printed T-shirts with pictures and words were made. I had one belt and a few pairs of socks. And that was enough. When I was a little bigger I had a pair of leather shoes, of which I only remember that the heels would wear down at an angle from walking in the city and I nailed little metal taps to the parts that would wear down. I liked the clicking sound the taps made when I walked. I knew about how blind people would hear the tapping of their white canes on the pavement and were sensitive to how those sounds would bounce off walls and parked cars helping them to be aware of buildings and the edges of a sidewalk. And how bats would use echolocation to avoid flying into anything.

We moved from cheap little hotel rooms to the apartments of friends who let us stay while they were somewhere beyond the city on vacation. Back and forth. One hotel room we were in had colored neon light flashing across the ceiling from a bar below our window that I first thought might have been from a fire in the building. It must have been every place we stayed in had the clanking of radiator pipes and the occasional whistle of hot steam emitted by radiator safety valves. Those were the sounds of indoor city living, what crickets and mice and the soft hoot of owls might be to country living.

I actually didn't mind our moving from one hotel room to another and to the apartments of friends. Our mother was with us more then than she had been before our nine months in Mexico when we were living on our separate floors of the brownstone on 56th Street. I didn't mind living out of suitcases with very few pieces of clothing and no toys at all.

One time when we were staying at Hotel 14 (14 East 60th Street) Addie Herder and Allan Lewis came to visit us in our room, walking through the small lobby with empty suitcases, and they left with their suitcases full so we could later slip out without paying the bill. For me it was a series of adventures living like that when there was no money for rent. Anne said we were like Gypsies.

I didn't understand how things worked in the real world. We were children. The city was home to me and Peter and we spent a lot of time on our own. We fished for sunnies in the 59th Street pond in Central Park and threw what we caught back in. Our fishing lines were tied to the ends of thin bamboo poles, with a hook and a worm and a red and white plastic bobber with a spring set wire that held it to the line and little lead sinkers that were attached to the fishing line. I didn't like waiting for the bobber to be tugged under. I think Peter liked fishing more than I did, but it was something we could do on our own to pass the time.

We often went to the zoo by ourselves. It was walking distance from wherever we were living. I liked how a zoo with all kinds of animals could be right across the street from tall apartment buildings on Fifth Avenue. There was a yak in the zoo we would visit that had one horn curved under its head, ground down by the pavement on the underside from when it ate, and the other curved up over its head. Long brown fur down to the ground. It had a sad, kind face. It was our friend. I say it because with its long fur I couldn't see if it was male or female.

When we were children left pretty much to our own devices in the middle of Manhattan, to occupy ourselves our mother suggested we start a stamp collection. As a family, we had no money beyond what it took to put food on the table, so she suggested we go to foreign consulates and ask if they had a few stamps from envelopes they were putting in the trash, and we did that. We asked and we were given a few stamps from letters received that day. It was a nice way to pass time. We would soak the stamps off the pieces of envelope and let them dry face down on newspaper and then organize them by country. We had the list of foreign consulates in New York torn from a Yellow Pages directory. That started our stamp collecting.

Peter continued collecting and eventually became well known as a philatelist in his narrow field of expertise that was mostly Egyptian stamps. His own collection was primarily second issue Egyptian stamps printed from lithograph stones from 1867 to 1869. Working with stamps in blocks of four, some of which still had the white border attached along one or two sides, he was able to reconstruct the positions of each minutely different hand-drawn second issue stamp to form a complete sheet for denominations that no longer existed in full sheets. It was like code breaking, or like working the most challenging jigsaw puzzles. And he searched for rare cancellations on envelopes mailed from places where few such cancellations were still to be found. Eventually he published a book on Egyptian and Sudanese revenue stamps.

Anne had no respect for Peter's philately. In her mind, stamp collecting didn't come close to the print collecting one of her art historian friends was expert in. I saw the two as being very similar, both being about research and collecting and the market value of images printed on paper. I thought the best 19th century stamps were as beautiful as some of the prints my mother's friend collected.

When we began collecting stamps, I would sometimes go with Peter to a small store on the southeast corner of 64th Street and Madison Avenue, which a stamp dealer shared with a man who sold antique furniture. Peter would take a long time sitting at the desk going through stock books as this dour looking man patiently answered his questions and watched Peter who would finally buy only three or four stamps that cost almost nothing. I liked how we looked through a magnifying glass at stamps held by stamp tongs.

I liked glassine hinges and crystal mounts, and how a drop of Carbona on a stamp placed face down in a little rectangular black dish would reveal a stamp's watermark. I liked that among our few possessions, we had the paraphernalia belonging to a profession. It was the oldest stamps from any country that I liked best. They were the single color stamps that usually had a portrait within an oval or a rectangle, surrounded by intricate borders, within which might be the word POSTAGE and numbers as both numerals and words, all in a most elegant design. To me they were very small, very fine engravings. But I didn't buy stamps with the few cents I had and I soon stopped collecting.

We went around to banks collecting free calendars when it was close to the new year. We did things that didn't cost anything and would occupy us in our idle years of childhood. I got a few cigar boxes from the corner cigar store for the odd little things I collected. I liked the fancy paper labels on the boxes and the color of the mahogany they were made from, and I liked the cigar smell the boxes had.

It was in those years that I started making my own toys, and drawing all the time. I made a house out of a shoe box, cutting windows and a door in the sides. The top was removable so I could see inside. The house was for a little porcelain Japanese dime store figurine. I made a car from stiff paper and wrote FOFT on the front, thinking I had written Ford. It would have looked more like a Jeep because I couldn't bend paper in complex curves. That was when we didn't have a place of our own and I had practically no toys at all. Looking back on that period, I think how we lived when my mother had no money to speak of probably contributed to my resourcefulness. I think it was better to have few toys than to be surrounded by toys the way many children are in our culture today.

One day Anne brought home a notice for a drawing contest, something from a TV show for children. We never had a TV of our own, only sometimes there was one where we apartment-sat. I made a drawing on a page from the newspaper using a black magic marker and Anne sent it to the contest address. My drawing was of an invented monster, lots of black lines on top of want ads evenly printed in columns of small type. My drawing won a prize. They sent me a $50 Savings Bond, which I kept for many years un-cashed. It was the single thing I kept for the longest time before I was in college. Along with the savings bond they gave me a little plastic Pez candy dispenser, a sponsor's prize. Something to keep in my cigar box.

One time when I was wandering through Central Park near 59th Street, I stopped to watch a group from the Art Students League drawing trees and paths and benches, and their teacher paid me 10 cents to stay still a few minutes while the students drew me. That was well earned money for a boy in the middle of Manhattan, where there was no such thing as a paper route, not that I ever had a bicycle before I was a Cooper Union student. The time I remember getting more than 10 cents as a boy was when Peter and I, one Halloween evening, went through all the floors of an apartment building, knocking on doors saying trick or treat. Not expecting any children to knock on their upstairs apartment doors, the tenants wouldn't have candy ready to give us so they gave us a coin or two. We got $11 that evening.

I liked the smell of Noxema and how when turning the top of the blue glass jar it would slide in a way others didn't. I liked the deep blue glass of the jar. I liked the unique smell of Packer's Pine Tar Soap that I used to wash my hair when I would find it on the shelves of a store. The package was beautiful and unlike any other soap package, with its flags that seemed not to be known flags, or meaningful flags, but gave the label design a look of something important. I remember liking the smell emitted by the air vent of a dry cleaner as I walked past. And the smell that lifted from the bridal path around the reservoir in Central Park when the sun heated the horse manure and what I thought must have been crushed volcanic lava.

New York City had a serious soot problem caused by the burning of heavy heating oils. The soot was part of the air we breathed, and window sills would be gray with the soot that would come in even through the cracks around closed windows; it would stick to women's faces if they wore makeup and to men's faces when they sweated. It would dirty the insides of white shirt collars in a day.

One year my mother enrolled me in a children's class at the Museum of Modern Art. It was probably a Saturday afternoon class. There was a little interview at which I was asked if I copied my drawings of knights in armor. My mother answered that I had drawn them from the movie *Ivanhoe*. In other words from seeing a movie, from memory. The only thing I remember from the class is that the teacher said I should paint the background right up to the edges of the figure, not to leave a gap of white paper between figure and background. A useful critique. That was when I was quite small, before I was going to museums on my own and knowing artists by name. Before knowing the studios of my mother's artist friends.

In my memory I can still see some of the characters who peopled those days that long ago. There was a man who stood outside Bloomingdale's on Lexington Avenue and 59th Street for years. He sold pencils from a coffee can he held in his right hand and he sold comic books that lay at his feet, one or two clutched against his body by his other hand. His hands were crippled. His face was deeply cragged, and I thought sad. His body was twisted like a marionette hanging limp from tangled strings, the way every marionette's strings are. I didn't know the man but he interested me in that he was always there as an integral part of that piece of the city. I wondered what he was thinking about all those hours and days while he would stand there with his comic books and pencils. It seemed to me he didn't change at all over years. Then after I was no longer there to see him, he must have gone.

* * *

Soon after my parents' separation, my father stopped paying alimony and child support, and we were poor for a few years. Anne would sometimes discover Randy's whereabouts from a mutual friend, who didn't know he was hiding from her and she would get a lawyer to try to get him to pay what he owed. And Randy would disappear again.

For a few years, our father sent me and Peter Christmas presents. The first I can remember was a Lionel electric train set we shared. That was nice.

After that, Peter and I would each get separate but identical presents. I remember two little overnight suitcases not much bigger than a briefcase, one beige and one gray. Another year we each got a wallet that had a pad of paper and small pen. What purpose would a boy have for a man's breast pocket wallet? They had the name "Jiffy-Jot" on them. I could see even then that those presents amounted to no more than a few minutes shopping at a five-and-ten-cent store, or some place like that, to buy presents for the two boys my father hardly knew at all.

Another year we each got a camera for Christmas. A camera was nice. But because film and developing cost money, I might only have used my camera a few times. It had a little round red plastic window on the back to see the number on the yellow paper backing of the film. Black numbers and black arrows were staggered in such a way they would fit the positions of the little red plastic window of any camera that took that size film. I liked opening the camera and carefully attaching the film and its yellow paper backing to the empty spool, then shutting the camera and advancing the film to the first number, and cocking the shutter mechanism before clicking a picture. I liked the sounds the camera made when doing those things. That said, I can only remember one photograph from that camera and I didn't think I had taken it. It must have been taken by itself, by accident. It was of an outdoor cage at the zoo, but the picture had no animal in it and the cage was tipped at an odd angle.

I don't remember any other Christmas presents from our father, nor any birthday presents at all from him. No letters. Nothing more. If my father ever felt deep sadness about not being a real father to his two sons, he didn't say it, not even in a lie so far as I know. I still, even now, feel the ache of being an abandoned child when I see a father and son together in a beautiful loving relationship, in films or in life.

Withdrawing into an inner world where what I might create was more exciting than reality no doubt had a part in shaping the artist in me. I wasn't the boy who kicked a ball around, running and laughing through childhood as I saw other kids do. I have almost no memories at all of my father before the separation when I was about six. I remember only one photograph of him, crouched down to be on the same level with his two little boys, actually sharing a moment of intimacy, believe it or not. But that was a photo seen years later. And only one. Other than that, among the few family photos my mother kept, she had cut off my father's head. Randy was away when he was there, and then he was gone. And no other man in Anne's life in those early years showed any kind interest in the shy withdrawn little Alan.

A child needs to be loved. And more than anything else, lack of love is what I remember of my early years, the cause of all the anxieties I was to know so well and be so helpless to deal with. Long before parental separation took my father from me there was a climate of change among educated people in America. My parents thought they knew better about child raising than their parents' generation did, and there was a kind of disconnect where there should have been a beautiful natural, nurturing home environment.

Too often Anne's love felt insincere. It would be there and then it would be denied, as though it was never there at all. Conflicted and contradictory behavior was what I knew from my mother, a recipe for disaster in a child's life. Later on, I began to believe that my mother tried to shift her parental responsibility to others and expect them to solve the problems that troubled me. One time, when I was a painfully shy kid suffering from chronic stomach aches, she set me up for some weekly sessions with a psychiatrist or psychologist at a free clinic in the city. It didn't succeed in doing anything productive because I didn't understand what it was about and I was virtually silent. The very nice doctor took me out for a slice of pizza and a soda two or three times and no conversations were had at all. And it was soon over.

We lived at the Hotel Croydon a short while so that Peter and I could qualify to attend PS 6 on Madison Avenue, a block from the Metropolitan Museum. PS 6 (Public School number six) was the best public elementary school in Manhattan. For lack of money we couldn't remain at the hotel or anywhere within the school district, so we had to pretend we lived with a friend of my mother's who did live in the district.

I have memories of being a boy alone in the Metropolitan Museum and almost no memories of the school other than looking out the big windows of the classroom daydreaming. There was a boy in my class named David Hamner, whose mother was an actress. We went together with her to see a war film she was in, and David showed me his mother there with the soldiers. I still remember a scene in which American GIs were cooking in their upturned helmets on a campfire. I remember walking on the street with David, and he was singing "Oh my PaPa, to me he is so wonderful...," and how the sadness of those words stayed with me many years. That is the strongest actual memory I have about the pain I felt as a boy in those years, David Hamner's "Oh my PaPa."

※ ※ ※

The Metropolitan Museum had three large Etruscan terracotta pieces that I loved when I was a child. Two standing warriors and a colossal head in a helmet. I often visited them and I made drawings of similar figures in Etruscan armor. In 1959 the Metropolitan's three Etruscan figures were proven to be fakes made by Italian potters who had broken them into pieces before firing them in a kiln too small to accommodate them whole. After the firing, they buried the pieces before unearthing them and claiming them to be Etruscan.

The way some artworks could be accepted and highly valued until they are discovered to be modern fakes interests me. What does that say about the works themselves, that they could go from masterpieces to objects of no value only because they were not authentic, because they were not centuries old? The objects didn't change, it was their story that changed. That has to do with scholarship and the market. The art itself is next to irrelevant. I understand it and I don't understand it.

I felt at home in the Metropolitan Museum. At home in that I was comfortable and better than at home because I didn't have a home to be at home in. Not in the way a kid should have a home. And the museum was so wonderful in all its collections, and it welcomed me as though it was there for me, the way the city was home to me, only better. Nobody was telling me how to behave or what to think. In the museum, I could be entirely myself, feeling protected in the sense that people there were quiet and respectful of me as much as of anyone else. I would stand in front of a painting and look into the soul behind the eyes of a portrait for as long as I liked, wondering and thinking and not being judged in any way because it was a painted face I was looking at and not the face of a person who would turn and leave, or ask me what I was looking at, as though I had no business looking at that person. I understood that looking into the eyes and into the soul of a portrait is only looking at a painting, but it was something I liked to do. The paintings that had that depth to them were magical. I wonder if, already as a boy, I was thinking I would like to make paintings like that one day.

There are very few bits and pieces of knowledge that I remember from childhood. The Möbius strip is one that comes to mind. I liked it because it was something pure in its simplicity and also something oddly barely comprehensible. I thought of it as useless other than as what it was, which was an idea, or a fact, if a thing can be that. And in a sense, is that not what art is, or what anything that has no practical function is, which is most of what interests me?

I can remember Peter and I once amused ourselves by cutting a golf ball open with a hacksaw and found it had what seemed like an endless rubber band wrapped tightly around a small black hard rubber core. Another time we filled the end of our Electrolux vacuum cleaner hose with as many cigarettes as it would hold and lit them and turned the vacuum cleaner on to see how fast the cigarettes burned down. They were cigarettes left by one of my mother's boyfriends. And one time we were on the roof of 58 West 57th Street flying a kite, and it came down on a roof across Sixth Avenue. I waited on our roof while Peter went down to the street and after a few minutes reappeared on the roof of the other building with the superintendent of that building, Peter pointing to our roof with me standing there looking at them, and then disappearing, and then being next to me again with the kite. We were amusing ourselves and we were learning, satisfying our natural curiosity about all kinds of things by doing things we wouldn't have been encouraged to do.

I remember we were told one could soak a dollar bill in water until it softened and then starting at a corner, carefully separate it into two pieces, a front and a back, one thinner paper than the other. We did that a few times. We glued them back together one side upside down to the other and spent them, wondering whether anyone would notice that one side was upside down to the other. We heard some people used to do that with a ten and a twenty-dollar bill, gluing them and passing them off as two twenties. We didn't do that. That would be like counterfeit. We knew that. Peter and I fantasized about running away from home. There was a sheath knife we saw in a store window, labeled as a "Black Forest Hunting Knife," with a claw holding a ball at the end of the handle. We thought if we had that knife surely we could survive in the forest. We weren't serious about running away, but maybe the idea says something about our childhood.

One day we bought a piece of dry ice from where ice cream push carts were dispatched to be situated on neighborhood sidewalks. We found that pressing a coin against the dry ice made a strange whining sound, and putting dry ice in a pot of water produced a cloud of fog. In the same period we discovered that blowing through the goose neck tube from a lamp made a sound that varied in pitch according how hard we blew. It has to do with the spiral, but I don't know why the speed or force of air spiraling through a tube would change the pitch. We made whistles from the little hollow wooden cylinders that were handles for packages some department stores gave customers. A wire that went through them hooked onto the cord of a bound package. We cut an angled notch near one end of the tube and glued a wedge shaped piece of dowel stick inside to direct the air blown through the tube past the wedge of the cut notch. A longer piece of the dowel stick sliding in and out of the open end of the tube varied the sound made by blowing into it. In essence it was a little toy version of a recorder and a slide trombone combined. I don't know how we knew how to do that.

Peter and I were leaning once out a hallway window onto a fire escape a floor above the sidewalk and we dropped a nail, timing it to hit the ground just behind a man walking by below. We did it a few times behind different men. Each time the same thing happened. The man would hear the nail hit the sidewalk and would stop and turn and check his pockets as he looked around him for what he dropped. And then he would walk on. Because he didn't have a nail to drop, he ignored the nail and kept looking around for a coin or a key or something he could have dropped. Remembering that time, I am reminded of when Jeff Bridges says in *The Fisher King* that New Yorkers don't look up.

One summer we were in a day camp for city kids. We were taken to a pencil factory and to a plastic toy factory somewhere in the city. Another day we went to an outdoor public swimming pool in the Bronx or Queens, just like the pool in Scorsese's *Raging Bull*. That film brought back a memory of women sitting in their one piece bathing suits, and the water and the buildings close by. I was there, I knew that place.

There were remembered moments that in retrospect were significant, or were just those that hadn't slipped out of my mind altogether. Those years seemed long and hard to endure before my brother and I eventually outgrew childhood. I remember there were pictures of ice cream sundaes and banana splits displayed over the counter in drugstore soda fountains. Round swivel stools bolted to the floor. I didn't have the 25 cents that a sundae cost, and for some years I longed to sit at the counter and order one. And then, one day and I don't know when that was, I realized that I could buy one, but at that time I no longer wanted an ice cream sundae. The idea of having one was enough to enjoy later, when I knew Norman Rockwell and Edward Hopper images emblematic of those childhood years. There were shoeshine guys at the train station, with their raised seats like thrones and brass foot rests. I liked watching them apply a creamy polish to men's shoes and brush them with two brushes simultaneously, and buff them with a cloth held in both hands, pulling it tight across the shoe, hands moving up and down fast in opposing directions. And they would snap the cloth in the air and continue their buffing and the shoes would shine like new. And there were barber shops with their red, blue, and white spiral barber pole out front. Men would stop by to be shaved and have their hair cut, holding still with their bodies under white cloths while listening to the stories and the gossip spoken by barbers whose trade was another of those with elaborate procedures that were part of the daily life of businessmen. For me, they were there to be seen as theatre because I didn't have the money to have done for me what I could do for myself. For most of my life I cut my own hair. Then, gradually, things that used to be so integral to city life were changing imperceptibly and I was hardly aware that they were slowly disappearing and being replaced by things I would come to see as lacking in charm.

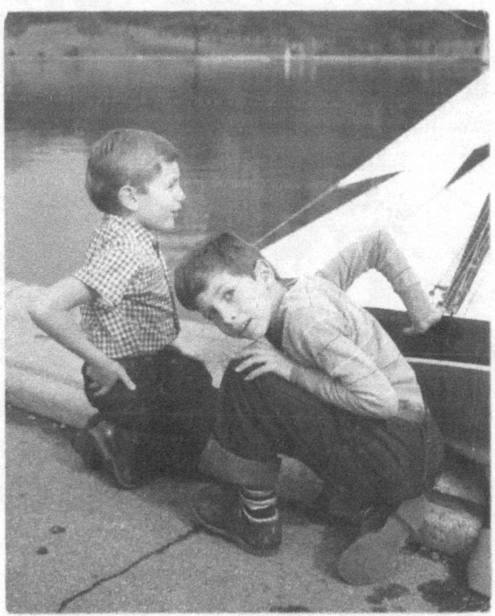

Peter (left) and me in Central Park, 1950s

5

SHERWOOD STUDIOS

In eighth grade I was in another public school, this time in the West 50s. I remember one afternoon following a classmate home. I wanted to be her boyfriend but I was helpless to do anything to allow that to be. We got to her apartment with me following behind her. Knowing that I was following her was how I let her know I wanted to spend time with her outside of class, hoping she would initiate something. When her mother opened the door and saw me, she invited me in, but I was too embarrassed and too shy to say anything at all. That was very uncomfortable. It was a foolish failed attempt to have something I so wanted but was unable to have.

I don't remember what we were being taught that year, but that was a long time ago. I do remember a classmate named Armando sang "La Donna è Mobile" from Verdi's *Rigoletto* standing in front of the class, and I envied his self-confidence and ability to do something I couldn't begin to do. Another boy in my class told me his uncle was George Gershwin, a famous composer. I remember walking to school and passing a small frame shop and stopping to look at a frame leaning against the wall in front of the shop that the framer was in the process of gilding. I was fascinated by the way so thin a leaf of gold it was that the slightest breeze would set it to fluttering where it wasn't held down where gold leaf size had been applied. I liked watching skilled workers. I have always had great respect and admiration for skilled workers of any sort. I was already certain that I wanted to be a maker of things.

In this period, my mother rented a studio apartment in Sherwood Studios, on the SE corner of 57th Street and Sixth Avenue. I think I was eleven when we finally settled down there. Our studio consisted of one large room with a big north facing skylight and a sleeping loft where Peter and I slept above a small kitchen and bathroom. Anne bought a used refrigerator from the superintendent of an apartment house down the street. She slept in the large room on a couch bed. We had very little furniture and only a few dishes and mismatched water glasses. After a young man came to visit my mother, he had a box of six proper wine glasses sent to her. Maybe that, along with a bohemian lifestyle romanticism, taught me to almost prefer jam jars to crystal wine glasses. Poverty afforded a kind of unconcern, or a disdain for what I have heard referred to as gracious living. The stability of that being the first place of our own after a period of constant moving about was really good. It was the first time I had the feeling that a *place* belonged to me. It was different from East 56th Street because I was no longer a small child and I was outside more, able to explore on my own. There was the Automat that Peter and I often went to for lunch, half a block west on 57th Street. It was one of a few Horn and Hardart Automats in the city. Unlike any other restaurant or cafeteria, the Automat had a long wall of glass fronted boxes through which you could see what you would take after putting coins in a slot and turning a knob that opened the little door. I remember liking the casserole of baked noodles and cheese.

There was a very small watch repair shop on Sixth Avenue between 57th and 58th Streets that stood tiny between two tall apartment buildings, its doorway too narrow for a large person to fit through. Across the street was a drugstore, and Lun Far, a Chinese restaurant where we sometimes ate. We ate more often at a much smaller North Chinese restaurant on a side street a few blocks away. They had tofu and I hadn't eaten tofu before. Anne described tofu to a friend as being like Roquefort ice cream. I suppose that was a fair description. When a boyfriend took my mother to dinner it was sometimes to the Russian Tea Room on 57th street. We couldn't afford to eat at the Russian Tea Room so I may have eaten there only once.

The south end of Central Park was right there at 59th Street. I could walk over to the park and be in the country with trees and rocks and ponds, with curving roads and footpaths, a place where people went to stroll or to sit quietly to read, or to watch others. There was a sort of reflecting pool where men whose hobby was making elaborate model sailboats would float their boats, circling the water holding a long stick with a hook on the end. Children would launch their little toy boats and watch them. Some days I would see a man who whittled things of wood like what sailors used to make to pass their time on long sea voyages. A ball held within a sort of box frame, and pliers, each of them made from a single piece of wood and having moving parts. He was probably a sailor who later in life whittled those things hoping to be asked about why he was doing what he did on those days. There was a man I more than once walked behind crossing Sixth Avenue. I didn't know who he was but I remember being interested in the shirt he wore. It was hot summer and his shirt I thought of as a fishnet shirt. A friend later explained that such a shirt protected someone from being sunburned because the strings and the gaps between them would shift as a person moved so that what was shielded from the sun and what was exposed to the sun kept changing. Maybe so. I saw him many times, crossing Sixth Avenue at 57th Street. Our corner. In the game I sometimes still play with myself, trying to decide what the national origin people I see on the streets might have been, I decided this man was German. In that period, when I was an adolescent boy, and I can't say why or even how I knew who he was, I rode in a taxi with Leó Szilárd, the Hungarian physicist who worked closely with Albert Einstein, Enrico Fermi and other physicists to establish research in nuclear fission for the US government, which led to the creation of the Manhattan Project, and ultimately the inventing of the atomic bomb. Szilárd then tried to discourage dropping atomic bombs on Hiroshima and Nagasaki, believing a test explosion on an uninhabited island witnessed by the Japanese could bring them to surrender. I didn't know anything about Leó Szilárd at the time, when we rode a taxi together in New York. I only remember liking him very much, and soon after, reading his book of short stories called *The Voice of the Dolphins*.

Often I would see Moondog on Sixth Avenue, silently listening to the sounds of the city. Moondog was a blind composer and poet who stood still for hours dressed in a most fantastic way in clothes he fashioned himself that made him look like a Viking warrior misplaced in time and location. He had a long gray beard and hair down to his shoulders and his eyes were often hidden by a triangular piece of leather that was part of a head covering that had cow horns pointing outward from above his ears. He held a long staff with a spearhead that pointed upward. His feet were covered in folded and tied leather, and in winter he wore cape-like blankets. The Museum of Modern Art was right there on 53rd Street and I often went there by myself. Milt Herder would lend me his membership card to go in. I liked watching films in the basement auditorium. I remember the auditorium would have a muffled rumble I would feel through the floor and the seat when a subway passed nearby underground, like an earthquake beneath an otherwise stable city. One film I saw there that I thought about for many years was called *The Mudlark,* about a ten-year-old street urchin who finds a cameo with the face on it he is told is Queen Victoria, "The Mother of all England." Fascinated by this, he is obsessed with the desire to see the Queen and he finds a way to sneak into Windsor Castle through a coal chute. I remember him hiding under the dining table inside the tent made by the tablecloth, surrounded by legs and feet, fearing being caught. I identified with the boy for his loneliness and his wanting to experience things he was too little and too disadvantaged to know.

Anne already knew Sari Dienes and Milt and Addie Herder who lived at 58 West 57th Street. Sari was born Sari Chylinska in Hungary in 1898 and moved to New York in 1939, unable to return to Europe after the outbreak of World War II. Her French mathematician husband, Paul Dienes, remained in England and she never saw him again. Peter and I were like studio assistants to Sari, I more so than my brother because Sari's studio was the first artist studio I knew well and it enchanted me. I practically lived in Sari's studio in those years.

Milt was also very important to me then. He was like a father to me, the father I had missed in childhood. Milt was the first man who took serious interest in me. He was not like Randy, or the men my mother dated, who were barely around, and then not around, in and out and only on the edge of my silent and introverted world. Sari in her way, and Milt in his, were my art teachers before I started art school. They were kind and were generous with their time. I remember very clearly when Milt made a model airplane with me and Peter. Actually he didn't make a model airplane with us, he taught us to design and build an airplane, first sending us out to buy balsa wood and piano wire and the ribbons of rubber that spun the propeller, and Duco cement in little tubes. He knew the theory, and he explained it to us. He taught us how the shape of airplane wings, curved in a certain way on top and flat on the underside, created lift, and how thin piano wire, bent precisely with two small pliers, could fix the wings to the body and how to shape a propeller and attach it to the nose with the piano wire and little glass beads to reduce the friction between moving parts. We used tissue paper to cover the wing ribs. The fuselage was a simple beam of narrow wood stiffer than balsa. And when it was finished we triumphantly flew the airplane down the long hallway of Milt's floor in the building. It was a strange apparition almost like a flying praying mantis moving slowly through the dimly lit hallway.

* * *

That was our first apartment following the separation of my parents, and it ended the period of moving from one little hotel room to the apartment of a friend of my mother's to another little hotel room, back and forth like that, living out of our suitcases. In those years I had only the few toys I made for myself, and no books of any kind. But that didn't seem to matter much because when I wasn't sitting in the back of a public school classroom daydreaming I was in the city streets and the art museums, and Sari's studio, and those were the places I knew best and was happy in.

Sari saw beauty in everything. To Sari things had a poetry to them, no matter how commonplace they were. Much of her art was made from discarded objects found in the streets of New York. Her sensibility may have grown out of knowing the work of Marcel Duchamp and his Readymades and the Dada artists' work, but it was different, a little closer to Joseph Cornell's poetic lyricism, but also not like that either. Sari's assemblages were more pure, and more raw. The things she brought into her studio had the patina made by rain or rust or having been run over many times by cars and buses that could turn rusted cans into what looked like leather. In the objects themselves Sari saw a transformation so they could be left almost as they were, or they could be combined with other found objects in ways that together they would become poetry. Her pieces were far more interesting to me than Louise Nevelson's sculptures in the Museum of Modern Art that had already become much more famous than anything Sari ever made. It was the predictability of Nevelson's pieces and that she painted them all a single black, or occasionally another color, that made them less beautiful to me. There was no individual story to the elements in a Nevelson, and having so many pieces to them detracted from any possible meaning in my mind. For me they have no soul.

Peter and I made a wall of storage shelves for Sari by bringing in and stacking the wooden shipping crates put out to trash in front of Salamander Shoes next door on 57th Street. And then I worked with Sari handling years of all kinds of accumulated things, sorting and reorganizing everything. Sari talked as we worked together. I was absorbing something of how, in the hands of an artist, objects can suggest ideas which then shape how we see, and how things can take on a new purpose.

Sari had a rib and a vertebra of a whale in her studio. They were big and mysterious and had they not been in Sari's studio, or in the Museum of Natural History, they would have been altogether incongruous in the middle of the city. Sari had an Audubon print on her wall depicting two red-tailed hawks and a rabbit suspended in something more like a free fall than flight, absolutely fixed in weightless immobility. And that image made a deep impression on me. It was something I looked at many times. I was moved by the power such an image could have, being silent and still, while portraying a moment of great drama.

When I first worked together with Sari, she was making prints she called Sidewalk Rubbings, working on long rolls of rice paper using printmaking inks and soft rubber rollers. Peter and I went with her in the early, early hours of morning when there were almost no cars yet moving. We helped Sari carry her glass palette and rollers and tubes of ink. Rolling her inked rollers on the rice paper placed on top of things that had a raised relief surface, Sari printed overlapping manhole covers and iron grates and the textures of the city streets. We would return to specific places where the street or sidewalk surfaces interested her and were saved in memory to work from. Robert Rauschenberg and John Cage sometimes went with Sari out in the night to help her in making these rubbings. I remember being around Bob Rauschenberg and Jasper Johns, and John Cage and Merce Cunningham on occasions when they would be at one of Sari's parties at 58 West 57th Street. One such party was given in the honor of E. Power Biggs following one of his organ concerts at Carnegie Hall, a block west of our building. Sari had me moving about among her guests offering them wine in glasses fitted in the round holes of an antique wooden stocking stretcher.

Sari also made very beautiful textile patterns with the same intuitive sense of design her rubbings had. And in that period she was making what she called her bottle gardens, that were various kinds of glass bottles of different sizes and colors and shapes fitted together, some upside down, some right side up, completely filling glass fish tanks that held them in position. Peter and I would carry the fish tanks in the elevator up to Sari's studio from where they were stacked in the basement, leaky and therefore no longer of use to the pet shop around the corner that shared the basement with our building. In our side of the basement sometimes a couple of off-duty policemen lifted weights. There, in a dimly lit and mysterious space beneath the city I could hear the sounds of clinking iron that are particular to weightlifting. That basement may have been the origin of reoccurring dream spaces I have visited many times and still dream about now. I dream of attics and cellars, passageways to derelict rooms, and cars that have broken down and don't run any more awaiting a mechanic who is nowhere to be found. They are my lonely dreams that in some way must be about aspects of my childhood that still linger in my subconscious.

* * *

I was sixteen when I saw Robert Rauschenberg's Combine titled *Monogram*, 1955-59, when it was first exhibited at the Leo Castelli Gallery in New York.

Rauschenberg made *Monogram* in the period when he and Jasper Johns used to visit Sari in her studio, in the same period when I was spending a lot of time with Sari, before I was an art student. Rauschenberg's *Monogram* was probably the single work of art that spoke to me most meaningfully at that time about what a work of art made in the 20th century could be, and what my life might be like if I were to become an artist. From knowing Sari I was predisposed to see beauty and potential in found objects and in the odd things I might see in junk and antique shops that I couldn't afford to buy at the time. Those were the things Sari and Rauschenberg worked with. I liked how such things had elusive meanings that were subtle and poetic and suggestive of things that might live in one's subconscious mind.

Monogram is a very long-haired taxidermy angora goat with paint on its face and a car tire around its body, standing on an abstract collage painting. The goat, once a live animal, seemed to gaze out calmly through glass eyes from a head smeared with paint, making it look as though it had survived some dreaded violent mishap that left it ensnared by a rubber tire to become transformed into something new and strange and mysterious that stood in the middle of a New York art gallery. Rauschenberg's *Monogram* has since become one of the most famous iconic works of neo-Dada and Conceptual art.

Another of Rauschenberg's combines, *Canyon*, 1959, has a dark, dusty, stuffed eagle with outstretched wings and a pillow hanging from a rope below. I had seen that eagle many times, wings spread wide, atop a wall of cabinets just inside the door of another artist's studio next to Sari's. Whoever lived in that studio often kept his door open, almost inviting me to peek around the barrier to see what was beyond, but the eagle in its place high above was foreboding in that dim light of the hallway where I stood. I didn't know the man behind that wall and never went inside his studio. After the man died, Sari got the eagle and gave it to Rauschenberg. *Canyon* is in the Museum of Modern Art.

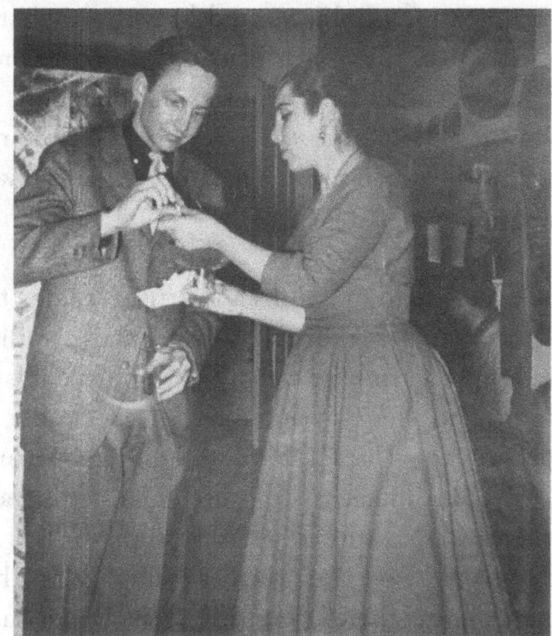

Anne and Robert Rauschenberg at one of Sari's parties, 1950s

Everything in an artist's studio, in one way or another, has a purpose specific to the work he or she makes. A studio might have things like old taxidermy and bones, and things found and things bought that serve as still life props or might themselves be incorporated in what an artist makes. Studios will have easels and sculpture stands, brushes and tools and bottles containing substances known to the artist alone. They might have paintings in racks with only their edges showing, that together could make a museum retrospective of years of work, if they were given such an opportunity. I loved how artist's studios were so unlike the museums I had known, where things were on display, catalogued and identified and expertly lit and made precious, and made do-not-touch public. The studios were where I was able to be me, and feel good about who I was. I was witness to the creative process before knowing what those words might mean, before understanding what it was to transform something seen or found into something new and personal, and meaningful. I sensed it, but without the explanation that I would be introduced to later. There was for me, way back then, the beginning of this nonverbal communication of objects, and I saw how what artists made meant so much more than things manufactured for commercial use. Years later when I was an art student aware of the interpretations art historians attached to such works, those explanations did not begin to mean as much to me as being with the work in a studio in a silence that allowed something unspoken to move me.

It was that early exposure to museums and artists' studios that made me who I became, in a manner of thinking. I saw in those studios something of a life I wanted one day to have for myself. Still silent, still observing what was around me and being shy and timid among people, it made sense that I would turn inward. The complex and unique mixture of parental distance and a rich and stimulating exposure I had starting at the breakup of our family when I was six turned out to be right for me. And, perhaps inadvertently, that would have been the best thing my mother could give me. Circumstances put me there at her side so the things that were about her, and for her, I could know and be nourished by.

We had David Douglas Duncan's book of photographs of Picasso, titled *The Private World of Pablo Picasso,* among the very few books in our studio apartment in that period. Duncan's photographs of Picasso instilled in me a great desire to make art and to live the life of an artist. Picasso seemed to be the most playful grownup I was aware of when I was an adolescent boy. I wanted to be like that. And I wanted to travel to other countries. I thought nothing would be more wonderful. But that would have to come later.

I was already very interested in what I had seen of the collages and assemblages by Dada artists and by some sculptures made by Picasso. His *Bull's Head*, 1942, was made of the seat and handlebars of a bicycle and nothing more; put together they became not just an object that looks rather like the head of a bull, but a very wonderful sculptural interpretation of a bull's head. Another is Picasso's *Baboon and Young,* 1951, cast in bronze from an assemblage he made that had two toy cars, one upside down to the other, that become a wonderfully characteristic head of a baboon.

Sometimes Peter and I would go to the Automat for lunch with Sari. We liked the Automat because it was a place where we could sit as long as we wanted without any interference by waiters. It was half a block from us on 57th Street and felt as though it was our place while at the same time around us there would be people we didn't know. Sari told me that when she was sitting alone in the Automat writing a letter to a friend, she looked up at the window to check the spelling of Automat, and saw the word spelled backwards to be read from outside. She saw, in nice big letters, TAMOTUA. So she wrote it that way, and from then on, among her friends, who were also our friends, the Automat came to be called the Tamotua. It was a good indication of the playful way Sari's mind worked.

Sari showed me a teacup she brought back from Japan that was small and simply made and in every way the antithesis of a fine English porcelain teacup. She told me the man who made her cup said what he was trying to do was to recreate in his pottery the smile of an infant. I don't remember exactly what the teacup looked like or exactly how Sari explained what the maker of the cup had said to her, but I never forgot the beauty of what those thoughts meant, which was that we can strive to make something that intangible, that sweet and pure and quiet and meaningful, something that would be that much in touch with the essence of a truly felt experience. And that in itself can be the purpose of, or the reason for, something we make.

After our studio building at 58 West 57th Street was torn down in 1961 Sari moved to the Gate Hill Cooperative at Stony Point, NY, a community where a few artists of various kinds were given studios to live and work in. There she would find things on her walks in the woods where John Cage had taught her which mushrooms were safe to eat. The found object sculpture that Sari made that I liked most was a leather shoe that had been out in the rain and sun for years, with its stitching long since disintegrated and its sides curled outward so it resembled an iris. She mounted it on a thin iron rod above a small block of wood under a glass dome the kind old clocks had. She called it *Shoe Flower*. That was all. Pure visual poetry. Another was a glass dome over a desiccated mouse that she called *Mausoleum*. Sari had a wonderful way of playing with words and their meanings. I must say

I owe the ways I view the world largely to having spent a lot of time with this wonderful eccentric Hungarian artist who, decades later, in the years when Lani and I would visit her, was washing her beautiful white hair with Woolite, still brushing it out so it looked like something between a halo and an Afro. She told me if Woolite was good for sheep's wool it was good for her hair. A friend of hers told her she looked like a dandelion. And it was so. Her hair was like the seed head of the dandelion every child has blown into the wind.

Sari was saving the round flat coffee filters that had been folded into the conical top of her coffee maker. Flattened out and allowed to dry, each one was unique in its brown coffee grounds stained image. They were a sort of self-made drawing that fit well in the context of everything Sari did. I thought they were like sepia ink landscape drawings. And in the 1970s Sari was making necklaces from things she collected on her walks. They were more breastplates than what we think of as necklaces, each an assemblage that might have incorporated bone and glass and plastic and metal. When Lani and I were first together, she spent a few weeks with Sari at her Stony Point studio while I was teaching in Washington. And Lani began to make wonderful necklaces in direct response to those Sari was making. It meant a great deal to me that Lani could also know Sari and learn from her the way I had when I was young.

On some of our New York trips, Lani and I occasionally stayed in Sari's bedroom in what she called the Crooked House. Soon after meeting a young composer named Richard (Rip) Hayman in 1971, they bought a tiny house above an Irish pub that opened in 1817 on the far west of Spring Street, close to the Hudson River. The stairs up to the two bedrooms were crooked from the land under it shifting years earlier. In 1977 when Richard bought and reopened the bar below, he changed the neon sign from Bar to Ear by covering the two curves in the letter B to become an E. It became the Ear Inn, a bar and restaurant that hosts weekly jazz performances and poetry readings and the like.

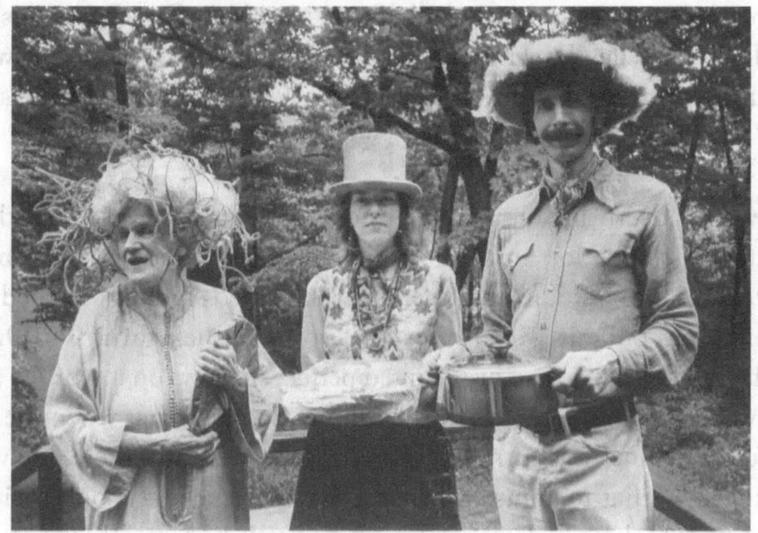
Visiting Sari with Lani, 1975

* * *

Milt Herder was the first surrogate father of three who were very important to me becoming the person I am. Milt was helpful for what he taught me, not only in his ability to make things but also in discussions about art. Three years or so after helping me and Peter to make the model airplane, Milt took me to the Cloisters Museum in Fort Tryon Park, overlooking the Hudson River in Upper Manhattan. The Cloisters, part of the Metropolitan Museum, was built in the 1930s from elements taken from five French and Spanish medieval abbeys and has a great collection of tapestries, paintings, sculptures, stained glass, and manuscripts. What Milt talked about in front of paintings and objects, even the architecture of the Cloisters, became new interests for me. Being in the Cloisters was the closest thing to being in Europe that I had yet known.

When I was looking at a website about the Cloisters recently, I read that it was the philanthropist John D. Rockefeller, Jr. who purchased the 66.5 acres he made into Fort Tryon Park and then created the Cloisters Museum and its gardens and put together the medieval art that is the core of the

Cloisters collection and donated all of it to New York City. It was this man, John D. Rockefeller, Jr., who my taxi driver grandfather was on his way to assassinate after the Ludlow Massacre in 1914, if, in fact, that was true. What a terrible, terrible thought.

Milt was an advertising design man by occupation, but he also built things. He built a sleeping loft in their studio apartment, made possible by the high ceilings in the studio apartments of Sherwood studios. I learned from watching him build it. He also restored some of their furniture. On one piece he showed me he had just painted perfect shadows on top of the actual shadows cast from the hinges of the cabinet doors, so that when the lamp next to the cabinet was turned off the shadows were still there. He would do things like that to amuse himself. I may have been the only visitor in his apartment who ever knew about his painted shadows. Things like that fascinated me. Milt could paint trompe-l'oeil as well as any I had ever seen. His practical making ability and the pleasure he got from everything he did for himself this way opened up a whole new world that was especially meaningful to me. My mother had no practical or mechanical abilities to speak of, and though she had many artist friends, she didn't make art. She was all in her head. She knew things from books and museums and talking to people. I doubt that she had a sharp kitchen knife or that she ever sharpened a knife. I don't remember that she owned even the most basic tools like a hammer or a screwdriver. In our Sherwood Studios apartment, she had a heavy mirror of beveled glass and she hung it on the wall using a stick-on hook that was obviously only adequate to hold light weight pictures. And I don't know how many days later it was, the gummed back picture hook failed and the heavy framed mirror fell to the floor with a loud thud. Old wall paint was stuck to the hook's backing.

We hardly celebrated holidays other than Christmas throughout my childhood. Christmases were simple. A few years Peter and I had a tree we carried up from the sidewalk in front of the grocery store around the corner on Christmas Eve, no longer to be sold. We had few ornaments to hang on a tree and few presents to put under it. One year Anne brought home a roll of cotton from the drugstore for us to tear into little strips to lay on the limbs of the tree to look like snow. And though it didn't look at all like snow to me it was a sweet idea. Christine Magriel had proper Christmas parties. Those are the ones I remember, with eggnog and the warmth of spending Christmases among friends. Christine was one of my mother's closest friends through my childhood. Her two sons, Paul Magriel Jr. and Nicolas Magriel were my closest childhood friends. In those early years Peter and I used to watch television at Christine's apartment with Button and Nicky. Button was Paul's nickname. Christine would make us cheeseburgers and we would watch *The Lone Ranger* and *Hoppalong Cassidy*. The good guys in white hats and bad guys in black hats, on a black and white TV. Silver bullets, cowboys and Indians. Button went on to become a chess champion and a champion backgammon player and poker player and lived in Las Vegas. Nicolas became a master of Indian music, and lives in London.

My mother didn't host dinners. It may have been because we didn't have money enough to buy food for more than ourselves. It could also have been that among my mother's friends, such occasions weren't common. My mother could cook, though I don't remember that she ever baked a cake, or any kind of bread. In the oven, she cooked chicken and acorn squash cut in half with butter and brown sugar. She scrambled eggs. I remember frozen vegetables, and frozen orange juice that we added water to in a pitcher. Maybe my mother didn't entertain, or rarely did, because for years we didn't have a place of our own with a kitchen. And then when she rented the studio apartment at 58 West 57th Street, for a while she didn't have a table big enough or chairs enough to seat more than four. Dinner parties were not part of my life until I was with Lani and we were hosting dinners and had close friendships. It's strange to think how what is now so much a part of our lives was new to me until I was a young man.

6

STOCKBRIDGE

There were two years before high school that I was in boarding school. The first was Cheshire Academy in Connecticut and the other was Tilton School in New Hampshire, with public school in between. New England towns were vastly different from New York. They were quiet places that had a Main Street and overhead telephone and electric wires strung from pole to pole to houses. There were trees and there were lawns in front of some houses. White picket fences and rose bushes. They didn't have manhole covers emitting steam, or yellow taxicabs weaving in and out of traffic with their honking horns. They didn't have people walking fast with briefcases and they didn't have soot. On the coldest mornings going outside after a shower my hair would freeze. Snowflakes on my eyelashes. The air an opaque gray silence. Long winter months. At Cheshire one teacher's eyes were the same pale blue color as his jacket and I thought that indicated he was narcissistic, though I didn't know that word when I was 10 years old. I don't remember what he taught, just that he stood in front of us and talked with his pale blue eyes and his jacket of the same color. Another teacher used to squeeze his teabags out after lunch in the dining hall and wrap them in his paper napkin and put them in his jacket pocket. He also collected pencil stubs left behind by students. I thought that was interesting. I don't know what he taught either.

At Tilton I remember an older student lifting weights in the gym and trying to start me lifting weights. He said I should ask my mother to buy me a set of dumbbells but I knew I couldn't ask her to buy me anything that wasn't absolutely essential. I remember trying to do something on the parallel bars but I wasn't strong enough to do what some of the boys could do. I was aware of my inadequacy at things that were completely new to me. I didn't have a father to interest and encourage me in sports of any kind. That made me different from the average American boy. At schools or at summer camp I preferred to be by myself. I did a little running and a little swimming. I might have liked team sports had I been at all good at them. I didn't even know the basic rules of baseball. If there was a point in playing baseball I didn't know what it was and didn't care so long as I was left alone and could find other ways to exercise. Physical work made sense to me. I am that way still. It was at Tilton that I measured six feet tall and one hundred pounds. I remember that well. They were round numbers memorable in how they described me at that age. I could see all of my ribs in the mirror. Some of the older boys tried to get me to eat more to gain weight. I tended to eat a lot whenever there was a lot to eat because I wanted to gain weight and because we had those years when money was so scarce. I never left food on my plate. Still don't.

Anne hoped a boarding school could work some magic on me that would turn me into a little scholar. But then there was the other side of it. I saw the possibility that my mother might want to be without the chore attached to the constant everyday responsibility for raising her two sons. I saw how her life had been more neatly lived in my absence than when I was there on the fringes of her life, accepted but maybe not received the way I would have wanted. It wasn't an easy childhood, though at times it was very interesting because when I was with my mother and her friends, her artist friends in particular, that was good.

When I was a little older, a couple of summers I was at Grace Church Camp outside the city where boys could enjoy swimming and canoeing and making lanyards of plastic gimp. Making lanyards out of colored gimp was obviously a wonderfully meaningful skill to be taught. Just kidding. I was a good swimmer. There was one boy who the others thought was the best swimmer at the camp. And I could see he thought that himself. One day there was a swim meet with kids from another camp and he and I were paired off. He swam the first lap under water. I could see him beneath me like a blurred shadow of myself, both doing the breast stroke as though intentionally in unison. I beat him by a few seconds, my hand touching the wood at the far end of the swimming crib just before his touched. And I remember how the boys were surprised because I was the skinny kid who wasn't interested in sports.

I liked the nature classes. Animals always interested me. I liked canoeing. I learned to control a canoe well, and how to empty most of the water from within a capsized aluminum canoe by thrusting it nose first down under the water so it would come back up and right itself with some of the water already sloshed out into the lake and then grasping a gunwale in both hands from outside forcing it to rock from side to side splashing most of the remaining water out with each thrust, a bit at a time. Then we could climb back into the canoe and it would stay afloat. I liked learning survival skills when I was a kid, never having been a scout.

A few years earlier I had seen a poster that showed a row of boys from Cub Scout through Eagle Scout and to me their uniforms looked like Army uniforms and I wanted nothing to do with that. I knew from newsreels what war was like and I hated it. Movie house newsreels showed the Korean War and I remember seeing soldiers using flame throwers to burn huts and that scared me.

* * *

For my ninth grade, Anne enrolled me in the Stockbridge School in western Massachusetts, and as it was with the other boarding schools, with a scholarship based on financial need and my mother's ability to charm people. Stockbridge School was founded by Hans Maeder and based on global humanitarian ideals. It was unusual among boarding schools in the 1950s for being coeducational and having an international and interracial faculty and student body. And it was established with what seemed to be a new concept that had students doing the work that in other schools was done by employees. We did the setting of tables and the bringing out of meals in the dining room, the clearing of tables and the dish-washing. We pushed sweeping compound made of sawdust impregnated with green wax across classroom and hallway floors with wide brooms. We collected trash from the various buildings and drove it to the dump in a big old pickup truck. Every morning before breakfast and all morning on Saturdays we had our various assigned weekly rotating jobs to do. Dining room and dish-washing, unlike the others, were done three times a day.

The United Nations flag was hung under the American flag in front of the school, and raising the flags before breakfast and taking them down at sunset was one of the jobs we had. I still remember two of us fumbling to hook the metal clips into the grommets on the flags and raising the flags to the top of the flagpole with fingers numb, almost frozen on some of the coldest mornings of a New England winter.

Bill Coperthwaite was a teacher at Stockbridge School for the first of my three years there, and he was the second of the three men that years later I came to think of as my surrogate fathers. Although Hans Maeder and Bill didn't agree on educational approaches and Bill only stayed that one year before moving on to teach at Quaker schools, he and I remained close friends from that year until he died in 2013.

Bill taught biology and a class in geography he called Map. And he ran the woodworking shop, and he had informal Sunday afternoon gatherings with a few of us who were interested at which he would read from the writings of Kahlil Gibran and Gandhi, among others, and we would discuss non-violence and his ideas regarding work and life. As a conscientious objector, Bill had done community service with village people building houses in Mexico before he taught at Stockbridge School. And as an alternative to the school's organized sports, Bill led a group of students in clearing dead trees and underbrush and thinning the healthy trees in the woods behind the school. There was a significant difference in the work Bill did with us from the usual assigned jobs. For one thing, Bill worked side by side with students on his volunteer woods crew.

With Bill, work was a privilege and it was something we enjoyed and took pride in. I was glad to have spent three years in a high school where work other than our studies was part of our education. Bill's teaching was a crossing of disciplines, interrelating ideas and enhancing the ideas through practice, which meant figuring out solutions to actual problems and working with one's hands. Bill treated me as an equal in that he had respect for what I might think or do. It didn't matter to him that I was a boy with little experience in the things he knew. That respect was very important to me.

During my three years at Stockbridge, I started to catch up with classmates in my studies in spite of being a slow reader with an easily distracted mind that made studying more difficult than pleasurable most of the time. I was still reading at the speed of the spoken word, hearing the words in my head as I read them and all too often not listening to those words that I heard in my head while I would read. My thoughts would wander to somewhere else. I smiled when I recently read that William Butler Yeats wrote in his *Autobiographies, Memories and Reflections*, "Because I had found it hard to attend to anything less interesting than my thoughts, I was difficult to teach." Like me, Yeats had not learned to read until after the age most children could read, but that did not deter him from becoming one of the most celebrated Irish poets and playwrights.

Having become aware of my poor reading ability, a new teacher took it upon himself to try to help me to read more easily and to concentrate better on what I was reading. If my reading problems were due to being somewhat dyslexic, as I suspect was the case, dyslexia wasn't well recognized in those years. A kid was thought to be bright or to be stupid, to whatever degree, and distracted boys did as well as they could. I should have appreciated that young man's offer to help me, but the book he chose to read together was Shakespeare's play, *Titus Andronicus*. And it reads like this:

> Romans, friends, followers, favorers of my right,
> If ever Bassianus, Caesar's son,
> Were gracious in the eyes of royal Rome,
> Keep then this passage to the Capitol

> And suffer not dishonour to approach
> The imperial seat, to virtue consecrate,
> To justice, continence and nobility;
> But let desert in pure election shine,
> And, Romans, fight for freedom in your choice.

It goes on that way for 320 pages and is violent and bloody and convoluted. I remember only that I couldn't make sense of names and an antiquated language in a story that didn't feel relevant or interesting to me, and I let go what might have been a good opportunity to be helped with my reading problems.

Embedded in my memory ever since reading Chaucer's *Canterbury Tales* later that year are the beginning words: "Whan that Aprille with his shoures soote, The droghte of March hath perced to the roote..." I liked the musicality of the Middle English. And mis-pronounced as I had them, the sound of those words would play in my mind unexpectedly every now and then, even until today. Another piece of our reading that does that for me is "Wee, sleekit, cow'rin, tim'rous beastie..." from a Robert Burns poem that was given to us as an example of onomatopoeia.

Our English teacher was Bill McCue, a flamboyant one-armed man whose passion about writing enlivened any discussions we had. I remember that he would throw pieces of chalk at students if they were talking to one another and not paying attention. And he would read with different voices according to whose voice it was in a book. I don't know if any of us ever found out how he lost his arm. We had a math teacher who didn't seem to know how math might be taught better to those of us who found it hard to understand. And he couldn't see that we might never have a reason to use algebra. I would have liked to have been taught the basic concepts and logical structure of mathematics at some point in my schooling so I might be better able to do what I would need to do with numbers in school and later in life. I liked Alex Perkins because he was able to explain, in his elegant English accent, how history was about those who did and those who didn't have wealth and power, and how history could be understood in terms of people, place, and work. He made interesting and meaningful a subject that history teachers in my earlier years presented as names of events and their dates to be memorized and tested on.

I was becoming less shy, and my three years at Stockbridge were long enough for me to make lasting friendships. Those were the years when boys were thinking about girls and about sexuality for the first time in any real sense. We talked among ourselves about losing our virginity, and my roommate Sam did lose his virginity with one of the girls one night in our boy's dormitory. I was there on the other side of the small room, politely pretending to be sound asleep.

Unfulfilled dreams and desires were always among us, overshadowing the things we were meant to be doing. I can remember being besotted with one girl who was cute beyond belief. She had a boyfriend and all I could do was to try my best to contain my feelings. I did have a few innocent boyfriend/girlfriend relationships, but they weren't very meaningful.

Saturday afternoons we could go to Lenox or Pittsfield if we wanted to. They were outings that broke the monotony of weeks of more or less repeated uneventful days. Sometimes there would be too many of us to find a seat on our yellow school bus and I might have a girl sit on my lap. I look back on my memory of those trips and smile at the thought of how much I liked having a girl sit on my lap on the bus. I liked that I didn't have to ask a girl if she would like to sit on my lap because it was simply how we filled the bus for short trips. I liked that who it might be who would sit on my lap was left to chance and it might be a girl who wasn't in any of my classes, who I had barely known.

I sometimes went to the Goodwill Industries Thrift Store in Pittsfield. Those were my first thrift store shopping experiences. I bought a pair of leather riding boots one time. And I bought a hand-knit sleeveless sweater that was quite unlike any I had seen before or since. Laid flat it was a simple rectangle with a half square neck hole. The stitching that held front to back ended part way up the sides to allow for the armholes. It had to be something knit by a beginner who hadn't yet learned to knit curves. But I liked that it looked a little like chainmail with its horizontal rows of knots. I also had a long and heavy fur coat that I have no memory of how I obtained. It was a man's coat that I thought of as a Jack London *Call of the Wild* coat.

One exceedingly cold winter day while I was walking in the woods behind the school wearing my heavy fur coat and riding boots and enjoying feeling like someone other than myself in some other time and place, I encountered my Austrian roommate who also happened to be walking alone in the woods. And then we talked as we walked together. But it was hard to form the sounds of some words because of the extreme cold. We sounded like two bumbling fools. So for fun, we devised a sentence we thought would be the hardest to say. I still remember it was "Where were we when we were wet Wheaties?" We could slowly barely speak it. We laughed at our silliness. Misha spoke German, French, and English fluently, and at home in Austria he had learned to ski and to ride horses well, and for those things I admired him.

Those were three years in which winter seemed too long. There were many, too many weeks of gray, below freezing weather and not a lot to differentiate one from the others. One late night Pieter Ostrander and Sam Annino and I walked off from the school along the small road in the dark. We ducked behind a thicket of bushes when we saw approaching headlights. After a few miles we were no longer hiding from the occasional drivers on the road and we were stopped by someone who guessed we were from the school and brought us back. That resulted in Pieter and Sam being sent home for a couple of weeks, but because my mother was in Moscow at the time, I wasn't sent home. I was only reprimanded by Hans Maeder in his office, which I didn't like. I thought Hans's concerns were more about how to instill within students his ideals of moral and social behavior to right the wrongs in a troubled world than how to understand and deal with the emotional problems of the adolescent kids in his care, and I thought he could have been less rigid.

After a holiday break, one boy brought back a box of oranges that he had injected with vodka which I thought was quite clever. Sam added sugar to a gallon jug of fresh apple cider he bought on an outing to the agricultural fair in Great Barrington. Knowing that the fermentation would cause a build up of pressure he kept it uncapped under his bed, but a few days later it overflowed bubbly and fermented onto the floor. Once I saw Sam swig the near pure alcohol of Acqua Velva aftershave. What we were doing on those occasions was escaping from the confines of what was allowed and what was expected of us. We were aware that such pranks were common among boarding school kids anywhere and were part of a tradition that we wanted to partake in ourselves. We wanted the challenge of doing something that might be a little dangerous and in some ways risky. We wanted to be free the way we might be a few years later when we would no longer be high school students.

I worked with Sam one summer renovating a house in Springfield, Massachusetts that his mother had bought to rent as two apartments. Sam was from Springfield and knew other kids from before Stockbridge, so sometimes we got together with them at the end of the day at fast food drive-in parking lots. I felt like an outsider in small town America where kids drove cars and congregated in such places after dark because they were the places that weren't their parents' homes. Sam had a red Jeep he kept at his mother's house during the school year. Growing up in the city, I didn't learn to drive until way past the age most people learned. I wasn't like other boys who could look at any car and know its name and make and year and know what kind of engine it had under its hood. I got my first driver's license when I was at the American Academy in Rome at the age of twenty-eight.

Other summers I spent in New York, except for one when I was at the Jerry Farnsworth School of Art in North Truro, on Cape Cod. Farnsworth took me on as a monitor doing odd jobs like sweeping the floors and stretching canvases for the students in exchange for having a little bed lofted above one end of the studio. I liked having a job that gave me responsibility and I found it exciting that I was sleeping there on my own when no one else was in the school at night. No parent, no roommate. Some evenings I babysat for one of the student's two little girls while she worked nearby as a waitress. At sixteen I was by far the youngest student in the school. It was the first time

I painted in oils working from still life and from models. I had a borrowed bicycle and sometimes I bicycled to Provincetown. More often I bicycled to the oceanside to walk along the beach. I loved having my toes in the sand and the wind in my hair and looking out at the sea and dreaming of things I have no memory of anymore.

Pieter and Sam were my closest friends at Stockbridge. When Pieter and I were in New York during school vacations, sometimes we would go to the Five Spot Café where Thelonious Monk and Ornette Coleman performed. Pieter already played jazz trumpet and he went on to Juilliard to study music composition while I was at Cooper Union. After high school I would see Pieter more often than Sam because Pieter was then married and had an apartment on the Upper West Side and Sam was back in Springfield working.

Years later, Sam visited me when I was teaching in Washington and I saw that he had become seriously alcoholic and seemed to be depressed and needy. I thought it likely that his military experiences could have changed him in ways that he might do harm to himself or to his friends and that worried me, being a very real possibility for any of our generation who had served in Vietnam. And after that I didn't see Sam again until we were at a reunion at Stockbridge School many years later. It was the only school reunion I have ever gone to. I was in New York for an exhibition opening after having moved to Italy, and had been told about the reunion and thought it might be fun to see Stockbridge School again for what nostalgic memories a visit might conjure up. I was able to join a few former classmates who were driving there from the city. We were older than our parents had been when we were Stockbridge students. That was strange. Being at the reunion was difficult for me because I saw that Sam seemed to have sunken still deeper into drink and depression. He had not been teaching as he had hoped to do after getting a masters degree in art from Pratt Institute in Brooklyn. The war and whatever addictions Sam had succumbed to had destroyed what promise he had of making a better life for himself.

On the other hand, seeing Pieter again at the reunion was strangely fascinating. Almost without even saying hello, Pieter started to talk to me about aesthetics, as though we had left an ongoing conversation in mid-sentence a few minutes earlier. Pieter was fine. He seemed himself other than having lost the beautiful boy quality he had when we were younger. He and Belle had divorced and he was then married to a lovely Irish girl, and he was still involved in music.

At the end of my first Stockbridge year, Bill Coperthwaite stayed a couple of nights at my mother's 57th Street studio apartment in New York on his way to Venezuela. And he discussed with me and with my mother the idea of taking me out of school to travel in Europe with him. We would learn together all kinds of things firsthand. This was the kind of education Bill understood to be the most effective and would have been very exciting for me. But my mother believed it best for me to stay in school and then go to a good college and on to graduate school and to a career of some kind. Following that conversation, in talking to me, Anne started to refer to Bill as Saint Coperthwaite. I don't know how my mother could not have seen what that said to me about her own lack of devotion to my well-being. It wasn't that she didn't have time to be teaching me because she had to work for a living. I understood that, but rather that she could not comprehend, and she said so, why any man would choose to take on the education of someone else's child singlehandedly, and not as a paid job.

Bill's convictions about education needing to be challenging and meaningful by means of direct experience rather than through the inactivity of the traditional classroom fit beautifully with who I had always been. I knew that I was not the kind of boy who would become a scholar, and I had always been fidgety and restless when not trying to keep from dozing off.

A few years after I first knew Bill, I joined him in exploring the coast of Maine looking for a piece of land he might buy on which to settle and reshape according to his concepts, which would eventually grow to be the Yurt Foundation, set up for educational purposes. Together we took small ferryboats out to the islands with the interesting names of Vinalhaven, Matinicus, Wooden Ball, and Seal. I liked the deep throated sound of the boats' engines and the smell of diesel fuel coupled with that of the sea air.

From one of the islands Bill borrowed a rowboat to explore Hurricane Island. We were watching great blue herons, loons, seagulls, and the occasional seal that would raise its head above the surface of the water to look at us as we rowed. We were conversing, and listening to water dripping from oars in a world without people, as far from New York City life as I had ever been. Bill would sing as we walked and canoed or rowed during my visits to his native coastal Maine.

Bill was a maker of furniture and dwellings, using hand tools he collected, and tools he made himself, working with techniques he adapted from where the use of hand tools and traditional techniques had not yet been lost. He learned an ancient kind of knitting he playfully called witless knitting. He learned from Scandinavian knife makers how to make fine knives. He learned to make Windsor chairs using a pole lathe to shape the legs. He learned how to work with a drawknife and a shaving horse.

Bill was often whittling wooden spoons and making wooden bowls and plates when he visited us, using a curved knife he made after learning from Inuit craftsmen how they worked wood with curved knives. Bill was always trying to improve on the design of hand tools and hand-made dwellings and furniture, and after some years teaching at Quaker schools, he shared his knowledge through teaching workshops in which he also discussed his beliefs about social change and the problems he saw as counter to the working of a healthy society. Bill's strong moral code came out of Gandhi's writings and example, and from personally knowing Scott and Helen Nearing who, like Bill, had dedicated their lives to sustainable and simple living and concerns about humanity as a whole. Bill brought Richard Gregg to Stockbridge school to talk to students about the concept of nonviolent resistance Gregg had learned while knowing Gandhi in India.

I gained from Bill a self-reliance that came to me naturally. His world made sense because it was uncomplicated and I could see how one could live a life true to one's beliefs and be in almost complete control of everything day to day. But I was destined to be a painter whose life would be a mix of Bill's way of living and another that was about the making of art. Bill's making of things was function based, about design and how what we live with could be shaped by our own hands for personal use. His book, published in 2007 called *A Handmade Life: In Search of Simplicity*, is filled with photographs of his world and passages of his writing. The making of paintings is another kind of concern for design and beauty. In one way of thinking, the paintings I was making weren't utilitarian, and therefore they could be absent from a person's life. But to the artist, art is as necessary as shelter and food.

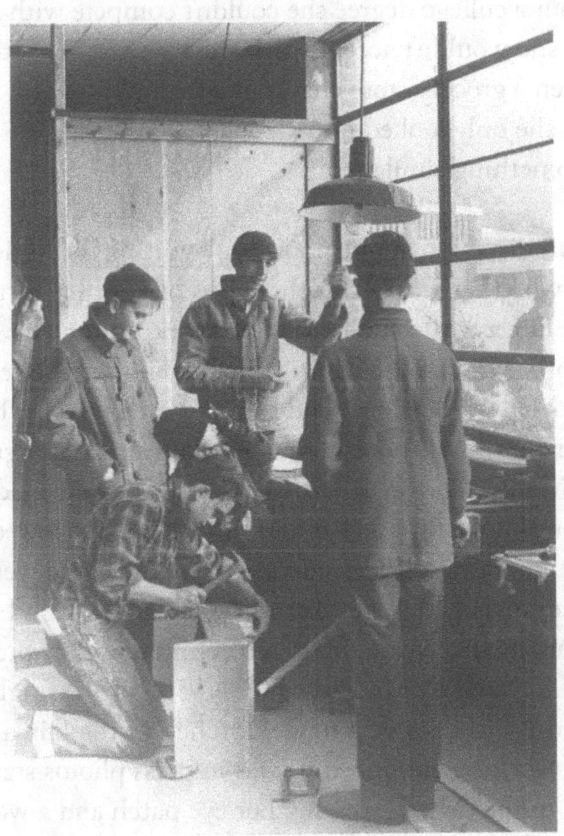

Stockbridge School, 1959

***

To be sure, the bitterness and hatred for Randy my mother held onto all through her life was more damaging to me than the poverty we experienced those years after they separated when I was six. Yes, she did sacrifice. She made sure we had food enough to eat. She looked for work and held jobs of one or another kind for periods, not being free to pursue a creative career that she would have liked but that might not bring in money enough to support a family. Only I didn't think of that as sacrificing; it was what we do for our children out of love and it is the responsibility that comes with having children. Pure and simple. Or not simple, but a basic given. As a woman without a college degree she couldn't compete with men who had degrees. And she wouldn't accept work she deemed beneath herself. She could have been a grocery store checkout person, I thought, how hard was that? But, no, she only looked for work that would use her skills in public relations or something similar.

She had a short-lived job at one point copy writing for Maidenform bras. I don't know why that was better than jobs of another sort, but she had her thinking. For a while she kept a job working for The Indian Trade Center promoting Indian textiles in American markets. She was involved in promoting Madras bleeding plaid summer men's wear, which had been made popular in one of those genius marketing campaigns that made the fact that Madras cotton wasn't colorfast into what made it uniquely desirable. I don't know if it was her idea or if she just followed a marketing campaign already initiated by someone else. And there were short term jobs my mother managed to get like when she and a friend teamed up to sponsor a company that made the stereo equipment they presented at the US Trade and Cultural Fair in Moscow in 1959. She was right there when Nixon debated Krushchev in a model kitchen at the fair, a spontaneous event that got world attention. Anne was in press photos standing among men listening to the debate, wearing her eye patch and a woolen suit she had designed and sewn herself, holding her portable tape recorder. She told me the battery in the tape recorder was losing power and the technician with her thought what it had recorded of the debate was so poor in quality it was useless, or he thought it would be counterproductive to the interests of the company Anne and her friend were representing if it was shared in any way, so he erased what was on the tape. Because the debate wasn't planned to happen, none of the others present had a recording apparatus, so my mother's had been the only recording.

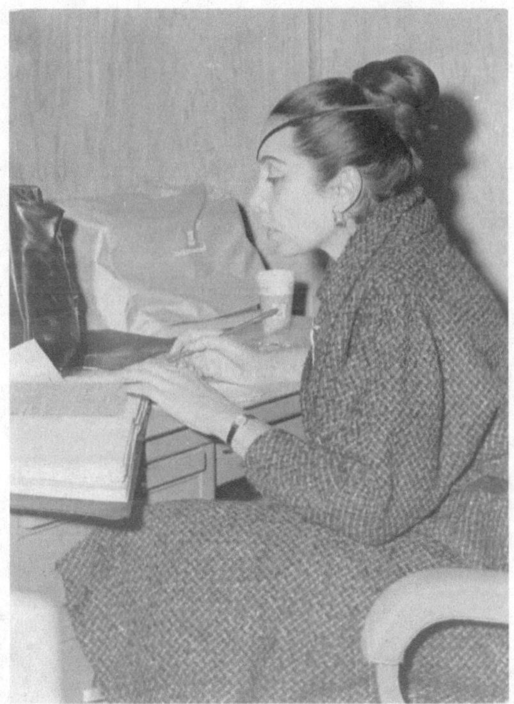

Anne in Moscow, 1959

EUROPE AT AGE SEVENTEEN

In 1960 my mother took me with her for the summer in Greece and the academic year in Italy, where she enrolled me in the Overseas School of Rome for my senior year of high school. My brother had dropped out of high school and was already living with roommates when he was eighteen and Anne didn't invite him to go with us to Europe. Peter didn't have a chance with Anne in his adolescent years or anytime later. She saw him as being like our father and there was nothing Peter could do to change that. My assumption is that if he was like our father, she might have been more to blame for that than she could accept. That Peter and I survived as well as we did was chance. It could have gone more wrong so easily. Or am I over-dramatizing in self pity? I can't tell. But I know that if Anne could look down from her afterlife and see what I just wrote, she would once again call me pitiful and stupid. And that, itself, would confirm that what I am writing has a lot of truth in it.

Anne was able to manage our travels with what money she had from her Moscow trip the previous year. She found someone to sublet our 57th Street studio apartment, we packed our bags, and she and I sailed fourteen days, from Brooklyn to Piraeus on a small Greek freighter named after the ancient Greek poet Pindar. The *Pindar* normally didn't take passengers and we were the only ones. My mother's cabin had a little sign above the door saying Owner's Suite, and over my cabin door the little sign said Two Cadets. We had our meals with the officers, separate from the crew members who slept below.

My mother had a brief affair with the young and handsome ship's steward who she described to her friends in the letter she typed during the voyage as looking like a Greek god. One night a crew member from below tried awkwardly to get into her cabin through the porthole onto the deck, and she scared him off with frantic reprimands in English before he was more than half-way into her cabin. In her ongoing letter she called that one "The Villain." We had meals with the twelve officers that included the captain, a radio man, and the Greek god. I don't remember who the other officers were. Probably they spoke no English. Of conversations during meals I only remember that the captain was concerned with the laundry getting dirtied by the smoke from the smokestack. I liked the transatlantic crossing with the vast open seas under our small ship.

In Athens we stayed briefly at the elegant Excelsior Hotel so that our heavy bags could be left there while we spent the summer traveling about exploring Greece. I loved the Bouzouki music and Retsina wine of tavernas, where men often danced by themselves or together in small numbers. I liked the sound of a language I couldn't begin to understand, written or spoken, and I liked the whitewashed towns and blue seas.

Anne attached herself first to a Norwegian man named Axel, and then to a young German man whose name I can't remember, and then to a very nice, very handsome Greek dancer named Giorgos Emirzas, who traveled with us for a while. I liked Giorgos. The only part of that summer that was not wonderful for me was that I was still the silent, shy boy tagging along behind his mother. I wanted to go off on my own but that wasn't a possibility. I was lonely for someone more my age and I wasn't entirely interested in Greek antiquities. After some weeks exploring the Peloponnesus and the islands, we returned to Athens, where we were again in the Excelsior Hotel to collect our baggage before heading for Italy. Our last evenings in Athens we went to tavernas with a little group of young people. There was an Australian boy they called Stralia and a beautiful androgynous Finnish boy with yellow hair and a few other boys I don't remember. And there was a very beautiful girl from New York named Susan Brockman. All of them were older than me and in my shyness I barely talked to any of them, though I wanted very much to know them. But I told Susan that we were about to go to Venice and then to Rome where I was going to be at the Overseas School of Rome. And in a day or so we were off to Italy.

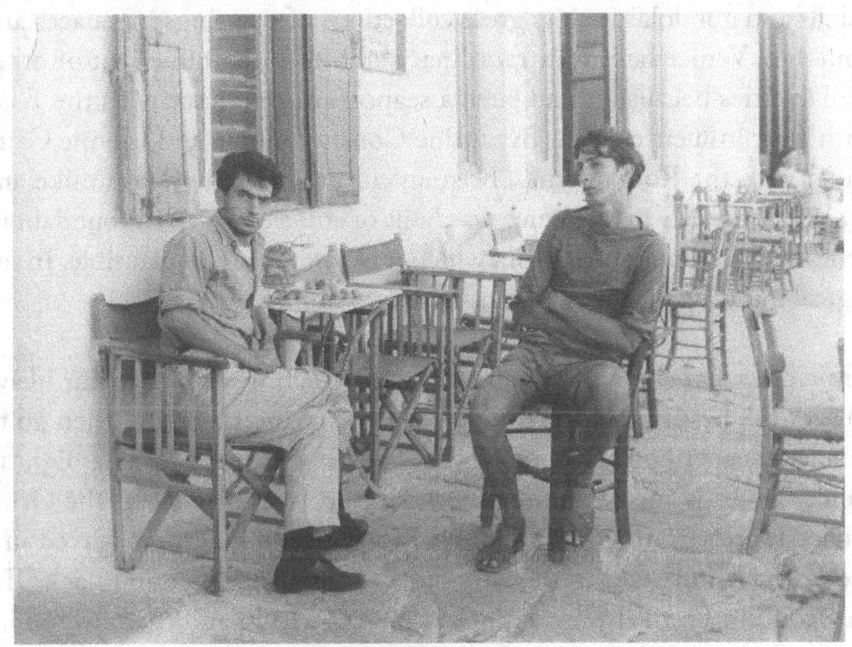

With Giorgos Emirzas, Greece, 1960

In mid-August we sailed on an Egyptian passenger ship from Piraeus to Venice. My only clear memory of that voyage is that there was a passenger I thought of as being like a character placed among us to add an element of interest to an ambiance that would otherwise not have been what I would think of as an ambiance at all. If that makes any sense. The ship itself was undistinguished, and nothing but open seas and grayness beyond it could turn one's thoughts to being elsewhere, in memory or in anticipation. He was a white-haired man who stayed always by himself and had the unkempt appearance of someone who has no friends and wouldn't like to meet anyone. I saw him a few times sitting alone making notes in a large book whose cover had a volume number on it under the single word PROBABILITIES.

The pages were written by hand. It was a book in progress that I guessed was the obsession of a recluse intent on discovering something important.

And then we were in Venice. I loved Venice. Venice was a city that truly sparkled. It was all sun reflecting off water, totally magical with its canals and gondolas and its great collections of paintings in palaces and churches. Venice has an extraordinary architecture unlike that of other Italian cities because it had been a seaport in commerce with the East, with clear influences from Byzantine Constantinople and Islamic Cairo along with the Roman and Christian cultures of Italy. And unlike any other city in the world, Venice was built of stone on wooden foundations beneath the waters of a lagoon, which was completely implausible. In my logical mind, Venice was a fantastic impossibility.

Anne did what she had done in Athens, which was to leave our heavy bags at the best hotel after a night or two staying there and then go to smaller cheaper hotels for a few weeks before returning for one night to collect the bags and depart for another place. In Venice it was the Gritti Palace Hotel, from which we moved to the Lido where we stayed in a modest pensione taking the vaporetto to Venice proper and back. The Venice Film Festival was taking place on the Lido and there were film stars and paparazzi around us. I liked the paintings I was seeing by Vittore Carpaccio, Gentile and Giovanni Bellini, Andrea Mantegna, Tiepolo and Tintoretto, and those by Canaletto and Guardi. But it was Venice itself that was most captivating. To be in Piazza San Marco with the music from the little orchestra in front of Caffè Florian was like being in the Venice of Visconti's film *Death in Venice*, based on the Thomas Mann novel of 1912. Although I was there that first time ten years before *Death in Venice* was filmed, my memories of Venice back in 1960 are about how I saw Venice and how it was portrayed in that beautiful film, which is set in 1911. In looking back to then, and to any subsequent visit, it is the romanticism of the place that I loved at that time and that I still love. Only now I don't want to go back to Venice while enormous cruise ships loom over the city and the streets are overcrowded with the tourists that those ships spill out every day.

One evening I was by myself on the Lido and I sat down in an outdoor café that had tables next to a dance floor with live music. Couples were dancing slowly under lights strung across the piazzetta. The sea was within a stone's throw. I wanted to dance with a young woman who was sitting alone at another table. I wanted to be able to touch a woman, to have her look at me, even if for a moment. So I asked her in English, not knowing what language she spoke, if she wanted to dance. She didn't answer. She didn't look up at me. We were two lonely souls, afraid to do something that would have been nice. She couldn't have known that I didn't know how to dance. She could have asked if I wanted to sit with her, but she didn't. In my mind, looking back and remembering my loneliness on such an occasion, I might let the possibilities that didn't happen become imagined scenarios of something beautiful.

We stayed three weeks on the Lido and then we were in Rome to stay until June. Rome was a wonderful place to be as a seventeen-year-old boy. I was happy wandering the streets by myself, exploring and discovering things new to me. I saw how ancient Romans were magnificent engineers and builders. And what they learned from the Greeks, they changed as it became Roman. The arch barely existed in ancient Greece. I had seen only one Greek arch in a photo in an art history book, as though it had been made by mistake and was never repeated. In addition to the arch, the Romans made the vault and the dome, neither of which had existed in Greece, and they invented concrete to hold together stone and brick, allowing for greater spans with more grand interior spaces. They made aqueducts with courses of arches, smaller ones on top of larger ones, three or four high extending for miles and engineered perfectly to supply Rome's water. I was intrigued by how in Rome the layering of centuries and cultures exists in a place where history is experienced as a continuum, very unselfconscious and alive. The art I knew from my childhood in the Metropolitan Museum was everywhere in churches and palaces and in streets and piazzas without the artful presentation of curatorial expertise. I loved how in Rome the sky would darken in the rainy season and then the sun would poke through and turn the earth reds and yellows of buildings golden against a backdrop of dark slate gray.

Ancient ruins have always seemed very romantic. The reason must have to do with how old they are and from thoughts about what life would have been like before whatever it was that brought the civilization that created them to an end. Some Roman buildings suffered from the pillaging of Christians stealing marble to incorporate into their churches in what was a disregard for the Roman structures and a total disrespect for the civilization that made them, in spite of how advanced that civilization had been. But those churches are very beautiful too. I loved their marble floors that had circles of different colors of stone surrounded by curving bands of geometric pattern. Rome was a place of temples and great baths and commemorative columns telling their stories in carved stone relief that spiraled around them from bottom to top. I saw stones with pieces of Latin inscriptions and fragments of statues that are part of courtyard walls along with marble sarcophagi made into fountains to water horses, now used for washing cars and for the watering of potted plants. I particularly liked the Baroque church facades with their curving, curling architectural forms that I hadn't seen before, and the Baroque statues on the Ponte Sant'Angelo I could see from the windows of the apartment I first stayed in. I walked into every church I passed because, more likely than not, it housed great paintings and sculptures and each church had an atmosphere of diffused daylight and the flicker and smell of candles burning under statues of saints and of the Virgin, or the scent of incense. They were places where I could sit for a while and let my mind wander in quiet, and find shelter from heat or cold or rain. On the streets outside was the bustle of people and markets and very small cars and scooters weaving in and out of traffic madly disorganized, or organized but in ways unfamiliar to a boy who grew up in Midtown Manhattan, where streets are parallel and numbered according to a master plan. I loved all of it.

One academic year at the school in Rome was not enough time for me to make friends with classmates. I liked some of my teachers. Miss Mitrani taught history through the history of Italian art, and what she taught worked hand in hand with my solitary explorations of the city when I was not in class. I liked my English teacher with her soft southern accent and blond curly hair, who I fantasized as my lover. Probably she had no idea of any of that, but it made the year more interesting for me. I passed the months drawing on the brown paper covers I put on my books, my mind wandering in and out of what was being taught. I remember the words SAT CLAW carved into the top of a desk in one classroom. Those two words intrigued me because I had no idea what they meant, or why some kid had carved them into a desktop, and into my memory for all these years.

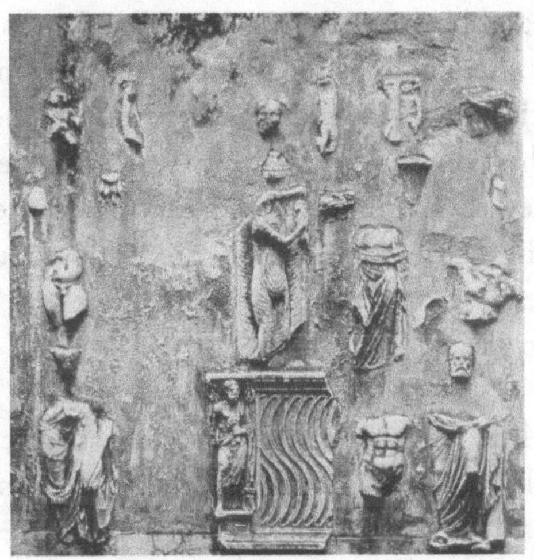

A courtyard wall in a street in Rome

There was the one brief but beautiful relationship I had with Susan Brockman who took a taxi from Rome out Via Cassia beyond the city to find me at the Overseas School after we had barely known each other in Athens a month before. Susan was a few years older than me. She had already finished college and had been working on a film in Greece researching costumes when we met. She was my first lover. I was too young and she was on her way back to New York so it was not meant to last more than a few days. Anne had flown back to New York to sort out the situation with my brother, who was in hospital after an appendix operation gone bad. I loved the experience of losing my virginity with so beautiful a girl in her pensione room on Via Gregoriana, off the top of the Spanish Steps, in so romantic a city. The little pensione was across the street from the facade of

Palazzo Zuccari whose windows and doorway are the mouths of gigantic grotesque faces. The palazzo was built in 1590 for a painter named Federico Zuccari. I have never been inside where that painter frescoed the downstairs rooms, but when I see that very unusual facade it brings back memories of being there with Susan when I was a boy of seventeen.

I loved the Spanish Steps for their Baroque grandeur and I was fascinated by the Fontana della Barcaccia at the bottom of the Spanish Steps, made by Pietro Bernini and his more famous son, Gian Lorenzo Bernini, in the form of a boat, but instead of floating on water, the boat and its surroundings are both filled with water. It was designed to commemorate the flood of Rome in 1598 when boats were the only way to move about, and after the waters subsided there remained a small boat in the piazza, far from the Tiber from where it had come. I only recently understood what that beautiful boat filled with water, spouting its water into the water around it, was supposed to mean.

Preferring things having that kind of strangeness to remain mysterious, I tended not to ask for explanations. I was never the scholar interested in researching things. It is the way light falls on surfaces, on carved stones and on stones worn smooth from the sliding of feet or from the wheels and then the tires of vehicles, that I might be interested in. And those things aren't the material history books discuss. It was enough to know that such things were there for centuries and whatever their story, they were part of the lives of the common people who didn't feature in the writing that research concerns itself with. What is the poetry of life if not a slowing down of time to see what something really looks like, and how that has meaning? It isn't that time is slowed down, for that is an impossibility, but that my mind is allowed to become quiet so that I can better notice what is there in front of me, or surrounding me, and not miss it entirely.

A few blocks from Piazza di Spagna, on Via del Babuino, there is an even more peculiar fountain. An ancient statue of Silenus was moved there and made part of a fountain in 1571. The marble statue has always been seen as a grotesque looking figure by anyone not knowing that he was supposed to be the mythological half man, half goat, old satyr god of drunkenness. His body simply looked deformed and ugly to most people, being covered in fur, that to me looked like moss that had covered him up to his neck. His face is that of an old man, never meant to be beautiful. The statue had long been called *il Babuino*, the baboon, and for that the street's name changed from Via Paolina Trifana to Via del Babuino. I didn't know any of that history. To me, that strangely ugly figure of an old man reclining on rocks that fed water into a rectangular basin oddly situated on a fairly narrow street in the center of Rome was just another of those unexplained strangenesses that I liked in a city that had so many stories and so many mysteries. I loved the incongruity of things I was finding in Rome.

I sent my Stockbridge School friend, Pieter Ostrander, a leaf from one of the big trees that lined the Lungotevere along the Tiber River. Pieter wrote back to me that he didn't know what to do with the leaf, but because it was from the trees along the Tiber and I had sent it to him, he chopped it up and ate it in an omelet. I bought Pieter a trumpet at the Sunday Porta Portese flea market. It was unlike the typical trumpet in form, looking something like a cross between a trumpet and a French horn. I sent it back to New York with Susan to give to Pieter, who played trumpet.

I learned some years later that Susan lived with Willem de Kooning through the 1960s. I saw her again only twice, only for a few minutes each time. The first time was when she was with de Kooning at the Porta Portese market in 1970, during my time at the American Academy in Rome, ten years after I knew her, and the other time was many years later when she came to one of my openings at Forum Gallery in New York when I was already living in Italy with Lani and our two boys. It would have been in the 1990s. I will never forget Susan. She will always live in my most treasured nostalgic memories.

* * *

I had a room in the apartment of an Italian family while Anne was back in New York seeing what was happening with my brother in the hospital in the same few days that I bought the trumpet at Porta Portese and when I was with Susan Brockman. The family had a connection to a teacher at the Overseas School and staying with them until Anne came back to Rome was suggested by the school. The couple had two very beautiful daughters. The older of the two, as the very proper English Overseas School teacher explained to us when she was arranging for my stay with the family, was preparing for holy matrimony. I don't think I had ever heard the term holy matrimony.

A day or two before my mother came back to Rome, I found us a room in a little hotel near Piazza del Popolo close to the Babuino fountain. I remember seeing the hotel desk clerk put two telephone receivers together on a shelf, the earpiece of one to the mouthpiece of the other to let an outside call be connected to the house phone in a room upstairs, and how clever and how antiquated that seemed.

Then, for the rest of the school year, my mother and I stayed in an apartment on Piazza Mazzini. I remember a long hallway and a small corner living room with a stained-glass window having a peacock design. The Marchesa widow who rented us her apartment secretly lived in a room just off the entry space within the apartment. I discovered that she used our bathroom late at night. She had framed photographs of her late Carabiniere husband in full uniform on the walls. The building's stairwell that wound around a caged elevator, typical of European elevator staircases, had a strange smell to it that I rather liked. I can't quite remember the smell to describe it. Maybe sour and damp at the same time. Always there. In my mind, it seemed to be the smell of a woman's sexuality. Because my mother didn't say anything about it, I figured my idea of what it was like was unrealistic. She would have talked about it if it was like the smell of a woman's sexuality. She would have complained to someone about it. But for me it was an interesting suggestion every time I was on the stairs or in the elevator. Perhaps for me that smell had acted the way pheromones act in nature. A strangely unlikely idea I have had.

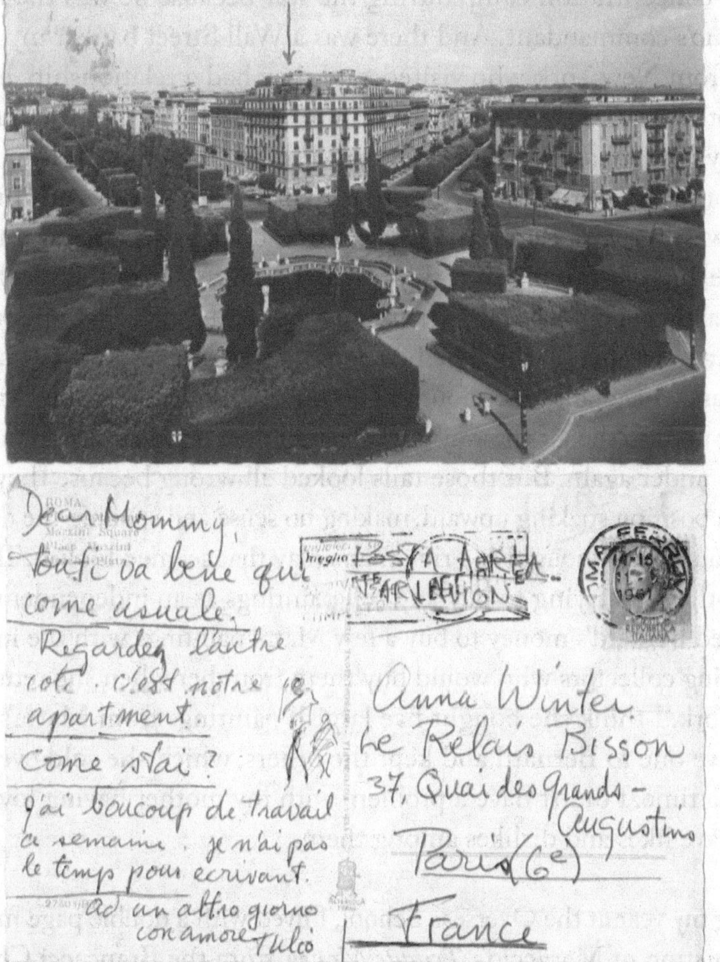

A postcard I sent Anne, telling her about the Marchesa's apartment I'd found
on Piazza Mazzini, which I highlighted in blue pencil, 1961

Anne made new friends in Rome easily. At an opening at Gallery 88, on
Via Margutta, she met a very good abstract painter named Alberto Sartoris,
and they became lovers. It was his opening we went to. I liked Sartoris
and I liked his paintings very much. I can remember one other Italian
lover my mother had that year who I did not like at all. And what little I
knew of that man's paintings I also didn't like. They were dark paintings

in every sense. He was the man who told my mother he had survived in a Nazi concentration camp during the war because he was the lover of the camp's commandant. And there was a Wall Street banker my mother knew from New York who visited, and they had a relationship. He took my mother to Capri for a few days, and they took me with them to Paris over my Christmas vacation. He was nice, but I thought he was too unlike my mother in every way for her to stay in a relationship with him. His name was Bernard. Bernard was pronounced with the accent on the first syllable, he told me, when it was a man's name, and on the second only when talking about a Saint Bernard dog. Bernard showed us a photograph of his catamaran, for which he had commissioned a sculptor to make two fiberglass whale tails, one mounted on the stern of each of the twin hulls, curling up into the air the way a whale's tail does after surfacing and about to dive under again. But those tails looked all wrong because they stayed fixed in position sticking upward, making no sense and spoiling the design of the catamaran. I thought it a rich man's play that seemed foolish. That year my mother was trying to buy and sell paintings as an independent dealer. She used Bernard's money to buy a few Matta paintings with the intention of finding collectors who would buy them from her when she returned to New York. I think she bought five largish paintings from Matta's studio. She gave one to Bernard and kept the others, which she sold eventually, one at a time. I didn't have a problem with my mother having lovers, but I did have likes and dislikes among them.

During my year at the Overseas School, I lived with a double page magazine reproduction of Masaccio's *Tribute Money*, from the Brancacci Chapel in Santa Maria del Carmine in Florence, and a couple of reproductions from Piero della Francesca's *Legend of the True Cross* frescoes in Arezzo. And I had a postcard of Niccolò Antonio Colantonio's *St. Jerome Removing a Thorn from the Lion's Paw*. I loved those images for the same quiet I found in the George Tooker paintings and Henri Rousseau's *The Sleeping Gypsy* I had known since childhood at the Museum of Modern Art in New York. They were paintings that spoke to me in a wordless language that I could sense without even knowing what was happening when I was in their presence. They would bring on a peacefulness within me. I began to know that I would have to paint such paintings, whatever they might be, that I couldn't yet begin to see.

When it came time to apply to colleges, what I wanted was to go to an art school because in my experience, knowing my mother's artist friends and spending a lot of time in Sari's studio, the life of an artist was the only life I could think about for myself when one day I would be on my own. I applied to Yale because my mother wanted me to apply to Yale, but I didn't have the requirements to be accepted in a school like that, and it wasn't what I would have liked. I wouldn't have had test scores any prestigious college would accept. The day our graduating class took the SAT test there was a large machine drilling a new well outside the classroom's windows where we were trying to focus on test questions. The pounding of the well drilling was very distracting and I had to reread questions over and over, and I knew I did miserably. The school offered no counseling at all on SAT test taking and I was totally unprepared. Fortunately, test scores didn't count for much in art school applications and I also applied to the Tyler School of Fine Arts.

When the semester finished and my high school years had ended, I took a ship back to New York on my own with all our baggage and stayed a few days with Anne in Bernard's penthouse apartment on Fifth Avenue overlooking Central Park.

8

TYLER & COOPER UNION

In September 1961, I started college at Tyler School of Fine Arts, a part of Temple University in Philadelphia, living in a dormitory at Temple University, where I worked evenings in the cafeteria in exchange for room and board. I enjoyed my classes in drawing and painting from still life and models and in sculpture working from a model. And I enjoyed my art history survey class and English class.

One day in English class, I told the teacher I was having trouble understanding what we were reading for homework in Sigmund Freud's *Introduction to Psychoanalysis*. And he said, "Alright Alan, show me where you can't understand what he's writing," and I found a paragraph and I showed it to him. He read it to himself a couple of times and looked up at me with a little smile and said, "You would find that!" Perhaps it was the fault of the translation, I don't know. I just didn't understand what it was saying. I liked that English teacher. He was very interesting and a little mischievous. He sometimes read things to the class no other English teacher I knew would have read. He sometimes read passages from Richard von Krafft-Ebing's *Psychopathia Sexualis*, a book of case histories of human sexual behavior published in 1886. I think he enjoyed seeing how his students would react to the stories. We wrote short themes for homework, and to learn to write better, we read George Orwell's *Politics and the English Language*. One line of that has stayed in my mind for all the years after reading it. It was the last line in Orwell's essay, in the third footnote, and it is this: "One can cure oneself of the not un-formation by memorizing this sentence: A not unblack dog was chasing a not unsmall rabbit across a not ungreen field."

Other than liking art school while yearning for an amorous relationship, my year in Philadelphia was most important for no longer seeing myself as a child living in the shadow of his mother. I was an art student among other art students interacting with teachers who were not the artists my mother knew, or knew about. I wasn't in a school where my mother would be inquiring about my life the way she had done when I went to the boarding schools, when her inquiries would have been as much to see if I was behaving in ways that would reflect badly on her as they would be to know if I was happy and doing well in my classes.

* * *

Although I was happy in Philadelphia, I wanted to be back in New York once again where I had spent my childhood years and where things made sense because I had grown up knowing them. I wasn't yet strong enough in my own identity that I could live elsewhere and hold onto the person I was. So I applied to Cooper Union as a transfer student. The application process involved taking what they called a Hometest, that in those years applicants sat for in the Great Hall of the school's Foundation Building. It involved making a drawing and a little plasticine sculpture on a theme that was different from those of previous years so that none of us could have had an advantage knowing what it would be ahead of time. Ours that year was a woman washing the floor, and I made my little sculpture like one of Degas' little sculpture sketches of nude women washing themselves on a shallow round tub on the floor, like those I had always liked in the Metropolitan Museum. When we all brought our sculptures up to the stage with our test papers at the end of the test period, I was able to get some idea of how I stood in comparison to the other students, being able to see the little plasticine sculptures other students had made, each on a board with their identifying name attached, sitting on the stage, and I thought I would do well. Another part of the Hometest was a standardized psychological test that might have been required for compliance with state funding or tax category laws. Or it may have been thought by the school that it would enable the admissions office to spot an applicant who might become a disruptive student. I found the psychological test absurd and amusing, and after taking it, I made up two questions that I liked for the fun of thinking them up. One was a simple question, "Which would you rather be, rich or ugly?" When I told friends I had made up that question they took a minute to think about how to answer it. And the other was a multiple choice question that was:

> Who invented gravity?
> a. Winsor Newton
> b. Isaac Newton,
> c. Abraham Isaac
> d. Fig Newton

I liked that it was who *invented* gravity instead of who *discovered* gravity. Art students would know Winsor Newton referred to a well-known manufacturer of art supplies. I was among the few transfer students accepted at Cooper Union that year.

New York was much bigger than the world my mother was the center of. She had her circle of friends and acquaintances, among whom were those who were her admirers as well as those who might find themselves in the same physical space and would look at her and want to know who she was. I could be myself on my own. In that way of understanding time and place and how I inhabited those, I was changing. I could then, for the first time, share an apartment with my mother, as I did for a period, and still feel independent. I had moved on in a significant way.

The summer between Tyler and Cooper Union, I was hoping to spend time with a folksinger named Alix Dobkin, who had just graduated from Tyler and was starting a career in New York. I went to the Gaslight Cafe in Greenwich Village where Alix was singing. Young Bob Dylan stopped in to say hello to Alix while I sat with her between sets. He told her about his first album that had just come out. That's all I remember of Bob Dylan.

Bill Cosby was performing at the Gaslight Cafe the same evenings. He had been a student at Temple University the previous year, where I'd first seen his stand-up routine, one afternoon at Tyler. At the time I thought he was very funny. It's disturbing to think of that now.

In September I was in school again. There were no tuition fees for Cooper Union students, and in the sixties one could afford to be poor in New York, before housing became outrageously expensive and Brooklyn started to become fashionable and became where students and artists settled. I already knew and loved the museums, and the school was in an interesting part of the city, on St. Marks Place and Astor Place, down at 8th Street, at the upper end of the Bowery. The Village is just West of there and the East Village and Lower East Side are right there where Manhattan gets wider. Little Italy, Chinatown, and SoHo are just a short walk away. I loved McSorley's Old Ale House and the Surma Ukrainian Book and Music store, both on 7th Street, half a block from Cooper Union's Foundation Building. I used to buy buckwheat honey at Surma. It was honey from the bees belonging to the founder of the store and his family and was by far the best honey I have ever tasted. They sold beautiful hand embroidered blouses and the elaborate Ukrainian folk-art pysanka Easter eggs and the tools and beeswax and dyes to make them. When I was in Surma I felt a connection to the Russian heritage that hadn't been part of my childhood. It was an interesting kind of nostalgia in that I was experiencing something that felt deeply related to my past without it having actually been part of my own life. And McSorley's was the other side, from my father's heritage, but I didn't feel the Irish connection in the same way because many generations of my father's ancestors lived in the United States and Ireland didn't have a place in any family stories I had ever heard. McSorley's was still a men-only pub when I occasionally ate lunch there. They served a good bowl of chili. A plate of cheddar cheese, crackers and raw onion was always on their limited menu because it was a favorite of McSorley. And, of course, they had very good dark and light draught ale. McSorley's opened in 1854. In the United States that was really old. Almost nothing had ever been modernized or changed in any way at McSorley's. The wishbones still hanging from the horizontal tubes of the lights above the bar that were once gas lamps were put there by boys going off to fight in World War I, to be removed on their return. The ones I saw were never removed because the boys never returned, so they are covered in the same patina of cigarette smoke and ale that colors what little you can see of the walls between framed Irish memorabilia from which nothing had been removed since 1910. Only the glass of the picture frames is ever cleaned. Surma and McSorley's and Cooper Union are part of my fondest nostalgic memories of being a young art student.

Our classes focused on understanding the structure in what we were looking at. We were learning to draw from observing a few objects assembled on a table in the middle of a studio or a model on a model stand in front of us holding still for some minutes, or possibly even hours. The objects we observed, no more extraordinary than things we knew in everyday life, were distinguished from their otherwise lack of importance by their placement and by our scrutiny. In time we began to discover other meanings, deeper meanings, in what we were looking at, and how the seeing was more significant in the process of drawing and painting than the identity of the things we were depicting. Objects can reveal stories, whether those stories are somehow inherent in the things themselves in an actual or symbolic sense, or are suggested through pictorial relationships. What we were observing could become utterly amazing if seen with the kind of penetration that comes with focused observation. The extraordinary, heretofore unnoticed quality of something is made evident in a work of art because the wonder of appearances and appreciation of how meaningful they could be is felt by the artist and made communicable. It can be about relationships of shapes seen and manipulated in drawings and paintings for their ability to become parts in a complex organization, a composing of what could be treated as abstract forms within the edges of the piece of paper or canvas. Even when we depict recognizable objects and persons, there is the element of abstraction that great works of art always have. An awareness of how things observed translate into a visual language as line and tone became more understandable, opening up a whole new world to us. The art we were looking at in slide lectures and in books and museums started to communicate on levels we were only beginning to know existed. And those works began to tell us how little we knew, and to hint at how far away and nearly impossible it would be to make something like those works we saw as great. The sense that I might arrive one day at that ability was very exciting to me.

I was involved equally in drawing, painting, sculpture, and printmaking as an undergraduate student. We had classes in two- and three-dimensional design and in typography and calligraphy. We shared our foundation year with students who then would choose to follow either in graphic design or studio art, and in our first year we had a beginning architecture class together with students who continued in the architecture department. Transfer students weren't given credit for studio classes taken in other schools so I repeated my first year of art school, but instead of taking a couple of academic classes that I had at Tyler, I could double up on studio classes. My program at Cooper Union was therefore a full four years which meant I did five years of undergraduate art school before my two years in graduate school.

The many teachers I worked with had their different ideas about the making of art. I took from each of them what I found meaningful and tried to understand it better. There were the museums and galleries I could spend time in that provided answers to questions I was barely aware of having in my head. And there was a library with art books and art magazines, and much talk among classmates. With the trends and the influences those trends might have on a young student, I had to steer a course for myself that would allow me to discover and remain true to what interested me. I was beginning to understand that my inclination was towards figurative imagery, and about a kind of silence that often had to do with melancholy, and perhaps with loneliness, though loneliness no longer seemed to nag and trouble me the same way it had when it was as present as my own shadow and never far from heart and mind. I was beginning to think that a sense of quiet and loneliness had to be part of what I make because that was what I knew; for me it was very real.

I could see no virtue in thinking about joining a fashionable trend in the art world. I could understand how it would have been easy, or appealing, for the Abstract Expressionist painters to form a movement with their backing of influential critics and their gatherings at The Club and the Cedar Tavern in New York. But, though those painters shared a non-objective premise, they were mostly unlike each other in their separate works. That was less the case with the Op and the Pop and the Photo Realist painters, who were becoming well known in the sixties. For me, the painters who were part of those current movements lacked a core essence in their work that wants to be individual, and would be recognizable as being personal. Of course, there are shades of truth and shades of untruth in such oversimplified statements as these, but that was how I saw it.

I wasn't interested in the permissive life of the sixties hippie generation, though I was in touch with others who were more a part of that scene. I wanted not to fall into the despondency that marijuana and drinking seemed to be about. Some of my friends were reading Beat Generation authors. I read some of Lawrence Ferlinghetti's poems and part of William Burroughs' *Naked Lunch.* To some extent I was able to identify with that generation of creative individuals unwilling to conform to a society I also saw as troubled. For lack of familiarity with the literature associated with philosophical ideologies, I wasn't able to discourse with others in such thinking.

There was something exciting about being a starving artist owning next to nothing in my art student days. We were immersed in our work. Later would come a lifestyle that more than ours included material things and the need to understand things like credit ratings and the responsibilities that came with marriage. Then it would be right to think differently and to make choices with greater concern for what they might entail. I was happy being an art student spending my days in the skylit studios on the sixth floor of Cooper Union's Foundation Building and going to the museums I knew and loved. But all that was overshadowed by a fear that the Vietnam War might suck me into its infernal depths and take from me everything I cared about and spit me out either dead or deeply wounded.

My friend Jean-Pierre Merle lived with his mother Ligoa Duncan, Isadora Duncan's niece, in what had been a men's gym on the Upper East Side. I remember their bathroom had tall floor standing urinals opposite toilets in separate stalls. I thought it an interesting place for them to be renting. Jean-Pierre was the only art student I can remember who carried a briefcase to school. Perhaps this oddity was because he was French. In that briefcase, he kept a box of teabags, two or three of which contained marijuana. I think he amused himself with the inventiveness of hiding marijuana among his teabags rather than that he feared being searched by the police.

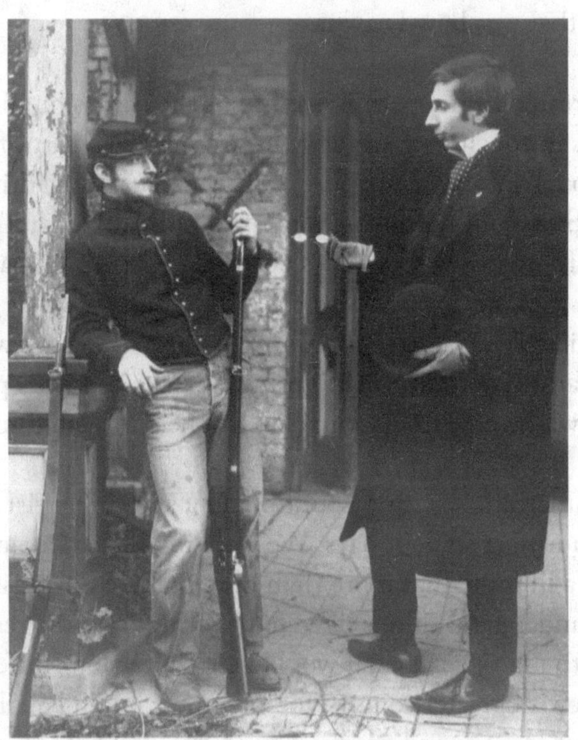

With Lazlo Kubinyi.
Photo taken by Jean-Pierre Merle, Welfare Island, 1965 or '66

I spent a day with Jean-Pierre and his friend Laszlo Kubinyi, photographing ourselves in Civil War costumes on Welfare Island with the backdrop of the abandoned hospitals and asylums that were still there before Welfare Island became Roosevelt Island. Laszlo was an illustrator a few years older than me and he lived in a little apartment near Cooper Union. In the photographs, Jean-Pierre and Laszlo are standing, wearing Union jackets and caps, leaning on muskets. Laszlo collected Civil War memorabilia. I wore a very long black coat that I found in a thrift shop. Laszlo wore a pair of antique wire rimmed glasses. After our Civil War photographs, we photographed ourselves wearing Russian shirts that Laszlo had. The wire rimmed glasses in Laszlo's hand were carefully positioned to reflect the light of the chandelier above a heavy antique dining table in Laszlo's sister's apartment.

* * *

At Cooper Union, Charles Cajori, Reuben Kadish, and Varujan Boghosian were my favorite teachers. What they taught me has stayed with me as an artist. And I valued them as friends. One day, Cajori took me and another student to an empty studio and had us draw from a few objects on a table against the wall. He directed us by telling us what to draw, one line at a time. One edge of something, then another, moving through the several objects. He showed us how what we saw, like the back edge of the table top that we knew formed a straight line, when overlapped by something else, especially when overlapped by something at a diagonal to the back of the table top, starts out one way, and then when interrupted by the object in front of it, would appear to pick up and continue on the other side from a position that is not what our logical mind believes to be right. That was the beginning of a new understanding of painting for me. It was an aspect of working from observation that was more than getting things right in a conventional sense. It was about what a painting could become, and what painting composition could be about that I had not yet been aware of. It can explain what happens in Cézanne's paintings, and in the Cubist paintings that followed Cézanne, where the forms or shapes we see can disintegrate the subject of a painting, leaving us with something that is more an abstraction than a depiction of something familiar. A Cézanne still life might have objects as ordinary as a few apples on a dish with a ginger jar and some drapery on a shelf or table, but his paintings are about something more than those things.

Cézanne is a painter whose unfinished watercolor paintings and pencil drawings taught me a lot about pictorial structure. From his first marks made by pencil or brush, he set up a tension and a relationship between those pencil marks or spots of color and the edges of the paper. Often he drew the spaces between forms, that if completed would describe trees or rocks or houses or figures. It might be the right side of one thing and the left side of another, neither thing having been completed. The shape made between objects is what we call negative space, or what Cajori called the interstices. Consciously working with those shapes will integrate the forms in a drawing or painting so that the picture becomes something whole unto itself, apart from what we think of as the subject of that work. It is one thing to appreciate a drawing or a painting for the image we see in it and another to see the whole of the image as a construct deliberately put together as a work of art, and not simply a depiction.

The late drawings by Giorgio Morandi are like the unfinished works by Paul Cézanne in how they are about the relationships between objects. To both Cézanne and Morandi the actual subject matter in a drawing or a painting was not more important than the interrelationships of the things they depicted.

Reuben Kadish and Varujan Boghosian taught sculpture at Cooper Union. Boghosian's assemblages fascinated me. I learned from seeing how he gently worked on the surfaces of things he would find or buy in antique shops and Italian flea markets, and then how he would combine those things to make his sculptures, and give them titles from mythology. It was teaching by example at its best. One day in class, while we were working on our own, he was very carefully sanding flat sheet metal birds he had cut out from an old store sign that had layers of paint and rust, watching as the color changed subtly under his sandpaper. He used antique Italian church mannequins and antique wooden children's blocks and ceramic marbles. The top of an old woodworking bench turned vertical became the back of a construction that had a Madonna mannequin with jointed arms and wooden balls along with other things, all of which were transformed through combining them into his own silent poetry. The delicacy of what Boghosian created stood apart from so much that was talked about in those years when Abstract Expressionism's Action Painting was still going strong as an influential force in art schools and Pop Art and Minimalism were replacing the more lyrical forms of art that I was most interested in.

Teaching art in those days generally didn't get into techniques, and fortunately my teachers didn't impose their own kind of art on students. It was a loose approach to schooling that suited me well. It is far better to encourage and stimulate students than to give them formulas for making art, as though art could easily be made by following instructions. Only in printmaking, typography, and calligraphy were technique taught because in those cases one had to know a process. Color was taught in 2-D design classes but color theory didn't make sense to me at all except as a way to explain one aspect of color to students, and that was about optics, about rods and cones and optic nerves. To a painter, color is something else and is personal. Only gradually do we begin to recognize what our own sense of color is. Art schools are important for how they prepare us to learn later what we need to know, and once we have the knowledge that allows us to learn on our own, learning never stops.

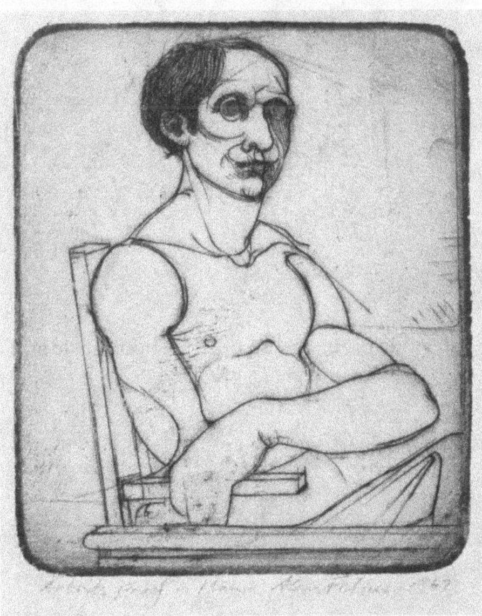

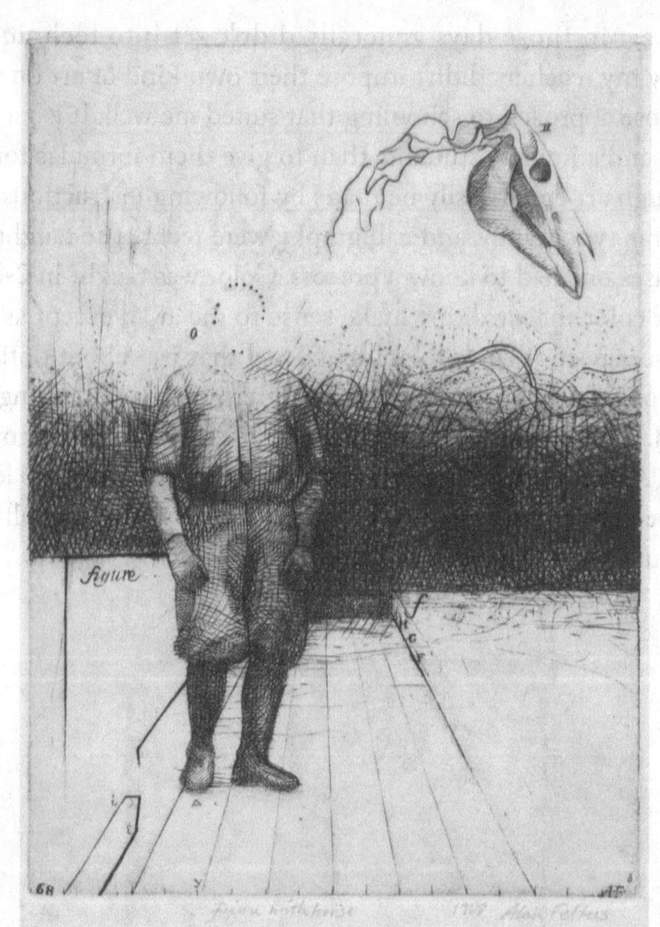

An engraving (previous page) and an ethcing, both made at Cooper Union

9

PROVINCETOWN

My first two summers while I was a Cooper Union student I worked in Milt Herder's commercial art studio doing whatever an unskilled person might do. When I wasn't running errands, I was learning to put together copy the office would get in the form of photostats having specified typefaces and sizes to make camera-ready paste-ups and mechanicals, a much more cumbersome process than what is now done more cleanly by computers in what I believe is magic. We were working with razor blades and rubber cement, preparing magazine ads and brochures for printing. I didn't have the experience to be good at making such things, but I did my best and it wasn't bad summer work. There was a man who worked for Milt who would sometimes say something absolutely absurd with a straight face and not let on that he was joking. He told me a blue whale is the size of a dill pickle, and that it is the salt water refraction that makes us think it is bigger. I loved that. And there was another man who was so good at the meticulous exacting work of preparing mechanicals that he could draw a perfect line a yard long with his ruling pen and liquid ink while standing and holding his breath.

Milt Herder once told me he could fall in love with someone he saw on a bus or on the street almost any day. I knew I was like that too. I assume most of us are like that, whether we admit it to others or not. Beautiful strangers have affected me this way my whole life. A girl on the Fifth Avenue bus who looked so sweet and beautiful in her vintage looking blue blouse, lost in thought. I wondered who she was. I wanted to know her. The young French woman at the airport who was seeing her mother off at the gate, standing beside me in the crowd and she took my hand thinking I was her boyfriend, or husband, who was somewhere nearby. I looked at her and for those two seconds when she looked at me and let me go, her beautiful smile, the moment was lived like a scene in a movie. I thought she could be a woman I would be happy sharing my life with.

In mid-August of 1964, I took a break from working in the hot city to visit Bill Coperthwaite where he had finally found and purchased a large piece of undeveloped land on the northern coast of Maine. Bill had with him a few students from the Quaker school where he had been teaching. I stayed several days, camping out in the woods and canoeing. And on one occasion, I swam in the ice waters of the tidal inlet along with one of the girls, followed by a rowboat. My body wasn't designed to do well in extreme cold and I had to spend that evening wrapped in a sleeping bag next to a couple of large stones heated in the cooking fire to stop my shivering. That was what I got for trying to impress a girl with my swimming ability.

On my way back to New York, thinking to warm up and briefly enjoy a different surrounding, I stopped in Provincetown, on Cape Cod, where a Stockbridge School classmate spent her summers. I slept outdoors on a hilltop from where no houses could be seen. While visiting Gabby at her parents' summer house, a friend of hers came by and he told me he knew of a couple of restaurants looking for help. Summer jobs were being vacated as students were returning to Boston and New York for the start of the new fall semester. I hadn't asked the boy if he knew of job openings because I planned to go back to Milt's office for what remained of the summer before classes began. But the idea of staying on a while in Provincetown seemed a good one. One of the two jobs the boy mentioned was at a restaurant called Sal's Place.

I knew that Sal was the same Sal from Ciro and Sal's, a very good Italian restaurant I had known when I spent the summer at the Jerry Farnsworth School in North Truro. I went to Sal's Place that afternoon and I was hired to begin kitchen cleanup that night. Sal's kitchen cleanup man had quit and the kitchen was being cleaned by the waiters, who were too exhausted to do a decent job of it after hours of serving customers. I moved my knapsack and sleeping bag from the hilltop where I had them wrapped in plastic tied to a tree and went to Sal's Place in time for dinner with the waiters and the kitchen crew before the doors were opened to customers. Without asking if Sal minded, I slept on a bench in the dining room hidden behind the tablecloths of two tables. Early on my second morning, while I was still hiding behind the tablecloths, the owner of the Inn at the Mews, where Sal was renting that summer, walked into the dining room and stood with his back to me looking up at the ceiling as though to see if there was a leak. I stayed still not wanting to be noticed by him. After that, with Sal's approval, I moved into the little boiler room/storeroom above the kitchen. A few days later the dishwasher also left and I was washing dishes during dinner and cleaning the kitchen after the last meals were taken out by the waiters. It was in my nature to do the best I could at any job I had, and I didn't mind at all washing dishes and cleaning a kitchen in a restaurant right next to the sea. It was like a vacation I couldn't have afforded without being hired by Sal, and it came with very good meals and friendship. I was soon one of the crew made up of Sal and his assistant cook and the several student waiters. I delayed my return to New York to the last possible day before classes began at Cooper Union, enjoying being in Provincetown and working at the restaurant while getting to know Sal and his family.

Descendants of Portuguese fishermen, who first settled in Provincetown when it was a fishing and whaling center in the 1800s, shared Provincetown with artists and writers who lived there, mostly in the summers, along with the vacationers and tourists. For a small town it was wonderfully creative and spirited. And because it remained relatively free of anything at all large and commercial, Provincetown and most of Cape Cod stayed extraordinarily beautiful.

Sal and Josephine Del Deo were among the small population that lived in Provincetown year-round. I returned for Christmas to stay with them and their two children. Sal's parents had moved from the island of Ischia, in the

Bay of Naples, to Rhode Island soon before Sal was born. I loved that Sal kept the family traditions he had grown up with that were from the Italy I think of as old Italy, the best of the Italy I had known from my year at the Overseas School of Rome and from early Fellini films. Every Christmas, Sal and his family made an elaborate *presepio* and had a candlelight procession around it to place the little baby Jesus in his basket, followed by a great feast of a dinner. I was their only guest sharing that marvelous Christmas with this family I had come to love.

Over the years Sal had enlarged their house, incorporating old ships' knees and beams turned silvery gray by the salt of the sea and the sun after winter storms had washed them up on the beaches behind Provincetown. During the summers, Sal and Josephine ran the restaurant and the rest of the year Sal painted in the studio he had made in the woods behind his house next to their vegetable garden and a fenced yard their goat lived in, near a piece of the old railroad track long ago abandoned.

After that brief period at the end of the first summer, I returned for three full seasons working at Sal's Place. By the start of my second summer, Sal's Place had moved back to the west end of Provincetown, to the property Sal had rented before being at the Inn at The Mews. He had purchased the property onto which he had a new dining room built on the wharf just beyond the kitchen, over the water at high tide. And with Sal's blessing, I was allowed to sleep in whichever of the three little cabins on the wharf beyond the new dining room or whichever small apartment above the restaurant had not yet been taken by paying guests. There was a little house next to the restaurant called A Home at Last that had a rental apartment upstairs, and a smaller apartment below facing the sea, and on the street front there was a storeroom where all restaurant supplies not needing refrigeration were kept. A Home at Last had been floated to that position from Long Point, where the lighthouse stood at the very tip of Cape Cod. In Provincetown, many houses were known by names and townspeople all seemed to have nicknames. I slept in the Home at Last apartments also, and once the summer was in full swing and all the rentals were occupied, I slept in the little storeroom on a folding bed that could only be opened if I shelved that day's deliveries to clear a little floor space. Boxes of Italian canned tomatoes and olive oil and wine and the like were delivered most days. What started as sleeping in the boiler room/storeroom at the Inn at The Mews became my right to sleep the whole summer rent free. I was the only one given that privilege because I was an exceptional worker. I did anything I was asked to do and anything else I thought might be appreciated, so much so that when I visited six years later, I found that there were people working at Sal's Place who told me they hated me because they couldn't live up to my reputation.

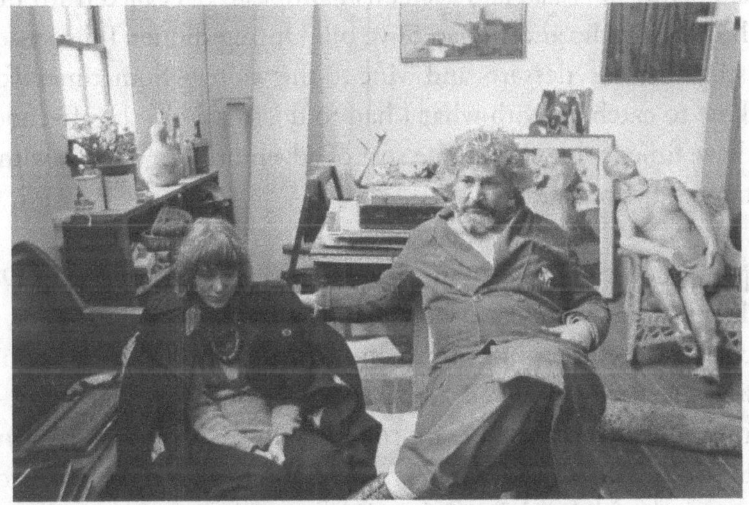

Lani with Sal, years later, in his studio in 1975

I would open the restaurant and work alone much of the morning. I made myself French toast from the leftover Portuguese bread of the night before, with a syrup of Marsala wine and sugar. I played music from Sal's open reel tapes. I often played a tape called *The Art of Rosa Ponselle* that had Rosa Ponselle with Ezio Pinza and a chorus singing "La Vergine degli Angeli" from Verdi's *La Forza del Destino*, recorded in 1928. Listening to that duet still brings tears to my eyes when I hear it even today. I turn the volume high and it stirs up all the nostalgia of those wonderful summers. I also played a tape of Marianne Faithful, who was then young and gorgeous. I was in love with Rosa Ponselle and Marianne Faithful, and with Amália Rodrigues for her singing of Portuguese Fado.

My daytime work companion at the restaurant was a boy named Tommy De Carlo. Mornings it was often just the two of us working in the kitchen. Tommy's parents had a house nearby. His father, Victor, was among Sal's painter friends. Tommy was a few years younger than me and he did smaller jobs, like peeling garlic and chopping parsley and grinding Parmigiano cheese in the antique grinder that reminded me of an old red fire engine. I prepared antipasto plates and salad and a shellfish antipasto Sal called frutti misti di mare, heavy in garlic and Italian olive oil. During dinner, I dispensed the antipasti and salads, desserts and wine to the waiters. Sometimes Tommy helped me to catch up with what I had to do, so that in the afternoon we might have time to go off on some sort of adventure, or go for a swim right there next to the restaurant.

Sal kept a canoe at the restaurant that was given to him by one of Donald MacMillan's crew members. MacMillan was an American explorer, sailor, researcher and lecturer born in Provincetown in 1874. That canoe had an impressive life, having been taken on at least one of MacMillian's 30 research expeditions to the Arctic. One morning Arthur Cohen was painting the shoreline of Provincetown from Sal's canoe, and to amuse ourselves Tommy and I prepared a full breakfast and took it out to Arthur on a sailfish, which without its sail was like a surfboard. Tommy paddled with his hands as I sat with legs dangling in the water, holding the tray to keep it from tipping. We gave Arthur the breakfast and left for shore, none of us saying a word. Arthur smiled appreciation. Another morning Francis Iacono, who was a waiter at Sal's and a close friend those summers, served breakfast to a man who walked in off the street and sat down by himself in the front room. We used to keep all the doors open for air. Generally people knew we were not open until evening, but this man wasn't aware of that. Without telling the man we weren't open, Francis just took his order and we prepared his breakfast. Diversions like those made one morning different from another during long summers without a day off.

Dinners could be quite interesting but we were usually too busy to have much to do with guests. Norman Mailer sometimes came with friends toward the end of an evening and they would be the last to leave. That used to irritate the waiters because they would have to stay until their last customers left before they could go for a beer somewhere to unwind. I sometimes went to the Atlantic House for a beer and to watch people. The A-House, as it is known among locals, was a lively dance club in a house built in 1798.

Tommy and I made up stories as we bicycled and wandered in our free time. One of our stories was about the Meatball Murders at Shank Painter Pond. We were eating sandwiches we made from meatballs and bread leftover from the day before, sitting at the side of the pond, off behind the houses not far from Sal's Place. We threw a meatball out into the pond to see if a fish would flip the surface of the water the way they do to get at the meatball. (Sal's meatballs were made with pine nuts and raisins and were very tasty). And a story started. I've forgotten how the story went. It was a fictitious oral history saga we kept unfolding through the summer. Tommy eventually took over running the restaurant when Sal retired from his constant and central role in the kitchen of Sal's Place. Then, in 1989, sometime after Tommy, by then called Thomas De Carlo, had moved on in his life, becoming an English teacher at the Burke Mountain Academy in Vermont, Sal sold the restaurant to his friend Jack Papetsas. Captain Jack, as he was known in my time there, had a fishing boat and took tourists fishing.

Sal bought fresh fish from an old, retired fisherman who took his dory out in the bay and caught sea bass. He would show up afternoons and Sal would weigh the fish and pay him and then it was my job to scale and gut the fish, cut their heads off, and put them on trays in the walk-in refrigerator. The bass were fairly large and I used a fork to scrape their scales off in the deep stainless kitchen sink. Captain Jack showed me how to use a fork for scaling, holding it perpendicular to the fish's surface. The drain of the sink would block with fish scales and the water would rise instead of draining. Repeatedly I would have to scoop out fish scales while those floating would be drawn down to the drain to block it again. I got tired of dealing with insistent fish scale drain stoppers and intestines and blood floating in the sink water too many afternoons, too many summer days. My days were already filled enough that often I didn't have a break from lunch time to late at night. Though I never complained, I got to disliking cleaning fish so much that I have avoided buying whole fish ever since.

Sal and Josephine would start work at midday. Josephine brought vegetables from their garden next to their goat's yard and we would eat lunch together. I decorated the walls of the street-front dining room in what was an ongoing project I gave myself. The varnished knotty pine walls Sal inherited from the previous owner weren't in keeping with a family run Italian restaurant, so I added lots of framed photographs Sal and Jo brought in from home: Italian things and things from Provincetown history and posters and announcements from artist friends' exhibitions. I hung what they had and anything else I could find that I liked. I got a beautiful vintage photograph poster of Amelita Galli-Curci from Lincoln Center, which I hung next to a large photograph of Enrico Caruso as Pagliacci, next to a vintage photograph of the Provincetown Town Crier in his Pilgrim costume.

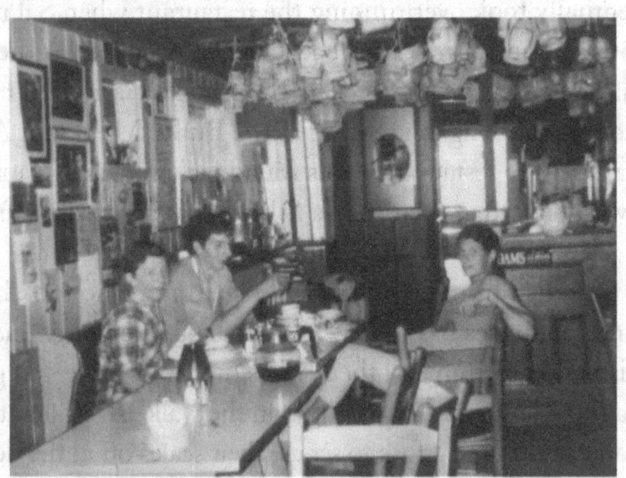

Sal's Place, Provincetown, 1965-67

When I started working at Sal's Place, the front room had empty Chianti bottles with straw baskets around them hanging from the ceiling in clusters. That was to help suggest Sal's Place was an Italian restaurant and not one of the usual Cape Cod restaurants, decorated with pieces of fishnet and painted buoys from lobster traps. I rigged one of the Chianti bottles with clear fishing line running through screw eyes on the ceiling so that from behind the counter at the kitchen end of the room I could lower that bottle just enough to be noticed and then raise it up again. That was very funny to do when families were sitting at their tables. One time I waited until only the girl, maybe she was about nine years old, was facing where the bottle would lower and I let it down to just below the other bottles. Then up again. She got very excited and wanted her parents to see what happened but I kept the bottle still until only the girl was watching and then let it down and quickly back up again. That was my way of helping to pass the evening of a long tiring day.

Salvatore Del Deo was the third of the three men who influenced me most in terms of how I have lived my life. The making of things with their own hands and living with what they made and what they chose to collect was something Milt Herder, Bill Coperthwaite, and Sal Del Deo all three shared. I owe that I have become a maker of things to their fine example. The beautiful and unpretentious lifestyle Sal and Josephine had created for themselves was very much what I wanted to have one day. Theirs had become my idea of the ideal family. Sal was a fine painter whose work showed both Italian and Provincetown influences. Of Provincetown painters, other than Sal, the one whose work I was most interested in was Edwin Dickinson. Dickinson moved to Provincetown when he was a young man to study with Charles Hawthorne, who was the first of the Provincetown painters, and Hawthorne's teaching was central to Edwin Dickinson's painting and teaching. Dickinson had a house in Wellfleet, not far from Provincetown, where he and his wife lived many years when he was not teaching at the Art Students League in New York or somewhere else. During my Provincetown summers, Dickinson would occasionally drop in at Sal's Place. One afternoon when he visited for a cup of coffee and a few minutes sitting with Sal, he left his hat behind. It was a simple cotton sunhat with brim circling around it. Sal had a small glass display case we sometimes used for cheeses that sat on the kitchen counter at the end of the front room, and I put Dickinson's hat in that, with a little note saying it was Edwin Dickinson's hat. And he didn't return to get his hat, so it remained in the box like a reliquary belonging to someone beloved by so many of us. Sal's waiters and kitchen crew were mostly art students like myself, and many of the restaurant's clientele were painters.

The summer between my two years at Yale was my last season working at Sal's Place. When the spring semester ended, I hitchhiked from New Haven starting early in the morning and got as far as Barnstable, at the base of the Cape. I was standing in the drizzling rain with my duffel bag hanging from my shoulder waiting for another ride when a car pulled in to the side of the road and a kid got out and walked over to me. He asked if I wanted a ride. I turned my head to see how many people were in the car when he hit me just above my left eye. I staggered back a few feet. He got back in the car and they drove off. It was evening, already dark, and still raining. I saw a bar a little farther with outside lights on and I walked over to it and started up the steps to the front door. I hesitated, fearing those boys might be inside, when the door opened and a policeman came out. He looked at me and asked what had happened. I didn't know I was bleeding because rain was running down my face. I told him what had happened and he handed me the coffee he was holding and turned my face toward the light. He said he would take me to the hospital to have a doctor check me and then he would stop by the hospital again and take me to the police station, where I could spend the night. I drank his coffee and went with him to the hospital. I got three stitches over my eye and spent the night in a jail cell with the door open. In the morning my policeman drove me back to the road and I continued on to Provincetown. The police were very kind to me. They were disappointed that I couldn't describe the car or the boys.

10

MARILYN

I met Marilyn Andre when she and I were working as volunteers at the same polling station in 1964, the year Lyndon Johnson won the Presidential election. After a few months I moved out of my mother's apartment and Marilyn and I shared a very small "bathtub in the kitchen" apartment on Second Avenue and 77th Street.

I saw in Marilyn someone who was lovely and uncomplicated, with her smooth skin and bright eyes, and something that I took to be a kindness that I attributed to the fact that she came to New York from Southern California. I don't know if I believed California made her what I believed her to be, or if knowing her made my idea of California what I believed that to be. I thought of the winds that blow across the country from west to east as having come from across the wide open ocean, clean and fresh.

Marilyn didn't try to impress me and she didn't judge me in any way. She was easy to be with and good natured and we enjoyed the things we did together living in the middle of a vibrant city. We went to museums. We invented stories about people we would see when we were out and about and we shared an intimacy that was beautiful when we were at home.

She was the antithesis of my mother, whose concerns were about having higher goals, or loftier purposes to strive for in life. My mother lived with a tension that was about her dissatisfaction with things that she believed not to be good enough for the person she thought herself to be. And she projected that thinking onto me. What my mother disliked about Marilyn could have been precisely what allowed me to be happy with Marilyn. Perhaps my being with Marilyn was an unconscious rebellion against the kind of pressure my mother imposed on me with her questions and her criticisms of those of my girlfriends she had met, with the possible exception of Diana Bryan who was an avid reader of all kinds of literature and whose conversations better lived up to my mother's expectations.

I spent my days at Cooper Union while Marilyn went to work as a secretary in an advertising agency in midtown. We stayed together a year and a half. It was my first experience living on my own with someone I had chosen to live with and the first relationship I considered making permanent. But when I was close to finishing at Cooper Union and was about to return to Provincetown for another summer before starting graduate school at Yale, I decided that for me it was time for us to go our separate ways. Marilyn didn't take my decision well. The one time I went with her to the office where she worked, she showed me a beautiful little set of baby clothes she kept in her desk drawer. That was very touching, and at the same time a worrying intimation of how much she loved me, and it made my decision to leave her all the more painful. But I thought I was too young to marry. And I had never thought about being a father. I believed I should be free again to be open to things unknowable.

A few months later, in my first year at Yale, I received a letter from Marilyn, mailed from somewhere in Europe. I wrote back to the address on the envelope saying that I was feeling unsure about having left her, that my leaving her may have been a mistake. But my letter didn't reach her and was returned to me weeks later unopened. I took that as a sign. I hadn't reached her, and at that point I thought it would be unfair to start up again with her if I wasn't ready to commit myself. I decided I was better off not rekindling our lost relationship and I didn't look for her after that.

11

GORKY'S MOTHER

Unlike when applying for undergraduate school, Yale graduate school applications were based solely on one's portfolio, and I applied only to Yale and was accepted. Whereas in undergraduate school I worked in painting and sculpture with equal interest, in graduate school I entered as a painting major. We can be both painter and sculptor and also many other things when we are working on our own later, but in graduate school it was necessary to limit what we did in order to be able to complete a reasonable body of work in two years. Part of my decision to choose painting was purely practical in that I had no place to store anything. I had no family home, and sculptures would take up a lot more space than paintings. But it was also that I figured painting would allow me to have a wider range of possibilities than sculpture. In the case of most sculpture, one can't control what is seen around and behind the sculpture itself. Contours change and relationships change with a millimeter's shift in viewpoint. Changes in the light that falls on a sculpture will alter completely how the form of the sculpture reads. And though this presents itself as a very exciting challenge, in a painting, on the other hand, we can have total control within the edges of a canvas. Everything can be pinned down and left unchanged forever after. I thought to have that ability would present enough of a challenge for me to deal with.

At Yale we were given a key to the building and could work in our individual studios any time, day or night. We had a minimum of actual classroom courses, like those in art history, that met outside the art building and were open to students from other departments. In painting we were assigned a teacher who we met with periodically for discussions and critiques of our work. At the end of a semester there were final reviews in which we put that semester's work in front of the full faculty to be evaluated. We dreaded those reviews, though only one student was asked not to return for a second year. That student was never seen, or I should say was hardly ever seen in his studio space by the rest of us. Occasionally we would notice something new there, but not much. For his final review, he bought a bunch of cardboard boxes from where they were made, and assembled them and stacked them in some way he thought might look as though it had meaning. He may have actually been influenced by Donald Judd, who had given a lecture at the school that year. Art of that kind exists and is sometimes taken seriously, but it meant nothing to me. Anyway, that student's accomplishments for his first year in graduate school prompted a few of us to talk about how, since we were accepted into the MFA program at Yale, we could probably invent a student whose application portfolio we would make and he would probably be accepted. And then the next year we could paint his paintings and leave notes for his teacher giving excuses for his not being able to be there for critiques. It was just to amuse ourselves that we thought that up, of course.

The kind of work we did in our studios at Yale was up to us. There were no still-life setups put together by a teacher, or models posed by a teacher for a class to work from the way it had been in my five years of undergraduate art school, and at first it was hard for me to make the transition from working within given structures to working independently. To avoid what I expected might be a period of floundering and inability to begin something meaningful, having never before been left on my own in a studio space I could call mine, and having no direction given by a teacher, I chose to give myself the assignment of painting a Gorky that Gorky never painted. It would be a kind of copy, but not a copy in the traditional sense because what I wanted to do was to interpret a photograph of Gorky with his daughter Maro on his shoulders standing in the landscape next to André Breton in the same way Arshile Gorky had interpreted the photograph of himself as an eight-year-old boy with his mother in two paintings and several drawings. The largest and most beautiful of the drawings had a tenderness that spoke to me about the love he had for his mother, who had died of starvation in the Armenian genocide in 1919, the year before Gorky sailed to America.

Gorky's painting *The Artist and His Mother* (1926–1936) was the one I could visit in person because it hung in the Whitney Museum in New York. I had been very interested in Arshile Gorky ever since I saw his Museum of Modern Art retrospective during my first year at Cooper Union.

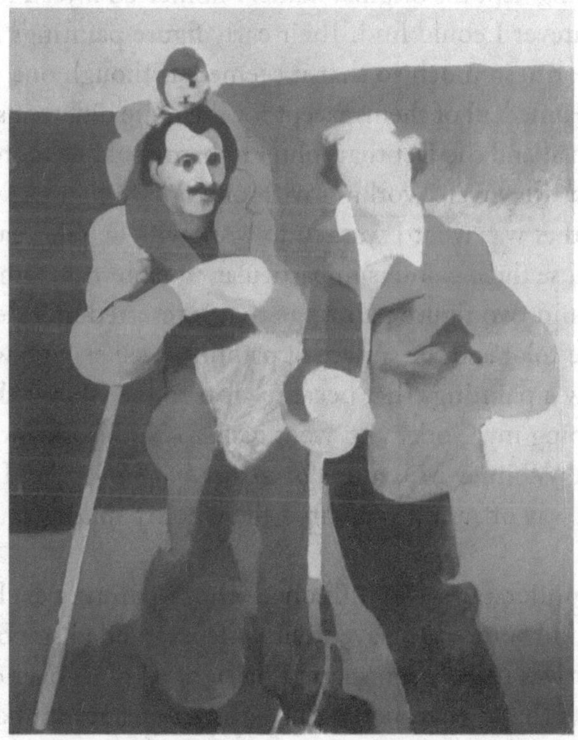

Gorky Study (The Gorky that Gorky Never Painted), 1966

Without being that conscious of what effect those images had on me, it is clear now that they entered into my inner being as feelings that related to my own boyhood growing up with my mother. I know that I still have a sadness that chokes me up every time I speak to someone about my childhood with my mother. So it is small wonder that I was to spend some months in graduate school immersed in that Gorky and his mother story as a painting experience chosen by myself.

I loved Willem de Kooning's early paintings and had just discovered the work of John Graham as I was deep in this self-imposed project. Gorky was Armenian and emigrated to the States when he was sixteen-years-old. De Kooning was twenty-two when he arrived in the US from Holland and Graham was thirty-four when he came to the US from Russia. Of the three, only de Kooning kept his original name. I immersed myself in the work of all three, whatever I could find. Their early figure paintings had a shared language of form, so much so that it seemed as though one person could almost have painted all of them, except for the quite different sense of color each painter had and the fact that John Graham could be more quirky than the other two. They were working with one or two figures, very carefully painted, and that was what I wanted to work with at Yale, learning what I could from those three painters in particular, though many other artists had made single and two figure paintings that interested me. Reproductions don't show the color and the surface of paintings well enough when we need to really know a painting. That became clear to me when I thought I was close to finishing my Gorky and went back to New York and stood again in front of the Whitney Museum's *The Artist and his Mother*. I realized that my color was way off, and I repainted the whole painting again.

I wanted to understand the influences those painters exchanged with each other, and I wanted to have their surfaces, sanded smooth like ivory. Gorky's color was made from scumbling lighter colors over darker colors with oil paints that by nature have a slightly translucent quality when in thin layers. Their drawing of forms was something that came from Ingres' paintings, which they carried further in its flatness and elegance, moving more toward abstraction. Most painters abstract what they paint in the sense that their paintings are something other than depictions of reality, the way a photograph might capture an image. Ingres' many portrait subjects nearly all have an anatomy that would suggest they came from the same rarefied family. They almost all have elongated necks and sloping shoulders and smooth skin with almost no surface disturbances made by veins and tendons and bones, and yet they are convincing in their realism because, unreal as his figures are, they were painted with great care.

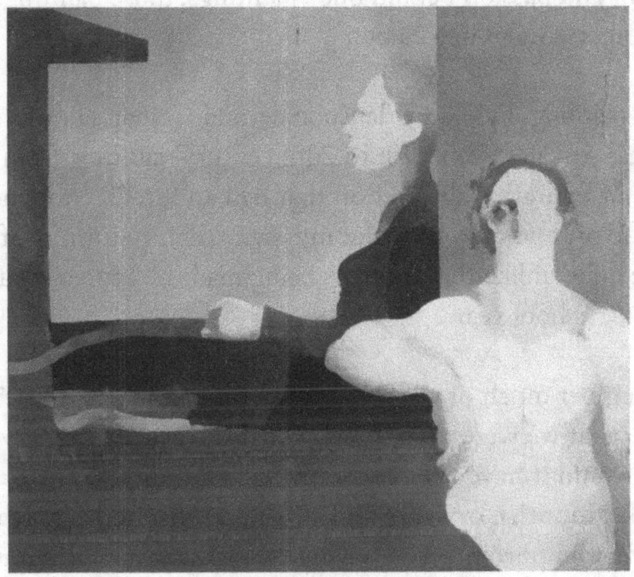

Lady and Torse, 1967

Gorky and de Kooning both started with a period of learning and searching to find themselves by imitating and absorbing all they could from the painters they admired. Gorky was, as he put it, "with Cézanne," making paintings strongly influenced by Cézanne, before he and de Kooning and John Graham were working in their beautiful figure painting period that had so strong an influence on my graduate school paintings. From there Gorky's paintings moved into a kind of abstraction that was rooted in his Armenian childhood memories and his interest in European Surrealism. His work didn't change abruptly as it moved from one genre to another. He kept his delicate scumbling of light color over darker color and his very elegant sense of form and line that allowed his paintings to flow and develop in a most natural way. And de Kooning's paintings also moved into transitions from his early figures influenced by Ingres and early European and American modernism into very related and very beautiful forms of abstraction no longer reading as figures, but having figure-like forms nonetheless, and then into a wilder and more agitated abstract figure period before losing the figure entirely and becoming completely abstract. When there is a true commitment and passion behind one's paintings, those paintings are going to be good at any stage in a career.

In the early paintings by Gorky, de Kooning, and Graham, I saw a logical and very personal passage from 19th to 20th century painting, from figuration into a kind of figurative abstraction that had an intelligence and elegance I understood and wanted to make my own. Their paintings of that early period were quite unlike the paintings being made by contemporary painters during my art school years.

I don't remember much of what was said by our teachers in their critiques focused on what we were doing that probably wasn't often very worthy of praise, nor would it have been indicative of what direction we might take in the weeks, months, or years ahead. The atmosphere of creativity was what was most important. And having two years of uncompromised time to dedicate to my own work was crucial in my continuing on the path that would become a lifetime commitment. What I was doing was teaching me a great deal, perhaps more than I realized at the time. It was much better for me that we were encouraged to find our own way than that we might have had a direction imposed upon us. I worked primarily with Lester Johnson and Jack Tworkov but I was also influenced by Lennart Anderson when I signed up for a six week seminar he taught concurrent with a small exhibition of his paintings at Yale. Of all my painting teachers, it was Lennart Anderson who, as a painter, was the closest to where my painting was taking me.

I was working with a reduced range of color and value, and a pervasive quiet. Fresco color is how Lennart described my color. It was a kind of tonality I had to have, unlike the chromatic qualities in my painting from observation in undergraduate school, when I was pretty much matching the color of the setups we were working from. Over the years the color in my paintings has gained in depth and richness. The stillness I had in my paintings back then, however, has remained always. I had to have that. It was something that all the painters I loved most had in common. I wanted to try to paint a silence that was more evident, or more subtly intrusive, than a sense of stillness. I thought about it as a piercing silence. Could a silence have the same power as a scream, I wondered. I knew Francis Bacon's screaming Pope paintings that had grown out of a still from Sergei Eisenstein's 1925 film, *The Battleship Potemkin*. I wanted to understand better what a painting could do to create what we might perceive as a sound, or as complete silence. I made a few small paintings of a head with its mouth wide open, as though screaming, but without the sound such an image suggests. And then I realized it was the painting itself that could become the silent scream I was thinking about, and not the head of a man painted as though screaming. It was a heightened sense of stillness that I wanted, that could be there when all the elements in a painting are carefully considered and repainted as many times as it takes for them to feel right in shape and color and in their interrelationships with one another.

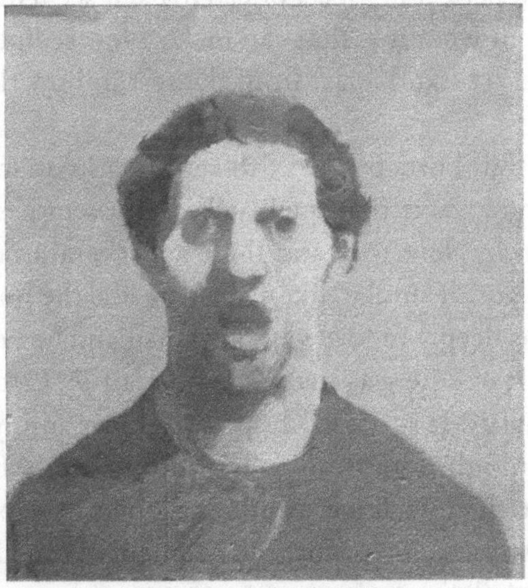

Open Mouth Scream, 1967

It interested me that in the same period, and in the same place, Dutch painters like Johannes Vermeer, Pieter de Hooch, and Gabriël Metsu could paint very serenely still paintings while painters like Jan Steen and Frans Hals were painting such turbulent and jocular imagery. Jan Steen painted drunken tavern scenes with dogs and people falling onto each other, and Franz Hals painted ruddy faces and had an agitated brushwork in his portraits. Their paintings were the antithesis of calm. That I saw these different inherent qualities as so much a part of the identity of those several painters living amongst one another helped me to understand how the nature of what we paint will reflect our own individual nature, and that realization reinforced my sense that the quiet in my paintings was more than just a choice I was making, but was something my paintings had to have, and I was happy to accept it as my own.

There was a bronze head of a girl by Charles Despiau in the Metropolitan Museum that I have often thought about for its extraordinary tranquility and particularly in the subtlety of planes and how they gently shifted one into another from under her eyes to her mouth. I find that the tiniest millimeter of a change in the features of a head, in position or in form, can make a face seem perfect in aspect or can make it seem disturbingly wrong. And I think about what it is that can make a few sculptures or paintings in the history of art stand apart from the rest in how they move me.

The marble portrait busts by the 15th century Croatian-Italian sculptor Francesco Laurana, have that quality. Two of them I had known in the Frick Collection in New York and there are several in various museums elsewhere. They are all similar, like sisters, or like the portraits made by a sculptor who was deeply in love with a woman and he kept recreating her no matter who it was he was making a portrait of. Georges de La Tour painted that quality. It is what I hope to achieve in my own paintings: this magical tranquility that holds within it a kind of strength that is something more than what we see in renderings or depictions of reality. In my best, most relaxed and focused moments I am able to create this beauty and tranquility.

As it had been in my undergraduate school years, the various art world trends emerging and gaining a following among students throughout the country did not interest me at all. Minimalism made no sense to me. It was a stripping away of everything I thought had a purpose in art to end up with something so simple it was pointless. Color Field stain painting was altogether too simple and decorative to interest me. Pop Art glorified the ordinary in a most uninspired way. I saw no virtue in that. Op Art was painstakingly executed design, and not very interesting design. And Photo Realism seemed to me to be about snapshots, the lowest form of photography, carefully copied in paint on canvas, and that was not something I was interested in. Painting had to be something more than all those trends that were becoming fashionable with the help of clever critics and curators eager to make a name for themselves. None of those trends were about the individual artist himself or herself. It required only a set of learned skills to enable someone to follow along in the footsteps of the few who were already well known. For me to fall into any of those movements would be to play the role of an artist instead of being an artist, and to busy myself with an activity that could only be a waste of time.

Paul Rudolph's Art and Architecture Building at Yale was an example of architecture created to call attention to the architect at the expense of those who would later inhabit it. It is said to be one of the earliest and best examples of Brutalist architecture, as though we should desire to be confronted by something brutal on a daily basis. I thought of it as a cruel building because its concrete walls poured in vertical corrugation and then hammered in alternating directions to create a rough texture of broken stones were as unfriendly as giant concrete rasps or cheese graters. Other walls, by contrast, were flat, and had the not so interesting distinction of being mildly honest because their unpainted surfaces of gray concrete showed the grain and knots of the plywood forms into which the concrete had been poured. It was a blocky, rebellious architecture, at odds with its surroundings and ill-suited for the purposes it was made to serve. Sculpture studios had low ceilings and painting studios had south light, if daylight reached them at all. North light has always been understood to be the best for painting studios because it remains relatively even throughout a day, without direct sunlight being able to enter and disrupt the work of a painter.

I liked going up to the little penthouse coffee shop above our studios. It was a convenient place where we could take a break to talk to each other over coffee and a pastry before returning to our paintings. The stairway that led up to the coffee shop had a ceiling so low that the spotlights attached to it had to be pushed up against the sloping concrete in order to be above the head of even a moderately tall man. Paul Rudolph was the Dean of the Architecture Department at Yale when he designed and built his famous A&A Building. He had to know how the scale of a person ought to be taken into account for the height of a ceiling in a building intended to be more than a sculptural object.

I think about architecture and art in similar ways. And I think of music also that way. When a painting or a sculpture has as its claim to fame that it is huge, or that it is confrontational, I have trouble with it. And I think of how much greater the achievement is when someone like Albert Pinkham Ryder or Albert York could become well known and appreciated for his very, very small paintings.

I rented a room in a house above a beauty salon my first year at Yale. A few other students had rooms in the same house, but mine was the smallest. It hardly had space enough to stand up in. I had a single bed, a chest of drawers, and a small closet. There was a shared bathroom down the hall and a small, shared kitchen on the floor below. I made my suppers and ate at the little table by myself, usually with a book of paintings to look at while eating. At the end of my summers in Provincetown, Sal gave me one of the long 20-pound boxes of spaghetti that Buitoni made available only to restaurants. The spaghetti was bent as it was twice the length of the box. It was a beautiful pale ochre color. One box would last me months. And with that very good spaghetti, I devised a meal that I would put together quickly. While the spaghetti was boiling, I mashed together a can of tuna fish, some chopped garlic, dried oregano, cream cheese and butter in a bowl. When I had fresh parsley, I would add parsley. That would be ready when the spaghetti was cooked so I only had to drain the spaghetti and pour it into the bowl and mix it together. That was it. I liked to wash the pot before sitting down to eat so I had only my bowl and a fork to wash after eating.

It was a place to sleep and not much more. I put a few postcard reproductions of paintings on the wall. On a little record player, I played my one Beatles record, and my Amália Rodrigues record. And I had a record of Marianne Faithful. I only had those three albums that I listened to continuously. My second year I rented a more attractive room across town and bicycled from there to the school.

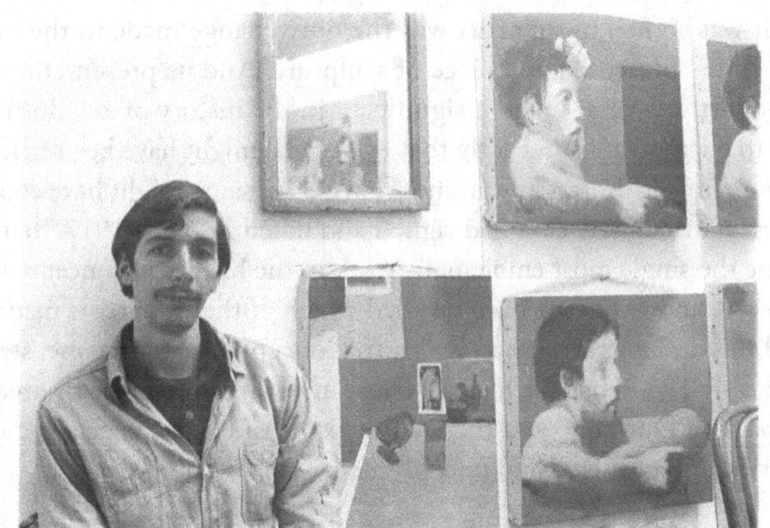

Yale University, 1967

I was continuing to better understand art in history and in practice, and to see how that understanding would inform my own painting. What we call Modern Art, the art that grew in the early decades of the 20th century in Europe and the United States, was the contemporary art that interested me most. It was rooted in what preceded it. It wasn't a dismissal of anything for the sake of breaking away in the name of newness, as some of the, to me, misguided movements that characterized my art school years had been.

I was interested in the Dada movement that emerged in Europe in protest to the horrors of the First World War. The art and the performances of Dada artists were new in the context of what is accepted as art because they were made as art by self-proclaimed artists. Dada art was new in name, and not in the sense that what was being made was entirely unseen before. It wasn't new. Dada was an art that incorporated bits and pieces of things from everyday living in assemblages and collages. The sounds of city life and spoken or written words were reworked into music and poetry Dada artists called their own. The simplest statements about what could be considered to be art were what Marcel Duchamp called his readymades. The most famous of Marcel Duchamp's readymades was a porcelain urinal lying on its back, titled *Fountain,* and signed R. Mutt 1917, in black paint. That it was signed by an artist was the only change made to the urinal when it was presented as a piece of sculpture. And its presentation as a work of art was what made it significant in the history of art. But it has come to be known just recently that this urinal might have been made by Elsa von Freytag-Loringhoven, and Marcel Duchamp might have coopted the actual urinal that Elsa had signed and dated R. Mutt 1917, that had become the single most emblematic work in the history of conceptual art. So far as I know it hasn't been decided which of the two artists made the urinal titled *Fountain*, signed R. Mutt. Conceptual art, in name, started in the early 1960s, but the idea that art can be anything made by an artist goes back to Duchamp and the Dada artists. And it had been around for centuries, unrecognized and uncelebrated.

From when I first spent time with Sari Dienes, I learned how anything can be seen as beautiful, and how found objects could be incorporated into what an artist made, and how in that process a transformation could take place. Sari was to me a Dadaist teacher by nothing other than being herself. The Dada collages of Kurt Schwitters and Max Ernst began to influence my work toward the end of my time at Yale and the years directly following. Using old portrait photographs and bits and pieces of imagery from old bookplates, glued down and painted into, led to an imagery that was more exciting than what I had been making in my paintings. I was trying to understand how my paintings might become more like my collages so that they, too, could have a figurative imagery situated within an unreal space. And I wanted to make better sense of abstraction within figurative painting because neither purely figurative painting nor completely nonobjective abstraction alone was what I was wanting to work with. Pure abstraction in painting is like instrumental music without words. Add lyrics and the music takes on more controlled meanings. And those meanings will be more or less specific depending on how they were written and how they are sung. Recognizable imagery is to painting what lyrics are to music.

I exhibited a few paintings in group shows here and there while still at Yale, and I had one large painting hanging in the library of the art building toward the end of my second year. I was also invited to join a new gallery in New Haven started by an architecture student. I left a few paintings with that gallery and put the rest in storage. From Yale I spent the summer in a sublet loft on West Broadway in New York. I had a teaching job lined up to start in September at the School of the Dayton Art Institute in Dayton, Ohio.

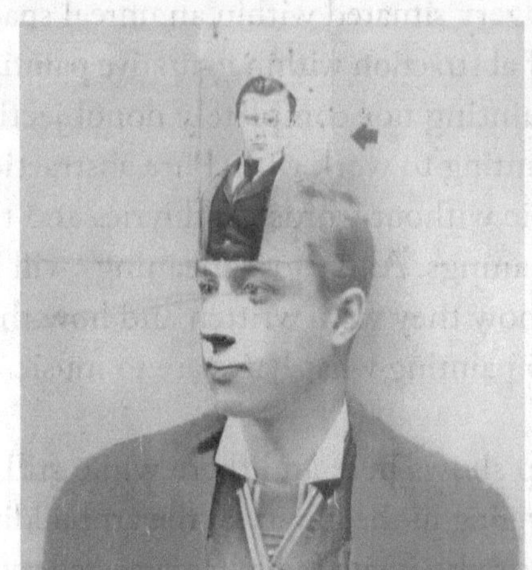

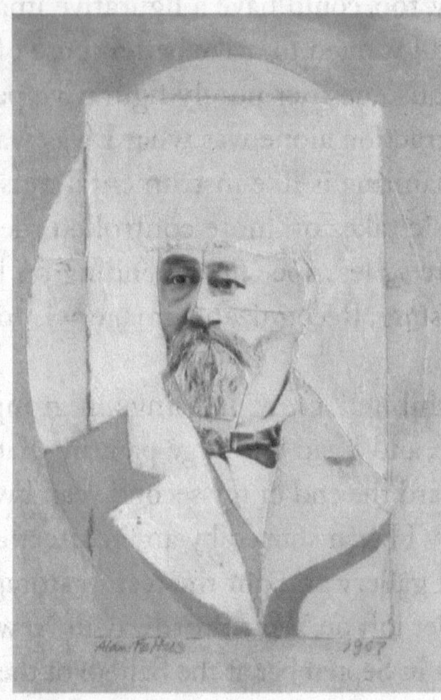

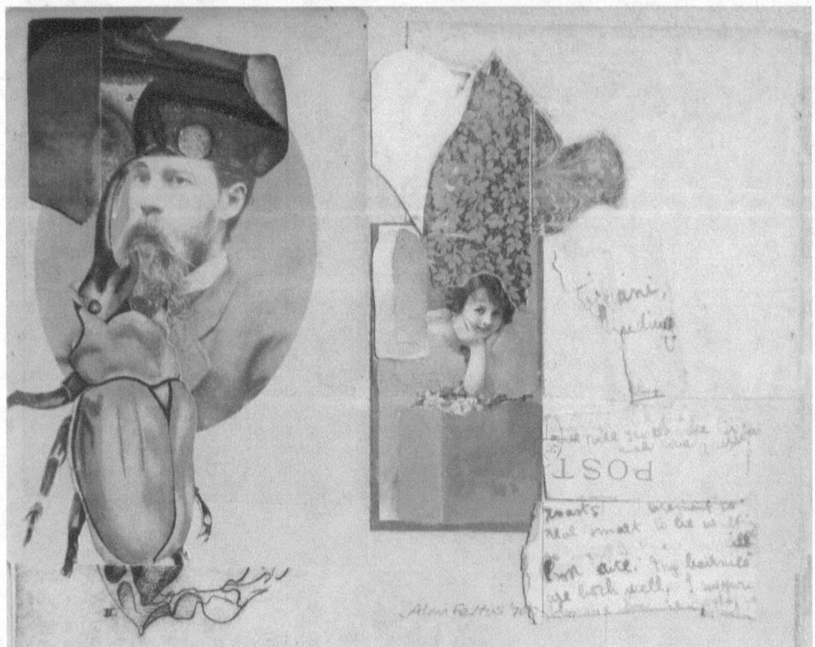

Three collages, 1967-1970

12

NINETEEN SIXTY-EIGHT

In May of 1968 I graduated from Yale with an MFA in Painting and married Toni Travis. After undergraduate school at Brandeis, Toni went to the Yale Summer School of Art in Norfolk, Connecticut, and then moved to New Haven where we met. We had known each other about a year and a half. Marriage could no longer keep someone from being drafted to fight in Vietnam and my student deferment had just then ended, but for some reason the idea that I could be called to show up for the draft physical didn't deter me from marrying. I was tired of dating and short-term relationships and the loneliness that was my life. And the fear of being sent off to fight in Vietnam made for a kind of thinking that anything I cared about, or identified myself with, might be taken away, and anything I might do at that time could have little long-term significance.

The wedding was a disaster. It was a small church wedding somewhere in Queens, New York, not far from where Toni had grown up after she moved to New York from Australia with her parents. I invited only four people, as I remember, because it was Toni's parents paying for the wedding and I had never been to a wedding and knew nothing about how they are customarily planned. I wrote to my mother to inform her that I was getting married, and she was there as well. She complained later that she had come "to perform at my wedding," as though I had insisted she be there or might have wanted her to do anything there. She had been in Hong Kong for I don't remember how long, for one last attempt to get my father to pay her

123

for child support or alimony, neither of which she was likely to get that many years after their separation, after Peter and I were grown up and on our own. My mother's thinking didn't make a lot of sense to me. She was acting out of vengeance rather than reason.

Mostly what I remember of the wedding is being terribly embarrassed in my awkwardness in front of expectant guests watching me fumble like a complete fool. I wore a rented tuxedo that felt all wrong to me. Any tuxedo would have felt all wrong to me. That was the only time I ever wore a tuxedo and it didn't fit me well in any sense of the word. And it wasn't until Toni and I were kneeling beneath the minister that I realized the pale leather soles of the nice black shoes I bought to go with my rented tuxedo were facing everybody seated behind me, and they still had the thrift shop price of $8.00 written large on them in black marker. I had asked Howard Vogel, a friend who played recorder and bassoon and was the director of the New York Baroque Ensemble, if his ensemble would provide the music for the wedding reception, but he said they couldn't because of union rules. This made no sense to me. Instead we had some band Toni's father booked. What I remember is only the awkwardness of it all. The bandleader said through his amplification "And now Tony and the bride will cut the cake". But Toni was the bride, and there was no man named Tony present. I wanted to be far away, not cutting a wedding cake at a reception surrounded mostly by people I hardly knew or had never even met. Me, ill-suited and suffering from hay fever.

Marriage would have been all right had I been able to know I was marrying someone I would want to share a life with. But almost before it came to be, I had doubts that I had made the right choice in Toni. I don't think either of us knew what love was. The marriage was like other things I did with the same almost passive acceptance as my moving through school, grade by grade, into and beyond college and then graduate school, and into a first teaching job.

Very soon after the wedding I was called to appear for a draft induction physical at a location down near the Battery at the southernmost tip of

Manhattan. I don't know how they knew that I was out of school and where to find me but they did. I had been safe only as long as I was still a student, which ended when I graduated with my MFA. The Vietnam War was raging.

I knew that the application I had sent to the Selective Service System hoping to be granted Conscientious Objector status, which might allow me to do alternative community service, wasn't going to amount to anything if I was interviewed. I had no religious background whatsoever and couldn't have made a convincing case for myself in an interrogation at which it would be assumed that I was just another miserable draft dodger. I didn't know what I could do and I feared what could be done to me. Some of my art school classmates put on crazy acts or homosexual acts to be let off. I would have starved myself to get my weight below the underweight disqualification point had I not been with my new in-laws in those weeks, even the evening before the nightmare of this physical. If I had been on my own in the preceding weeks, that would have been easy enough for me to do. I was still very thin.

I had dinner with Toni and her parents and decided to walk Manhattan through the night arriving totally exhausted at the examination center in the morning. I thought I would be suffering from my severe hay fever and look quite miserable with red itching eyes and a nose constantly dripping or sneezing. And that would help. At Times Square, I stopped a policeman and asked him if he thought it would be safe to go into one of the movie houses that late at night and he said no, don't do that. My thought was to find a war film that would instill in me the anger and fear that would somehow give me a better chance of failing the physical. I wasn't going to pretend to be something I was not. So I walked all night and saw how Manhattan becomes quiet in the very early hours of morning when only the garbage trucks are out and about. It was rather beautiful.

When I arrived at the appointed hour at the examination center, I felt quite good and my hay fever hadn't been acting up the way I expected. So there I was, one of what must have been a few hundred young men standing in lines in our underpants holding clipboards. At each part of the exam my papers were being stamped ACCEPTED. Only the one officer who was herding us through the chest x-ray part of the ordeal was nasty, and he scared me sufficiently that I didn't dare create a scene. The others were gentle with us, and I had not expected gentleness. I was helpless to do anything that might have made myself seem unacceptable. I envied a boy sitting on a bench who had thrown up on his feet and was crying. I couldn't do that. I saw one boy genuinely upset because he failed on some count. I envied his disqualification. Finally I asked to talk to the psychiatrist, and was directed to an office upstairs where I told the psychiatrist about the bleeding ulcer I was hospitalized for when I was eighteen, first at Temple University and then at Mt. Sinai Hospital in New York where I was sent from Philadelphia for the Christmas break. And he told me if I could get the x-rays that showed my ulcer sent to the address he gave me, I might be given a medical deferment. He wrote something on my forms and I turned them in and left. I remember leaving before doing the final test in case that would void my test results if my x-rays could not be found, in which case I might re-take the physical in Ohio and have more time to prepare myself for failing it.

Of all the hospital tests performed at Temple University and at Mt. Sinai, there was only one piece of evidence of the ulcer that caused me to faint for loss of blood one morning in the men's bathroom of the Temple dormitory. That was the x-ray I needed and I had no idea if it still existed in the records at Temple University Hospital from seven years earlier. But fortunately they still had the x-ray and they sent it along with their report to where it had to go. Based on the fact that I had suffered from a bleeding ulcer seven years earlier I was given a one-year medical deferment. The Temple x-ray saved me from being drafted. At first I guessed that what caused me to have internal bleeding must have been a little curl of metal I might have swallowed. I worked evenings in the cafeteria at Temple University, and I had seen that the big table-mounted can openers in the kitchen made sharp little curls of metal that I thought could fall into the can, and from there could end up in my stomach. That seemed more likely than that I had a bleeding ulcer caused by severe anxiety. Many years later I realized that it was much more likely that the number of aspirin I swallowed to ward off colds would have caused intestinal bleeding. Nobody had told me aspirin caused bleeding if taken in the doses I was taking. My life might have been saved by aspirin. That was an amazing thought. A year later the draft went to a lottery system based on birth date, but I was no longer one who could be drafted because I was 26 years old, the cutoff age for draftees.

13

DAYTON

Yale MFA graduates tended to go directly into teaching, but 1968 was probably the first year that not all of us who applied for teaching positions were hired by schools. I had sent about two hundred letters to art schools and university art departments with my then very short resume and a few slides of my paintings, asking if they had a painting and drawing position available. I went to the College Art Association meetings, held in St. Louis that year, where I was interviewed by a few school representatives but I was not offered a job. On my way back to New Haven, I stopped in Dayton, Ohio to visit the School of the Dayton Art Institute, from where I had gotten a positive response to my mailed application. I met with the dean, toured the facilities, and accepted an offer at the lowest salary I had heard of at the time, $5,600 that was raised to $6,200 when I started teaching in September.

Teaching at the School of the Dayton Art Institute was my first teaching experience and I was totally unprepared and scared of having to speak in front of a class. I was still shy and unsure of myself, and more so in the situation of being seen as the teacher standing in front of a room full of students.

As a college level studio art teacher, it was up to me to decide how and what to teach for the classes I was assigned. The biggest challenge was a 2-D design class because for that I had to create projects and explain possible approaches students would work with before I could go from student to student to discuss what they were doing. After a class or two, I devised a system that saved me from having to present projects in the customary way. I brought the assignments to class written out in marker pen on long pieces of butcher paper that I pinned to the wall. Students read them and took notes from what I had written. I used the excuse that because inevitably a student or two would come in late, this allowed all of them to get what I was presenting without missing anything. Critiques of their finished projects were easier because I could be facing the work lined up across a wall instead of looking at a room full of expectant faces. And after a few weeks, I was able to speak to the students without the fears I had on the first day.

I didn't have the same anxieties in painting and drawing classes since students could start working from the model or still life as soon as they found a place in the studio and settled in, and I could circulate and critique their work individually. One-on-one critiques of drawing and painting students wasn't that much of a problem except for the fact that I was not very confident in my knowledge about teaching art because, as a painter, I basically did what I did intuitively. I had not learned techniques that followed teachable procedures.

Gradually I became comfortable with group critiques and also presenting slide lectures which sometimes included my own work, discussing things that interested me most, like composition and color. I wanted to teach students about what I learned from other artists and how those artists' work had influenced my own. Overcoming my shyness enough to be able to teach was undoubtedly the best result of my two years in Dayton. That and becoming friends with Emmet and Edith Gowin. Emmet taught photography there for a few years before moving on to teach at Princeton. He was a born teacher whose slide talks were brilliant. Emmet's black and white photographs taken in Danville, Virginia in those years were extraordinary. Edith and her sisters, and their ancient grandmother and extended family were his primary subjects in that period and those photographs are as beautiful as any I have ever known.

* * *

The paintings I made in Dayton still had the visible remains of my Gorky-de Kooning-Graham influence, coupled with other influences, like that of Italian Renaissance portraiture. And they were also entering into something I related to surrealism. I wasn't interested in the surrealism of Dalí or Magritte or others of the Surrealist movement whose paintings I thought of as being illustrations of ideas. I wanted to make paintings that would have elusive implications somehow related to mystery and subconscious imagery. Our dreams evolve as stories, seen in our sleep like scenes in a film, but are more disjointed and illogical than what most films portray. They are experienced independent of willful thought. I believed to work with that kind of imagery would be more interesting than depicting the everyday things of the real world. But I thought it would be wrong to paint mystery in a deliberate, conscious way. Subconscious imagery lives within a person's mind on a subtle level and I would have to find it as I worked on paintings, allowing it to emerge almost by itself. I wanted an imagery that would work as an unreality in which things didn't have to make sense in terms of real space or the laws of gravity. I made a large painting of two horses based on the horse anatomy engravings by George Stubbs. One horse was a skeleton and the other, identical in position, was from the outer layers of musculature of Stubbs' running horse, seen in 3/4 view. It was dreamlike in its strangeness. Another of my Dayton paintings was a half figure of a man in profile holding a cigarette in one hand. Or he could have been holding a stick of white chalk. What interested me was the way the figure occupied the space within the edges of the canvas and the way the hand was painted. It wasn't important what the hand held. It could be one thing or it could be another thing. Visually they were the same. There was a curtain and a window and a table that were only half described. The painting had a kind of pinwheel composition, with each of the four elements radiating outward toward a different side of the canvas.

I was still making collages like those I made at Yale, using vintage portrait photographs and parts of illustrations from botanical books and anatomy books. I found an old first aid manual with black and white photos showing how an injured man could be carried and how wounds could be bandaged. I used a few of those images in my collages as well as a few small photographs from Eadweard Muybridge's *The Human Figure in Motion*. There was a particularity in those images that interested me within the context I was creating in my collages that was unlike that for which they were originally intended. I thought of my collages and my paintings as being separate, though both were part of my endeavor to figure out what I was doing with my work as a painter.

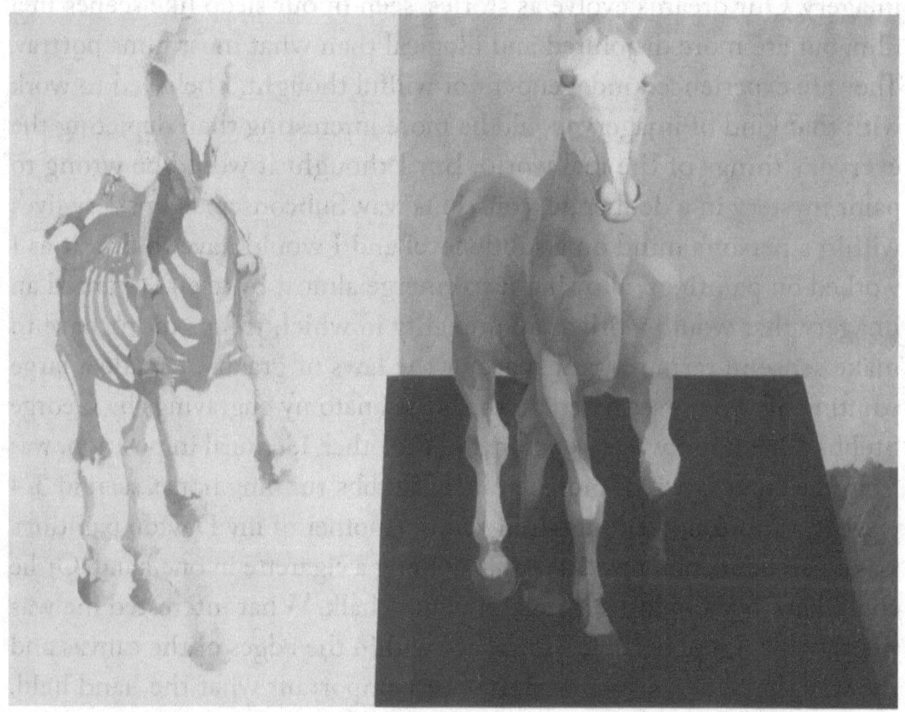

Horses, 1968

I liked the paintings I made in those two years but they didn't feel right in that they didn't seem to come into being naturally. I began to realize that as much as I was trying to avoid it, I had been imposing ideas on my paintings rather than finding an imagery that would result from a personal development that ought to evolve almost on its own if allowed to. I had been trying to force something to happen, and I had been impatient. I was beginning to understand how impatience isn't good, that it could not be part of my painting process if I was going to do anything I would ultimately be happy with. So I was beginning to reconsider my flirtations with surreal imagery in order to find what was most important to me and closest to my own inner being. That meant I was returning to things more difficult to deal with because I didn't really understand them yet, trusting they would become clearer to me in time. I had yet to know what kind of paintings I wanted to make.

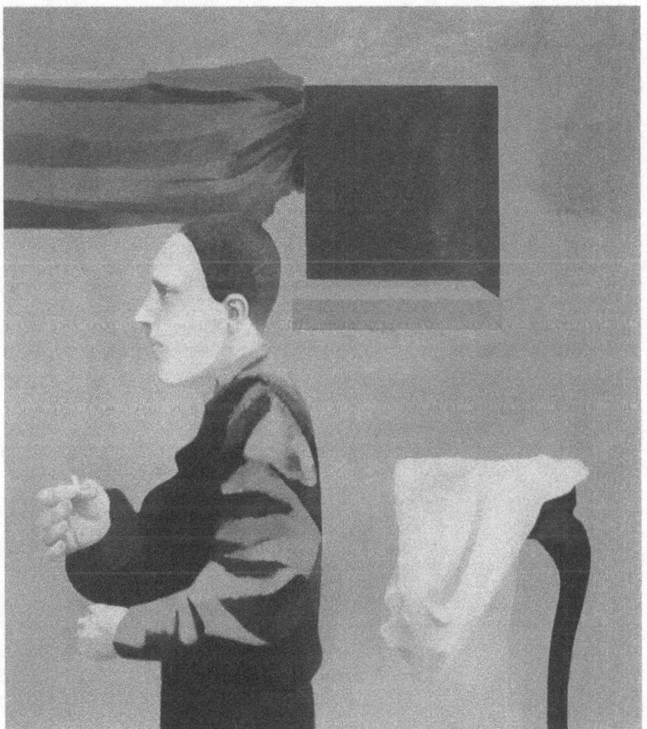

Man, Window, Table, Curtain, 1970

The summer between my two years teaching in Dayton, Toni and I were in Europe. I flew Icelandair, staying a couple of nights in Reykjavik before going on to Luxembourg, from where I took a train to Lisbon. A few weeks earlier Toni had gone to Australia to visit her grandmother and then traveled by ship from Australia to Lisbon, where we met up. From Lisbon we went to the coastal towns of Cascais and Estoril. It was early May and the beginning of the summer season, and on the beach of one of the towns we watched women and girls in a line that stretched from the edge of the beach to the sea, each seated on the sand with a basket in front of her collecting the parched cigarette butts and little bits of trash left there over the winter months. They sang as they slowly advanced across the entire beach. Portugal was like Europe before Europe became industrialized and modern and prosperous.

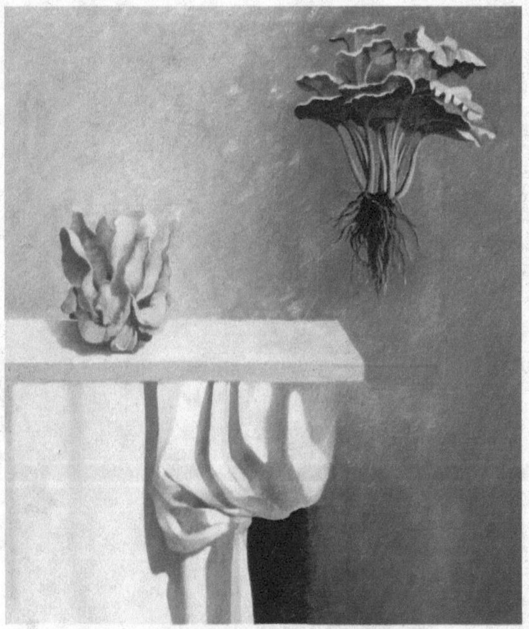

Saint Martin's Weed, 1970

We were only in Portugal a few days before going on to Rome, where I revisited the places I had known and loved from my year at the Overseas School. Lew Cohen was a Fellow at the American Academy in Rome at the time and Toni and I visited him there. I knew Lew's wife, Norah Pierson, from when I first started to work at Sal's Place. She was one of the waiters who was doubling as a kitchen cleanup person. I saw Lew and Norah in Provincetown when they returned the following summer to visit Sal and to give him a sign they had made to hang in front of the restaurant. It was a painted Neapolitan-styled sign on a cutout shape of rigid aluminum in the form of Sal wearing his white apron holding a large skillet of mussels and a fish, with an orange setting sun behind his head. Sal asked me to do the lettering across the bottom of the sign. I painted Sal's Place, Italian Restaurant, Quisisana. The word *quisisana* meant "here you cure yourself," and in this context translated to mean something like good health through fine food.

In his Academy studio, Lew was working on a life-sized female figure in clay that I liked very much. It was in Rome with Lew and Norah that I first met Gregory Gillespie. I had seen Gillespie's Forum Gallery exhibition in 1966 and was very interested in his work. A few years later, when Gregory Gillespie and I were both represented by Forum Gallery, we reconnected, but because we lived far from each other, regrettably I didn't have the opportunity to know him well.

When we arrived in Florence, Toni and I found that all the pensioni listed in our guidebook were full. Even back in 1969 Florence was overrun with tourists. I went from one pensione to the next, and other people were coming out of the front door of each building, passing me as I walked in, holding the same guidebook as I had in my hand, having been told there were no rooms available. So I asked at the desk of one such place if the woman, by chance, had a friend who had a pensione that wasn't listed in the guidebooks and therefore might still have a room. And she phoned a friend and directed us to a small pensione that was well hidden upstairs in a building only half a block from the back side of the Duomo. It had a tiny little indication next to the buzzer on the street saying Locanda Soggiorno Amalfi. We were given a nice back room from where the sounds of scooters and small motorcycles outside weren't heard. The woman lived in the apartment with her mother and her young son and kept a few rooms for guests. They served breakfast on a small rooftop terrace off the kitchen where they kept a tortoise that walked freely at our feet. It was perfect in every way. It was on their TV that Toni and I, together with the family, watched Neil Armstrong taking his first step on the surface of the moon, and heard him say, "One small step for man, one giant leap for mankind." Such a long time ago.

14

SUSANNA

During my second year of teaching in Dayton, I was awarded a Rome Prize Fellowship, also called a Prix de Rome. So in September of 1970 we put our few belongings in storage, said goodbye to our Dayton period, and left for Naples on an Italian ocean liner. As it had been with my first trip to Europe ten years earlier, I thought it was right that this adventure would begin with a transatlantic crossing by sea. When we arrived in Naples, we hired a taxi to drive us and our cumbersome baggage to Rome and to the American Academy.

I stayed two years at the American Academy in Rome in the company of an interesting group of Fellows, each on his or her own path within our various disciplines doing independent research or working individually in our studios. Anticipating something like what I faced when I began graduate school at Yale and wanting to immerse myself in painting without losing weeks floundering in a new studio, I had brought with me one of my Dayton collages, thinking to begin a painting based on its image. So my first Rome painting began with the partial figures of a couple of ballet dancers floating above the floor in a room. Their legs weren't in the collage. On the left was a grouping of bones on a table and on the right was an antique portrait photo of a girl on whose head I had put a vertebra that she wore like some strange kind of hat. The vertebra was in the scale to the girl like the whale vertebra Sari had in her studio on 57th Street, a bone out of place in a world that could only be within a dream.

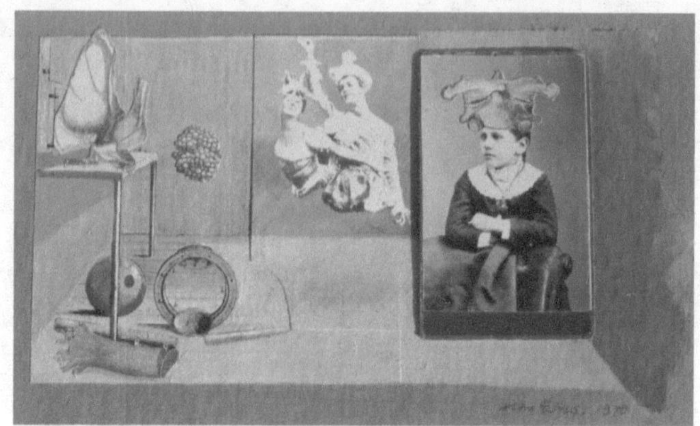

Untitled Collage, 1970

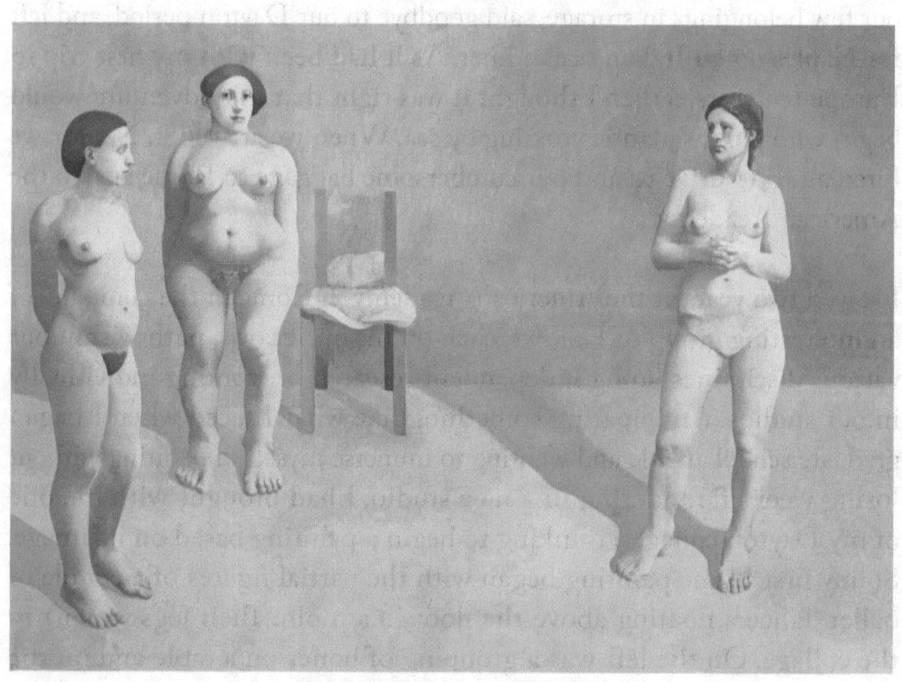

Three Nude Women and Chair, 1970

That first Rome painting measured about 6 x 8 feet. It was larger than anything I had painted before in workspaces that had always been small.

After getting most of the elements from the collage barely stated on the canvas, I was already making changes. Some painters work from completely resolved preliminary studies, but in my case a painting has to evolve through changes made on the painting itself over weeks or months, with little or nothing predetermined. For me painting wants to be an experience that is more than the rendering of an image. The two half-figure dancers came out first, then the girl wearing the vertebra as a hat disappeared, and then the table disappeared. In their places I painted three standing nude women and a chair on a yellow floor with a gray wall behind. In the end, the only thing that remained from the initial stage of the painting based on the collage was the horizontal division between floor and wall. The collage served to get me involved in the painting. The chair was part chair and part something more like de Kooning might have painted in about 1940. It was in form almost a creature, and the closest element in the painting to my playing with a more surreal imagery the previous year. I based one of the women on a photo I had taken of Toni and loosely based the other two figures on photos of Roman copies of Greek Venus statues. One of the almost Venus women I deliberately made heavier and less graceful than the contrapposto Venus figures of classical sculpture because I was concerned with the possibility that I might become too directly influenced by things I was exposed to in Rome and be caught up in a superficiality, or something that might be more decorative than substantial. I knew that to let that happen to my painting, at the uncertain place I was in as a young painter, would be like allowing myself to be lured by Sirens and to crash on the rocks and be destroyed. Or less dramatically, what I hoped to be able to make was something that could come in a natural way out of what I experienced living in Rome, the place I remembered from when I was seventeen as being layered in the factual substance of stones worked by chisels and placed and then displaced, buried, uncovered, sat upon, cried upon, left behind by each piece of history that was and is that great and romantic city. Eternal. Timeless. I couldn't know where that might take my painting. I couldn't get to where I wanted to be because I still wasn't able to envision what it would look like. It had to emerge somehow without too conscious an effort, as a result of things I had yet to know. And that was only just beginning to happen.

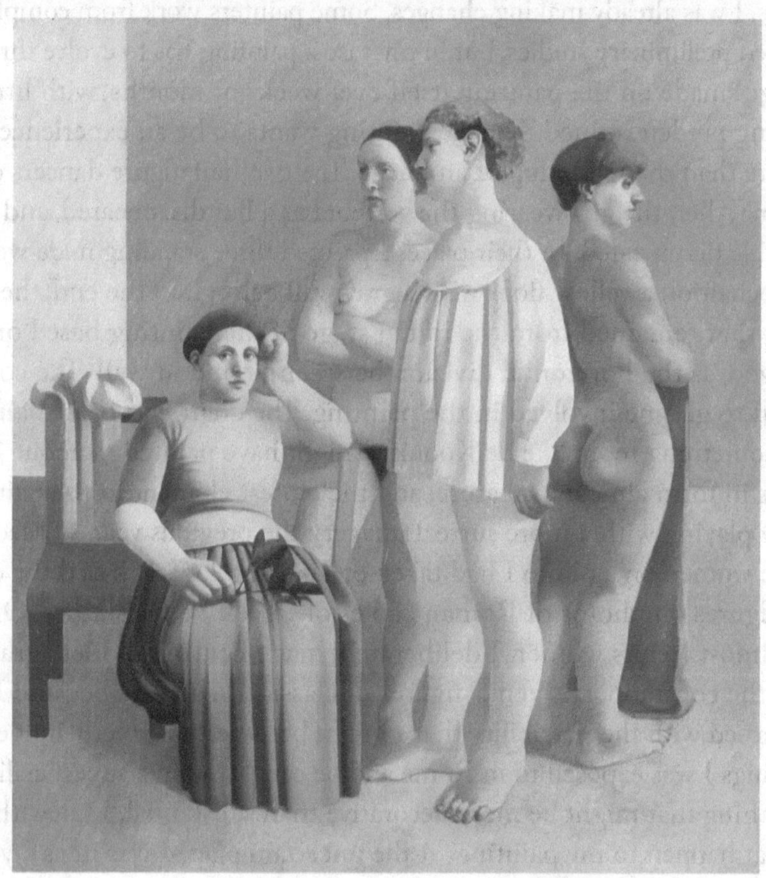

Four Women, One Seated with Olive Branch, 1970

My second Rome painting was also quite large. It had four figures, one of which was taken from a turn of the century family portrait photograph I found at the Porta Portese flea market in Trastevere. In the photograph there was a seated woman, the matriarch of the family that surrounded her, holding a few olive leaves in one hand on her lap. She wore a heavily pleated skirt that interested me for its fluted column-like form. I used her position and the pleated skirt and her hand holding the leaves. I painted her heavier and more classically stylized than the woman in the photograph, making her more like a Picasso figure of the 1920s. One of the standing women in the painting was based on a half-figure from an old postcard photograph, and another I made up without any source at all. The figure on the far right started as a man, but he soon became a very different figure, and a woman.

In that second Rome painting, I wanted a quality that I was seeing in early Renaissance frescoes where the figures, and particularly the legs of those figures, overlap. The frescoes were usually painted above our eye level on church walls so we don't often see the ground or floor surface. We see a density of legs of different colors and the spaces between the legs forming a continuous, almost abstract pattern across the lower part of the fresco. Beautiful examples of this are Andrea Mantegna's fresco of the Gonzaga family, (the one in which the figures are standing), in the Camera degli Sposi of the Ducal Palace in Mantova, and frescoes by Piero della Francesca in the church of San Francesco in Arezzo.

The direction I was letting my painting take had influences from Italian Renaissance painting and Roman sculpture along with traces of the early Gorky and de Kooning figure paintings I had been influenced by as a graduate student. And they had aspects of some of the paintings by Italian painters working between the wars. From those influences what I was painting was my own, not showing any influences in an obvious way.

There was one particular painting by an Italian painter hitherto unknown to me that more than any other single painting influenced me while I was working at the American Academy in Rome. I chanced upon it after nearly finishing my second Rome painting. It was by Felice Casorati, titled *Susanna*, painted in 1929. It is a painting of two people sitting together in an interior space. It is a perfectly composed painting having a quiet, contemplative quality I loved.

I first saw *Suzanna* when I was wandering through the rooms of Rome's Galleria Nazionale d'Arte Moderna e Contemporanea. Then and there that one painting stopped me and held me captivated. The other rooms of paintings that I had just seen disappeared from my consciousness. There it was, a painting that had everything I could want my own paintings to have.

One of the figures is a naked woman, sensual but seemingly unaware of her sensuality. She doesn't look like someone who has such concerns. She is comfortable in her body and she feels safe in the presence of the other figure, a man dressed in a gray suit. Perhaps the man is talking in whispers to her as they sit close together. She could be listening to what he is telling her, but we don't know that he is speaking. They could just as well be turned inward in thought. We don't know why he is clothed and she is naked. The one foot of the man that we can see wears a red slipper. It would be unlikely to be a red shoe, because few men's shoes would have been red like that when the painting was made. Slippers would suggest these two people are at home. I see it as an intimate scene, even though Susanna and the man might seem to be separate in their aspect. All we can assume is that this is a quiet, domestic scene that remains mysterious and is evocative of something unexplained that is about these two people. And that's all I would want it to show.

Realizing that this painting by Casorati might direct me in what kind of paintings I wanted to paint, I tried to understand what made that painting seem so important to me. What it helped me to understand was that a quiet painting showing two figures, in this case one being a clothed man and the other a naked woman, sitting on two chairs in an interior space, could have the kinds of psychological nuances and tensions that interested me in a painting. And that subject could be repeated endlessly in all kinds of variations without it being exhausted. Such paintings could have enigmatic subcurrents I don't feel I need to or even want to know. When a painting is mysterious, it is more engaging than when it is deadpan direct and simple, no matter how well it is painted. And I should add that after my two years at the American Academy, when I could no longer go down into the center of Rome to see the painting, other than my memory of it, I had only a small black and white photograph to look at. On subsequent trips to Italy I searched for a book on Casorati that would have that painting reproduced in color and only found such books years later when they were published to accompany a new exhibition.

Casorati was not a painter of highly refined, nuanced, detailed and polished descriptive surfaces. He was not a realist in that sense, but a figurative painter who described things well, without excesses of any kind. Susanna's knees, and her face, are described as specific and well observed anatomically correct forms made up of carefully placed spots of color. The contours of her legs are precise in how they reflect the way one's body will change with any changes in position, and the pressing of one volume against another. Susanna's thighs are made wider by the seat of the chair under them. But nothing is overdone. The turn of her head and neck and her collarbones and shoulders are beautifully described, but not over-described. Her breasts have weight to them, but they are hardly more than part of her body. Suzanna is not treated as an idealized goddess figure. Nor is she a model posing for a painter. She is simply a naked woman sitting quietly in the presence of a man fully dressed. And we know not why. To me, that is marvelous. As painters, we can create our own reality. Or our own unreality.

I studied the painting while thinking about how it might influence my own paintings. I saw three chairs and the molding of a doorway divide the surface of the painting with horizontals and verticals and diagonals, while at the same time they define the space surrounding the two figures. I saw how darks and lights are meaningful in their placement as they move from the back upper edge of the canvas to the bottom edge. Some newspapers spread casually under the feet of the two figures hold down the plane of the floor. Their laps and the seats of the chairs define a second horizontal plane above that of the floor. The painting is simple and it is complex, both in terms of compositional structure and in terms of narrative and how little or how much of a psychological content a painting might want to have. I still look at this Casorati painting, and each time I learn from it. That learning might come as a simple whisper that says, "Make what you are working on better." Few if any of us are capable of painting as well as those we try to emulate, but we try nevertheless. We compare what we make to what we consider to be the very best works made by those artists at the top of our personal list of the greatest artists of all time. That isn't a formula to guarantee failure. That isn't what it is about. It is a challenge we undertake that becomes something we live for.

I was already interested in how the paintings by Willem de Kooning and Arshile Gorky could seem to be so right in the measured placement of one or two figures within the edges of a canvas, and how that was enough to concern myself with in terms of content. The paintings Picasso made up to and through the 1920s were also among those that I was learning from in terms of what one or two or a few figures could do in a space that had little else. The simple elegance of the Metropolitan Museum's Greek marble relief carvings on funerary steles had interested me for years. I had known and loved those marble reliefs since I was a child. Picasso had based some of his best early paintings on their compositions. They were like the bare bones essence to which other elements could be added that would bring in layers of suggested meanings.

In the course of those two years in Rome, my paintings finally found a direction that felt right. I knew I wanted to make figure paintings that had in them everything I had internalized from the painters I most admired. I painted by the daylight that came in through the very large window in my studio and at the end of the day, sitting on my studio cot as the light diminished, I saw the gray wall behind the figures in my paintings disappear and the figures would seem to inhabit the deep space of my studio itself and appear to be quite real in that dim light.

The sound of the noon cannon somewhere in the distance always rattled the glass of my studio window in its iron mullions, breaking the silence I was working within, telling me lunch would soon follow. It was one of the things that characterized place and time in those most important two years while I was there. I liked waiting in the salone downstairs for the call to enter the dining room for lunch and dinner. The scale of the room was monumental, with a very large fireplace on one wall and a large painting of Diana on a hunt on the opposite wall. The wait was often accompanied by the sound of the clinking of billiard balls coming from the smaller room between the salone and the dining room. Fellows, residents, visiting artists and scholars ate together at long tables.

Visits and tours to places of interest were organized by the Academy throughout the year. I went on one such excursion with a few Fellows in the little Academy van to do what is called the Piero della Francesca Trail. Often simply the Piero Trail. The works of Piero della Francesca have the same narrative common to Italian Renaissance paintings, but they also have a grandeur that is unlike that of most Renaissance painting. Piero's paintings have a mystical presence that's hard to explain, being a subtle quality that doesn't easily fit spoken language. It is a gravitas we feel in part because his paintings are devoid of any excesses or decorative embellishments, and because in Piero's paintings there is an underlying geometry that creates a serenity and a monumentality that is fairly unique. Philip Guston and his wife, Musa, were with us. It is always a great privilege to be with passionate painters looking at the paintings they love most, and Philip Guston had been a great admirer of Piero della Francesca all his life. Guston's early paintings of children playing in city streets wearing paper hats and holding wooden swords and trashcan lid shields bear witness to the admiration he had for Piero della Francesca. They referenced one of the battle scenes Piero painted in Arezzo. I think even the last period of Guston's paintings, in a less direct way, and coupled with a measure of Fellini narrative, also have in them a poetic presence that would have something to do with the paintings of Piero della Francesca. We went together to Arezzo and Sansepolcro and Urbino and Monterchi to stand in front of Piero's paintings. Books can't equal what we gain from being in the places where these paintings were painted, seeing them in the original.

Philip Guston had been a Fellow at the American Academy in Rome when he was a young man, soon after the war, and returned as Painter in Residence at the Academy during my time there as a Fellow. Guston had just made a break from the Abstract Expressionist paintings he had been known for and was painting the clumsy, somewhat cartoon-like figures that had gotten unfavorable critical reviews just before he and Musa arrived at the Academy. Those new paintings started to be well accepted only following his residency at the Academy in 1971. I grew to like Guston's new paintings very much, as unlike my own as they were. In fact it may be that *because* his paintings were so very unlike anything I could ever make that I grew to like them very much. It could also be that because I liked Philip and Musa, I like those crazy paintings.

Balthus has probably been the single most important 20th century painter for me. He is known simply by the name Balthus, from his full name Balthasar Klossowski de Rola. I had known Balthus's painting titled *The Street*, (1933-35) since I was a boy going to the Museum of Modern Art in New York. Before Balthus had permitted books to be published on his work, which only started after his large retrospective exhibition in Paris that then moved to the Metropolitan Museum in New York in 1984, I would often visit the Pierre Matisse Gallery and the Wittenborn Book Store, hoping to find a new Balthus catalogue. None of the earlier catalogues that I found had color reproductions. I saw the Metropolitan retrospective in New York in 1984, and saw the Palazzo Grassi retrospective in Venice in 2001, the year Balthus died. And I saw his retrospective exhibition in Rome in 2015, which was divided between the Scuderie del Quirinale and the Villa Medici. Each of those major exhibitions was different in what it included and in how it was organized. Each was supremely important for me to see.

When I go to large retrospective exhibitions I often try to focus on one aspect of the work as I move from one painting to another. With Balthus, I would try to see and understand how every part in any painting has meaning and wants to be there in exactly the way I see it. Nothing in a Balthus painting is without purpose.

Between 1961 and 1977 Balthus was the director of the French Academy in Rome, in the Villa Medici, and was there while I was a Fellow at the American Academy. I would have liked very much to know Balthus, but I had been told that he was a very private man and not even the French Academy Fellows I had met had been invited to see his studio. I did finally meet him at one of the Villa Medici exhibitions he curated toward the end of my two years at the American Academy. I took the opportunity to give him the little catalogue from the show of my paintings that was currently hanging at the American Academy gallery. After a couple of minutes standing together amidst many others at the opening, that was that.

My American Academy in Rome exhibition in 1972 was my first one-person exhibition, and the small catalogue that accompanied it was the first publication that reproduced any of my paintings. I hoped the catalogue could work for me in some way. I wanted my paintings to be seen by people beyond the walls of the Academy, so I spent some time in the library looking at exhibition catalogues and books to see what names of collectors in Rome I could find. With a few names, I looked in the phone book for addresses, and I drove around Rome delivering catalogues to people I hoped would be interested. I only remember two of the places that idea took me to. When I was led into the foyer of the apartment by the servant of one of the collectors, while waiting for the collector to come in to greet me so I could give him my catalogue, in front of me there was a painting by Michelangelo Pistoletto. It had a life-sized figure painted on thin paper cut out and adhered to a mirror surface of stainless steel. It was typical of Pistoletto paintings but it was the first one I had ever seen. The idea was very interesting for what it did with the relationship between painting and reality, between what was within the painting and what was outside the painting. Pistoletto's figure was surrounded by a reflection of the room space the painting hung in. And that changed depending on exactly where the viewer stood, and the viewer could also be reflected in the mirror surface and therein be part of the painting.

The other person I remember going to visit with my exhibition catalogue was Cy Twombly. I was familiar with the work of Twombly and I wanted him to know who I was. Twombly had a magnificent apartment in a palazzo in the center of Rome. He let me in and graciously led me through a series of large, nearly empty rooms, one leading into the next, to the last one that was his studio. The high ceilings and the white walls with their tall windows had a starkness and an elegance that was very beautiful. One room had a marble Roman portrait head on a pedestal. And in that room, along with the Roman portrait was his bicycle and nothing more. In his studio, the painting he was working on was stretched out across the length of the longest wall, with part of it rolled on the left, like a window shade hung sideways, too long to be fully unrolled. The painting was something between calligraphy and a gentle, unpretentious graffiti. It was both playful and elegant.

During the two years I was at the Academy, I would walk down the Gianicolo hill on Sunday mornings, to wander through the weekly flea market called Porta Portese. At the near end of the market there were permanent sheds housing car and scooter parts and tools and machinery, and close to those there were several makeshift dwellings cobbled together from old doors or anything their occupants found put out to trash. They had chickens and other small animals in their yards. I stopped to look at one of those dwellings, early one Sunday morning and the man who lived there walked over to me with two fresh eggs from his chickens in his hand and offered me one of them. I said I didn't have a kitchen to cook in, and he told me the egg was to drink. And he cracked one and drank the contents. I liked that this man was not asking me for anything. He was just being friendly and generous to a stranger.

One Sunday, I was standing at a vendor's space in the part of the market where things of all kinds were spread out on the ground. And a young man picked up an accordion, turned it so he could see all its sides, and then started to play the most beautiful music. I felt as though I was in what seemed to be an early Fellini film. In Italy the look of a place, or something about a person, or hearing music like what I heard there that morning would bring back memories of those films I loved so much. Fellini was making *Roma* in 1971, while I was at the Academy, and one evening I happened upon a place in downtown Rome that was being prepared for filming. The white arrows and lines on the street surface had been repainted in new configurations, and groupings of posters that were made for Fellini were being put up on a wall according to the film's requirements. Everything was touched, changed in some way to be right for the vision Fellini had for his film.

Several years ago, in the monthly antique market in Perugia, a man picked up an accordion that had been half hidden among the usual clutter of objects on a table and started to play Gypsy music that was both elegant and passionate. And then a woman standing right behind him, next to me, who I think didn't know him, began to sing. And his accordion and her voice had the beautiful melancholic quality that we can feel deep within our bodies, that can transform a place, or transport us to another time. They are moments I love to experience in which life and art become one.

While I was at the Academy, there was a fuel strike, but it was known that one gas station in Rome was still operating at Piazza della Radio, in a part of Rome that we hadn't known. Toni and I went with another Fellow and his wife to get gas so they would have it the next morning. It was a cold winter evening just after dark. We found Piazza della Radio and were driving around it to find the gas station. John slowed down as we passed a scene as good as any scene in a Fellini film. There was a large truck parked with its open back end toward the piazza. And on the ground just below the dark square shape of the empty interior of the truck, a large prostitute was sitting on a chair with a fire at her feet. As we approached her she spread her naked legs, lit by the flickering orange light of the fire. We drove around the piazza to pass her a second time, but having seen that we were two couples in John's car she didn't spread her legs for us a second time.

The Academy encouraged Fellows to travel and we had a small Fiat for which I had made screens to fit the side windows so they could be left open at night while we slept at campsites. I also cut two pieces of plywood to span the dip in the front seats when they were put in the reclining position so that with two pieces of foam rubber on top of the plywood, we could sleep in our car as we traveled across Europe. I had to park the car on a bit of an incline, so the front was higher than the back which allowed the makeshift beds to be level. The campsites ranged from a small one on the side of the Danube in Austria next to a country inn, where we were the only campers, to larger campsites on the edges of cities that were fully functional and peopled. The strangest camping experience we had was pulling into a campsite one cool evening on the coast of Slovenia without knowing it was a nudist campsite until the next morning when nearly everyone was nude except for us. We sat at a table for breakfast next to the little store that had a window onto the patio, through which I saw a Yugoslav girl wearing a dress sitting as she added up the cost of items belonging to a nude man standing in front of her with his genitalia at her eye level. That seemed absurd and almost surreal.

One day, we were on a beautiful beach in Greece, aware of a few teenage boys splashing around in the sea not far from where we were sitting on the sand. There were several other people sitting nearby. Suddenly one of the boys ran past us along the water's edge, and moments later he ran back again in front of us together with a man and they ran into the sea and were swimming out to where the group of boys were now repeatedly diving under and calling to each other. At this point, it was clear to me that one of the boys had gone under and had not come back up. I ran into the water and started swimming toward them when, not halfway out to the others, right below me, I saw a boy with his arms stretched out, face down and motionless. I called out and dove down and brought the boy up to the surface and back to the beach. A couple of men took him from my arms and carried him up to the dry sand, where one of the men started to administer CPR while I massaged the boy's arms and hands, hoping that might help to get his blood circulating again. But it was too late.

The police took me to a teacher at the school who spoke English, wanting to find out whether I knew anything that might or might not suggest foul play. But I knew nothing other than what I had seen. That experience still haunts me to this day.

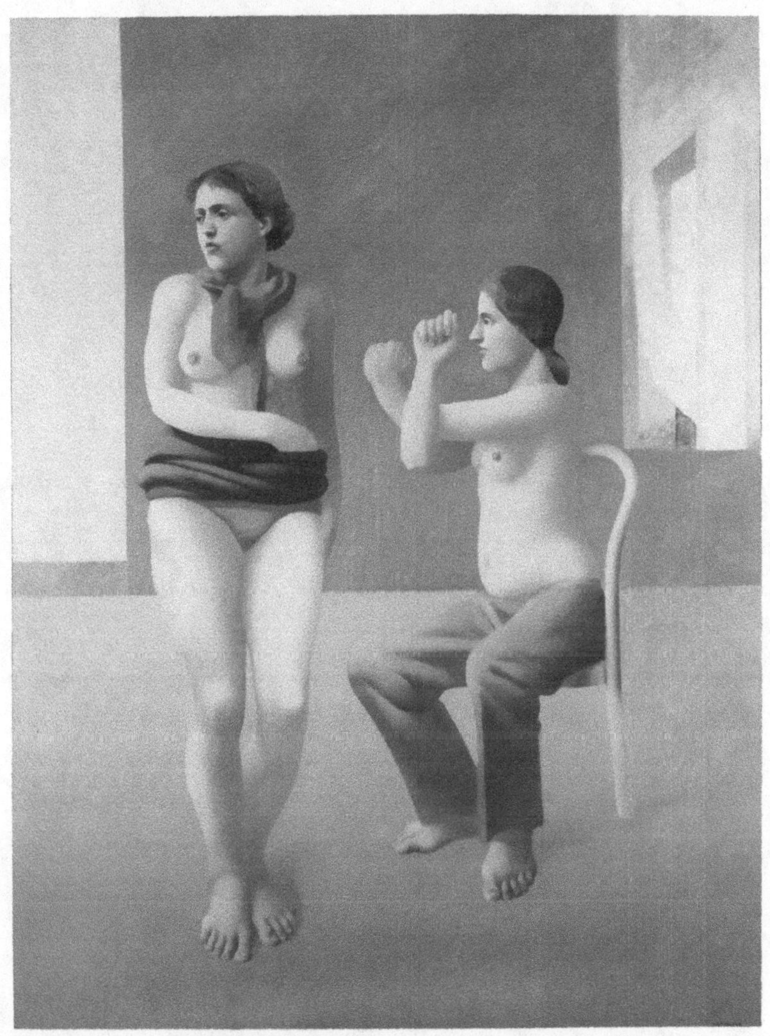

Two Women, One Seated, and Window, 1971

15

CHAGALL'S KISS

I had been offered a full-time tenure track position at American University in Washington, D.C. based solely on my painting slides and what at that point was a very unimpressive resumé. It was enough that the Art Department faculty at American University knew personally and had great respect for Jack Tworkov and Philip Guston, each of whom had written me a strong letter of recommendation. I had been hired before the faculty laid eyes on me. There was no interview and I had not given a slide lecture and critiques of student work, as seems to be required today. They had trust in me, and that was reassuring.

Jack Tworkov was the painting teacher I worked with my second year at Yale. At the time, Tworkov was painting very elegant abstractions, applying a veil of delicate fluid touches of subtle silvery grays on a geometric linear structure. Perhaps because I had told the Director of the American Academy that Jack Tworkov would make a very good Painter in Residence, Tworkov was invited to be Painter in Residence while I was there.

***

In the fourth year of my marriage it was becoming clear to me that Toni was not someone I could see myself being happy with for the rest of my life. I often felt Toni was unable to appreciate me for the person I was, criticizing me much as my mother had done. When I got the job in Washington, Toni expressed disinterest in again being the wife of a college professor, preferring to stay on in Rome. I paid for her to be able to use a small vacant studio at the Academy and to rent a small apartment nearby to live in. Both of us were willing to accept what might happen in terms of having relationships with other people. It was almost as if I was once again a single man, open to what might come into my life.

Washington was a good city in which to teach painting and drawing. It was not overwhelmingly large and there were great museums. And the Art Department at American University had a good reputation and a good faculty. So, strangely, in September of 1972 I found myself living and teaching in the city where I was born but had not visited since my infancy.

After two years of teaching in Dayton and the following two years at the American Academy in Rome, I had a greater understanding of some of the elements I considered to be important in painting and drawing that I wanted to share with students. An example: as a student at Cooper Union, I was introduced to a fascinating idea regarding composing figure paintings. The idea is that parts of one figure, when overlapped by another figure, could be explained, or continued by suggestion, in the overlapping figure. According to that idea, what is hidden wants to be explained in what is in front of it. It is not something we can easily find throughout the history of art, but when I find it I like seeing how it is. In Poussin's *Bacchanal*, in the National Gallery in London, for example, the face of a man in the back row of figures is seen in the elbow of a figure in the foreground. It is an elbow and at the same time it is a face. And half of the female figure in the center of the painting is completed by the demarcation between shadow and light on the same male figure with the elbow. And his arm doubles as her arm when we look at her. The leg of the female figure in blue shares a contour with the leg of the naked man of the obscured face, her upper leg even passing through the leg of the man in front of her to rejoin her lower leg. And there are a few smaller moments like those happening with other figures in the painting.

In the Caravaggio *Deposition*, also titled *The Entombment of Christ*, in the Vatican Museum, one raised arm of the female figure on the right is made in part by the shoulder and neck of another female figure, and both of those figures share the legs of the man supporting Christ's legs, even though that male figure is much stockier than either of the women. It is clear that both painters deliberately made that happen in those paintings. It is a kind of game a painter might like playing. Or, we could say, it is a complexity some painters create of necessity. There is a brief discussion about this in Rudolph Arnheim's book, *Art and Visual Perception: A Psychology of the Creative Eye*. And I have found other instances of shared parts of overlapping figures. Another good example is in the left side of Georges de La Tour's *The Fortune-Teller*, from the 1630s, in the Metropolitan Museum. The arm in the white sleeve visually could belong to either of the two women. And yet another example is in a pastel by Degas called *The Jewels*, from 1886, that is interesting in that what can appear as the arm of one figure is actually that of the other, and if it were the arm of the upper figure, as I first saw it, that figure would have a right hand where it should be a left hand.

What meant most to me as an art student was when a teacher showed how he or she saw paintings, a finger following a line or a direction between separate objects or figures across the surface of a painting in a book, or with a pointer across a projected slide on the wall. And in my teaching, I found that when I used books or projected slides on the wall and pointed out exactly how I understood things to work on a structural level, apart from the reading of the subject matter, students learned important things and they remembered what was shown to them.

It is Picasso's early work that interests me most. When I started teaching in Washington in 1972, I was glad to find that the National Gallery of Art has Picasso's *Family of Saltimbanques*, of 1905. And when I first stood in front of that beautiful painting, which was much larger than I had expected it to be (about 83 x 90 inches), I noticed something that amazed and delighted me. The painting shows a group of saltimbanques, or harlequin performers, in a landscape. I saw it as a balance between narrative and painting issues, like composition and the ways imagery can work in a painting without conforming to the logic we know in the natural world. I was very excited to see something I had never noticed before in reproductions of the painting.

I saw that the largest figure in the group of saltimbanques is missing his right leg. He is standing on only one leg, but he is not standing the way a one-legged man stands. This figure's considerable weight is not centered above his single supporting limb. If he were a real man, he would have fallen over. The little girl with her back to us stands in front of where below her skirt we would expect to see the right leg of the man in red. When I saw this it was as though I was with Picasso in his Paris studio in 1905 while he was working. I could see how the right leg of the man would have crowded the space the legs of the little girl occupied. With that one leg removed, the shape of the space between the leg of the young man on the far left and the little girl's leg was better than it would have been had it been complicated by another leg and foot. Picasso either painted out the missing leg or he never painted it to begin with. Either way, it had to be a conscious decision.

In two other examples I have found of paintings with missing legs, it is table legs that are missing. One is Degas' *L'Absinthe*, also titled *Absinthe Drinker*, from 1875-76. It shows a woman and a man sitting behind three tables in a café, she with her glass of absinthe in front of her. The tables beautifully define a tilted plane that moves diagonally up from the bottom of the canvas toward the left and then shifts toward the right. We see the legs and feet of the woman and the man, but there are no table legs to be seen. The other painting is by Balthus, titled *Solitaire*, dated 1943. There is a girl leaning over a table on which are the cards of her game of solitaire. In this painting one leg of the table is missing. In the same way Picasso's central figure is missing a leg and Degas' café tables have no legs at all, this missing table leg is absent because Balthus saw that the painting would be better without it. And in all three cases we can see how that would be so. I talk to students about learning from the old masters and making analytical drawings from paintings, focusing on forms and the directional lines they make and how everything works with the edges of a painting as abstract structure. I am most interested in paintings that have a balance between abstract composition and readable subject matter. Medieval paintings have that balance. In medieval paintings there is often an awkwardness in the depiction of figures and architecture that allows composition to have an equal place to the narrative. Those paintings, usually about Biblical subjects and the lives of saints, can have changes of scale and oddly unreal depictions of architectural space, and sometimes two or three moments in time within the one image. That kind of deliberate lack of adhering to what we know to be real makes those paintings particularly interesting. Renaissance painters a couple of centuries later became so able to render landscape and architectural perspective, and figures with their beautifully detailed drapery, that their virtuosity can distract us from seeing that their paintings are also about composition.

* * *

I was walking the hallway of the Art Department to give students some time to work before going from one to the next to talk about their drawings. I glanced into the office and gallery and saw a student standing between the desk and the doorway. I stopped and stood looking at her maybe for a minute, possibly longer. Time seemed to have slowed. She was a graduate student named Lani, finishing her Master's degree in painting. As a new young faculty member I wasn't working with graduate students and I hadn't yet spoken to Lani. But now, there she was. There we stood, me in the hallway and she in the middle of the department office and gallery, I looking at her and she at me. She was wearing a long Afghan sheepskin coat that had the fleece on the inside and a decorative embroidery on the soft suede outside. Her hair was tied in a small knot on the top of her head and her face was shiny with some kind of skin cream. She was like nobody I could remember ever having seen before. I was transfixed. Was she really looking at me or was she deep in thought, that I didn't know, though there was nothing else there in the hallway to see other than me and the white painted cement block wall between two classroom studios. Nobody other than me. She didn't say anything. I didn't say anything.

I thought about her for days, seeing her just like that, with her funny little topknot above her shiny pale expressionless face. What I saw was a sweet young person unaware of anything like the trends and fashions other students seemed collectively to share. She was unlike all the art students

I had known in my student days, whose nonconformity was as much a statement of protest as it might have been about having little money or little concern for what we looked like.

My mind made Lani into the incarnation of an ideal I had carried within me for years without knowing what she would actually look like, or if I would ever find her.

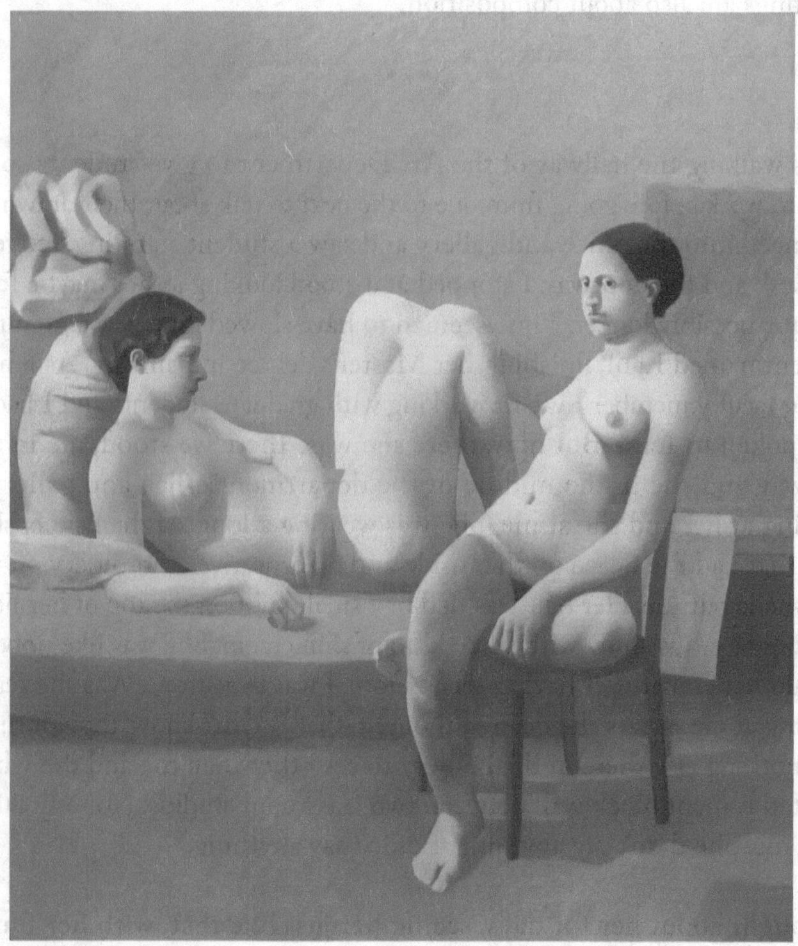

Two Nude Women, One Reclining, One Seated, 1973

***

I arrived in Washington without my Rome paintings. I had crated them and had obtained the paperwork necessary for shipping art out of Italy and left them at the Academy until I had an address in Washington they could be sent to. When I finally had the paintings, I invited a few graduate students to stop by to see them. Lani was among the students who came to my studio to see those paintings. She told me the following day that the experience of seeing them had kept her from sleeping. She said the paintings were for her a rare and impressive merging of the contemporary with the classic and were very personal and individual and intensely expressive.

Following this exchange about her feelings after seeing my paintings, Lani and I had very little contact, only occasionally passing in the corridors of the art department. I was occupied with my teaching and Lani was busy with her classes and studies. But I would think about her. Though I knew little about Lani, she had told me that after she graduated high school at age 15 in 1963, she and her family had lived in Naples. We shared a deep love of Italy.

When Christmas drew near, Toni flew to Washington from Rome. Maybe she thought we needed to see how we would feel about each other after the few months living apart. Probably her parents had asked her to return for the holidays and to the marriage she had left hanging. While she was visiting, I showed her the school and awkwardly introduced her to faculty members in the Art Department. I took her to museums. We were pretending to be a couple while it was clear, at least in my mind and heart, that the marriage was over.

Although I don't quite remember how it happened, Lani invited me to bring Toni to a small gathering at her house in Virginia on New Year's Eve. We were only four couples and it was a strange evening for me to be among people I either barely knew or didn't know at all, feeling uncomfortable because I was there with Toni, who sat with a pack of Gauloises held between her fingers, intended to impress the others, as if to say, "Look at me, I have European culture."

What no one other than Lani and her then husband knew was that she had told him that she was unhappy in her marriage and wanted to end it. There was a sweet sadness in Lani's eyes and demeanor that, although I knew nothing of what was causing it, I found alluring. Soon after that party, Lani moved out of the house she and her husband shared, taking her car and little else with her.

Toni returned to Rome and I was once again by myself in my little McLean Gardens apartment at the start of the spring semester. Lani was staying with a roommate in an apartment on Wisconsin Avenue, a few blocks down from my little apartment. One evening, she and her roommate invited me to dinner along with the secretary of the Art Department and her husband. When I arrived at the house, Lani came out the front door at the top of the steps looking very cheerful and without saying a word she reached up and kissed me. And for shy Alan who had no such expectations, that kiss was momentous in its effect. I see it in memory as Marc Chagall's 1915 painting of his first kiss with his wife, Bella, titled *Head Over Heels in Love*, also titled *The Birthday*. In the painting Chagall and Bella float above the floor of her room in a moment of extraordinary tenderness, real the way feelings will sometimes defy the constraints of everyday reality and take us to a place more beautifully real than what is possible. I lived with fantasies in my head and dreams in the night and by day that I only barely had control over. My fantasies accompanied my days without me directing their existence. But the kiss at the top of those steps on Wisconsin Avenue was something I had not fantasized. It took me by surprise as something I would have wished for, believing it could only be a longing living in my mind. I felt it in my whole being.

At dinner that evening, Lani and I sat with our feet touching beneath the tablecloth and our eyes meeting as though they were asking a question we could not ask in words. I was hoping what was happening between us was unseen by the department secretary, whose position would have been one of disapproval.

I know it was not love at first sight because we knew each other a little at school already. It was more like love at first believing I could possibly have found the girl I would spend a lifetime with. I'm not sure if I thought that at the time, but I did know that this could be love in a way that made all my previous relationships feel unimportant. What I felt at that moment was pure joy. It felt like something had welled up in the core of my body, as though it was an internally driven force that moved like a wave within me. I hadn't expected such intense emotions. I thought if this were to be the beginning of something really meaningful, I was fabricating a possibility on a supposition about who Lani was and what she might become in time. Not only that. I was going on trust about who I was likely to become as time passed, and thinking we could, perhaps, travel that road together. There were already moments when we were first seeing each other that were new to me and said to me that this was more special than what I had known before, like when Lani baked a cake for my thirtieth birthday, that was the only birthday cake I can remember ever having been made for me.

* * *

In the spring of 1973, Lani had been legally separated from her first husband and divorce papers had been filed, and I was fighting to be free of Toni, who was back in Rome. Lani's first marriage had only lasted two years and mine had been about five. Fortunately neither of us had children from those first failed marriages. As the rest of that year unfolded, Lani and I were spending time together. We discussed paintings and we talked about the Italy each of us had known and felt a longing to return to. We made trips to New York, where I shared with Lani the things I had known and liked most. I took her to the museums I had grown up knowing well and showed her particular paintings that had been important to me in the ways I was developing as a painter. This was the city of my childhood and my art student years, the city where I felt most at home. I took her to the Papaya King on East 86th street for their very good hot dogs and papaya juice, and we ate hot potato knishes and halvah on the street from Merit Farms. We stayed nights with friends and visited friends I wanted Lani to know. Sometimes we drove Route 1 from Washington, partly to save the cost of highway tolls but more because the drive, though much slower, would be more interesting. Instead of stopping at highway rest stops that were all the same on roads that were all the same, we saw things like an airplane that had been made into a roadside diner.

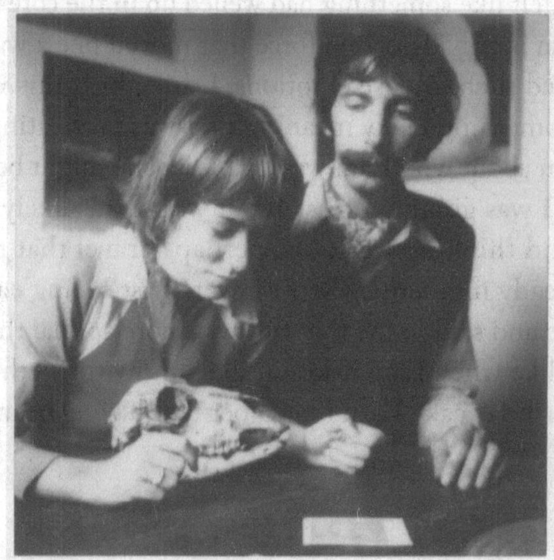

With Lani, 1974. Polaroid by Emmet Gowin

On our first New York trip together I waited until we were in the city before making calls from a phone booth to find a place to sleep. What I found had us staying in a completely empty apartment that a couple I had met at the Academy in Rome, and only barely knew, were having painted before they would move in from another apartment downstairs in the same building. Not only was there no furniture whatsoever, but there was a round hole in the door in place of a lock. Strange as that hospitality was, we liked the privacy it gave us, and the oddness of it didn't seem to matter since it was part of an adventure we were having. So we slept on Lani's Afghan coat on the bare floor of an unlocked empty apartment in the middle of Manhattan and were perfectly happy. Crossing the street after what seemed hours trying to find a place to leave the car, I picked up a five-dollar bill somebody had dropped between parked cars and we bought olives and beer for our supper. I took finding five dollars on the street to be an omen of good things to come. It seemed right that chance should make more of this first trip to New York together than if everything were planned from home at the outset.

* * *

Without a lot of effort on my part during those first months teaching at American University, I was invited to have an exhibition at the Jacob's Ladder Gallery in Washington in 1973, and in the same months I began the arduous process of taking my slides to New York galleries hoping to find one that would want to take me on. But I was one among hundreds, or maybe even thousands, of young artists seeking New York gallery representation. I walked from one gallery to another, asking if the director would look at my slides, and it was seldom that I was given the opportunity to sit with a gallery director. Most often a gallery assistant would tell me that they weren't taking on any new artists. Or I might be told I could mail the gallery a sheet of slides and a resume along with a self addressed stamped envelope. Art gallery directors didn't want to be confronted by an artist seeking gallery representation and I understood that was how it was, but I knew also that on rare occasions a gallery does take on a new artist and I believed sooner or later my paintings would interest a gallery director. I was able to accept repeated rejections, as discouraging and demoralizing as they were, because I understood both the artist's side and that of the gallery.

During a trip to Rome the year before, Bella Fishko, the Director of Forum Gallery, had visited a few studios at the American Academy. I had not been informed about her visit and therefore I missed what might have been a good opportunity. I already knew that Forum Gallery was one of the best figurative galleries in New York and it was high on my list of galleries to approach. So I wrote to Bella Fishko from Washington, explaining that I had missed her studio visits at the Academy, that I was now teaching at American University in Washington, and that I was hoping to be able to show her my work the next time I would be in New York. A few months later I was in New York and I sat with Bella Fishko in her office and showed her my slides. She was impressed by my paintings and decided to include me in a group show at Forum Gallery that summer that would be part of the New Talent Festival. The New Talent Festival was made up of about a dozen New York Galleries that had simultaneous group show openings of the work of the most promising artists who had asked to be represented by them during the past year.

After that Bella asked me to send her what I considered to be my three best paintings. When it was time to take paintings to the gallery for the exhibition we borrowed Lani's sister's truck. And after delivering the paintings to the gallery, that night we slept in the back of the truck parked under the street lamps in a quiet residential area three blocks east of the gallery. We saw the trip as an adventure and I was excited to have three of my paintings in Forum Gallery at the beginning of my career.

We spent the next day in the Metropolitan Museum, where among other things, I showed Lani one of my favorite Italian paintings in the museum collection. It was Fra Filippo Lippi's *Portrait of a Woman with a Man at a Casement*. It is a beautiful, double portrait, unlike any other Renaissance portrait known to have been painted at the time Lippi made it. In the painting, a young woman in profile facing left fairly fills what we can see of her room. A bit of landscape is seen outside a window on the back wall. Close in front of her the face of a young man is seen poking into her room through the frame of another window. They look past each other lost in thought. It is a painting about the intimacy of two young people in love. What draws me to this small painting perhaps more than to any other painting in the Metropolitan Museum collection is its gentle intimacy. Most of the paintings in the adjoining rooms are much bigger and more inclusive of every kind of detail while depicting momentous events of one kind or another, but as impressive as they are with their angels suspended above their Madonnas and whatnot, they lack the tenderness and the simplicity of this little Lippi double portrait, which speaks to me in whispers while I am in my studio, whenever and wherever that may be. I took Lani to the Museum of Modern Art and showed her Henri Rousseau's *The Sleeping Gypsy*, painted in 1897, that had been my favorite painting long before I had seen the Lippi, or Arshile Gorky's paintings, before I noticed Balthus' street painting also in the Museum of Modern Art.

I might have been ten or eleven when I first really saw Rousseau's *The Sleeping Gypsy*, in which a lion stands above a Gypsy asleep in a desolate landscape with a full moon above. Next to her is a mandolin and a water jug. What I loved about it was the silence it depicted. It was a painting about stillness, about the feelings I had within me all my young life. I was, even then, recognizing that the paintings that moved me most were those that depicted quiet and stillness. They were the ones that would center me and calm me. They seemed to say to me that I was safe in my shy and often melancholy being.

The museums were fertile grounds for my daydreaming. I hadn't yet begun in those years to think about one day becoming a painter, but looking back on my early years I can see how great a part paintings played in enduring the hardships of my childhood. I was fortunate to have had the Metropolitan Museum and the Museum of Modern Art as my home territory.

* * *

One thing that was different about time spent with Lani from time spent with any of my previous girlfriends, including my first wife, who fancied herself a painter, was the depth of our conversations about painting. When Lani and I were looking at books and going to museums together, our conversations were about how paintings were composed, and what they were about apart from their subject matter. While in the beginning of our relationship I was explaining to Lani what I understood about paintings, it soon became clear that we were equals in discussing what we saw. Among others, I was showing Lani paintings by Italian artists working between the wars whose work I had come to know while I was at the American Academy in Rome. With the exception of Giorgio Morandi and Giorgio de Chirico, those Italians had been essentially unknown to American painting teachers and their students.

* * *

Forum Gallery occupied the fourth and fifth floors of a small building at 79th Street and Madison Avenue. When we arrived for the opening of the New Talent exhibition, the building was experiencing an electric failure and visitors had to walk the stairs up to the gallery, which had no lights or air conditioning. However, nothing could have dampened my enthusiasm and excitement.

Soon after that I had my first solo exhibition at the Jacob's Ladder Gallery in Washington, which comprised of my Rome paintings and those I had made the following year. The reviews were very positive and a few paintings sold. It is possible that the show's success was in part because Joseph Hirshhorn had bought one of my three paintings from the New Talent show at Forum Gallery[2]. Hirshhorn was an avid and influential art collector whose collection became the core of the Hirshhorn Museum and Sculpture Garden in Washington, D.C., which was under construction and opened a year later.

At the end of the New Talent exhibition, Bella Fishko offered me, as she put it, a "guest one person show" scheduled for 1976. And following that exhibition she welcomed me into her stable, meaning that I was represented by Forum Gallery, and I have been with Forum Gallery ever since. From there my career as a painter began to unfold.

Following Bella Fishko's recommendation, I was very nearly on the cover of the October 1980 issue of *LIFE* magazine. One of my large paintings of four nude female figures had been delivered from Forum Gallery to a photographer's studio in New York. Photographs were made with me posed bare-chested in front of the painting in a position that mirrored one of the painting's figures. In the end the editors elected to use a photo of a Chinese girl that was part of an article about portraits of China for the cover of that issue. But six alternate covers were reproduced in the "Editor's Note" on page 4 and mine was one of them. Although my painting was not used for the cover, it was reproduced in an article about painting titled "The Lonely Look of American Realism," in the company of well-known figurative painters.

---

2   *Three Women (one seated wearing green tights)*, 1973, page 299

Unfortunately by 1980, *LIFE* was being published only monthly and no longer had the prominence it had had as a weekly magazine.

I mention this story because at the time it felt like a brush with success of the kind Jackson Pollack experienced following his *LIFE* magazine cover. Traveling to New York, staying in a chocolate-on-the-pillow kind of fancy hotel, courtesy of *LIFE*, and being photographed in a proper studio for the cover of a major magazine with a large readership seemed to bode well for the future. Over the years I have had many articles published about my work and have had paintings on covers of magazines, but none of those covers or articles had quite the romanticism of my *LIFE* magazine experience.

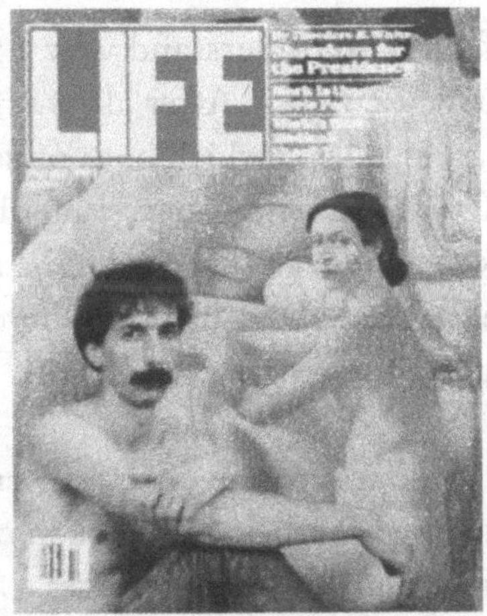

From the Editor's Note page in *LIFE* magazine, October 1980

* * *

In the early summer of 1973, Toni returned to New York in a very delicate emotional state. Her story was that she had fallen in with a few Fellows from the German Academy and in their wild partying, she had been slipped drugs, which resulted in her having a serious nervous breakdown. By the time her parents had received the phone call from the office of the American

Academy in Rome telling them of her condition, Toni was already in a doctor's care, taking heavy medications for depression and unable to fly by herself back to New York. Her mother and sister flew to Rome, and after some days the doctor permitted them to fly Toni back to New York.

Lani and I drove up to New York for a few days, during which time I went to Toni's parent's house in Queens in the morning and returned each evening in a state of despair so deep that only with the emotional support of Lani and the friend we were staying with did I have the strength to resist the pressures I was being subjected to. The sedated Toni I saw was not the vindictive narcissist Toni I had known her to be. Lani and I returned to Washington, and then began months of abuse from Toni and her parents that I am glad are all but forgotten.

It seems impossible for me to understand why I felt that I might not be able to end my marriage to Toni. After all, we had allowed ourselves those months of separation, during which both of us had been unfaithful. However, faced with Toni vehemently contesting divorce, I didn't think I had the right to be strong in what I then saw to be a selfish decision. My dilemma might well have been about having suffered in childhood from the dissolution of my parent's marriage.

Eventually Lani and I got our separate divorces, hers amicable and mine horrid, and we were happy together, giving each other the respect and admiration we hadn't found in our first marriages. Lani was an amazingly kind and gentle person I knew I would learn from as much as she would from being with me.

My version of courtship with Lani involved telling her the stories of the films I loved most that she hadn't seen, and introducing her to works by painters she hadn't known. I introduced her to those of my friends who had meant the most to me in my life. I took her to see films like Fellini's *La Strada* and Jean Vigo's *L'Atalante*. They were the films whose beauty and melancholy touched me most deeply. They were films by directors who composed their films masterfully, frame by frame, and interwove them with music in beautiful and magical ways. They were classic films of the black and white era that tied in with my ideas about how paintings could be composed and structured. I took Lani to see films by Eisenstein and Kurosawa and Buñuel and Chaplin and Fellini, shown in the two repertory theaters in Georgetown, one of which ran a retrospective series of double features every night pairing Fellini and Bergman, and a Samurai film series that had many Kurosawa films.

I have always been interested in films. When I was still a kid living with my mother, long before one could watch films at home other than those that showed on television, and we never had a television, occasionally we would go to watch a movie in a theater. In my childhood, that may have only been once or twice a year, but more than that later on. My mother would buy the tickets and we would walk into the theater at some random point after the film had been running and find seats in the flickering light of the screen. When the film would end, there would be an intermission and people would go out while others came in and we would stay in our seats until the film would begin again. Then, when the film reached the point where we had come in, we would get up and leave. Strangely, I didn't question why my mother had no problem seeing movies from somewhere in the middle to the end and then from the beginning to the middle. But she would do that and it was therefore normal for me to be seeing films that way, conditioning me in something like a kind of dyslexic contrariness that might explain why I might skip around and not finish reading a book. I do that sometimes because I'm interested in the writing itself more than in the story being told.

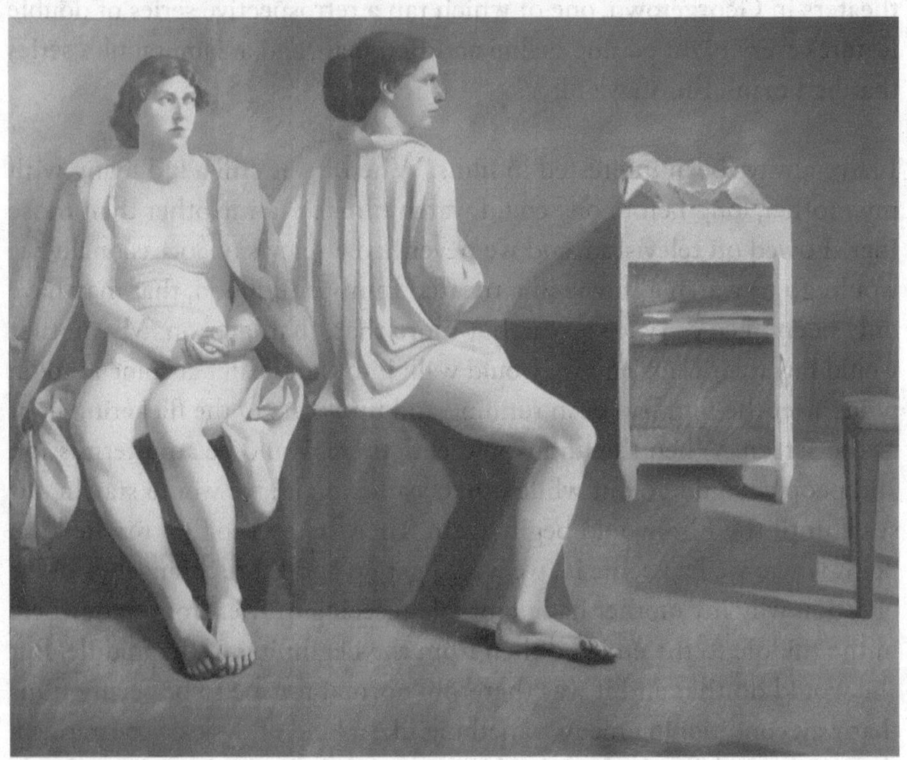

White Cabinet (Two Women on a Bed), 1975

16

ITALIE

In the summer of 1974 Lani and I flew Icelandair to Luxembourg. We walked out of the airport with our small shoulder bags and standing at the side of the road, I held a cardboard sign on which I had written ITALIE. It was not long before we got a ride with a Luxembourg businessman driving to southern France. He was well dressed in a tweed suit and seemed rather formal. There was little spoken between us until evening when he stopped at a country inn just outside Dijon. He told us he always stopped there for the night and offered to drive us farther the next morning if we wanted to take a room in the same inn. That evening in the restaurant of the inn, we had a most memorable chicken dinner, rich in Dijon mustard.

After breakfast the next morning, we continued as far as Lyon, where our driver left us at the side of the road to find our next ride. We discovered that in southern Europe, hitchhiking was not easy, and our ability to get rides slowed down dramatically. In Provence we were picked up by a truck driver who we assumed was French. And our ability to speak even poor French was very minimal, so we had little conversation until we stopped for coffee at a truck stop. I saw a truck there that had Italian tags and we asked our driver whether we could change to the Italian truck, whereupon our driver told us that he was, in fact, Italian, and he, too, was going to Italy. So we stayed with him.

The ride had been rather slow and plodding until we crossed into Italy, where on the curves of the Ligurian coast, our driver became quite another person, taking the road with ease and speed. When we arrived in Ventimiglia, he left us at a hotel where he knew the owner. And although it was late and the restaurant had closed, the owner shared with us a bottle of wine and a plate of cheeses and prosciutto. Gradually, after a couple of glasses of red wine, Lani began to remember enough of her Italian that she was able to discuss her nostalgic memories of living in Naples with this Neapolitan hotelier. In the morning we breathed the fresh sea air and went to the small covered market, and bought mozzarella and tomatoes before boarding a local train headed to Rome.

In our six weeks, we went to Rome, Orvieto, Todi, Assisi, Arezzo, Siena, Florence, and Venice. It was not easy to travel on five dollars each a day, but it was still possible if one loosely followed Arthur Frommer's guidebook, *Europe on Five Dollars a Day*. A pensione room without a bathroom cost about five dollars a night, which left five dollars for picnicking, and that wasn't bad for a young couple who dearly loved being in Italy.

* * *

Lani and I first saw Bendt Thoft Nielsen in the chapel with the Piero della Francesca frescoes in Arezzo. We introduced ourselves to each other a few days later when, in Florence, we and he walked toward each other on a narrow back street and came close enough that Lani and I recognized the young man we had seen sitting on the floor of that chapel in Arezzo, speaking softly to his friend in a language I thought might have been German. We knew they had to be artists because only artists would be as engrossed with Piero della Francesca's frescoes as they were, and out of respect for each other and for the solemnity of the chapel we hadn't said anything to them nor they to us. But then seeing this tall, handsome man walking up to us with his broad smile of recognition, one could believe we might have been destined to meet and to become friends. As it turned out, we would not just be friends, but friends who would share a great deal and whose lives would be changed as a result of our friendship. Bendt and his travel companion had come to Arezzo from Copenhagen and Lani and I had traveled at the same time from Washington to Arezzo. In a sense we were on the pilgrimage other artists had been on at varying times in history to see Piero della Francesco's frescoes and pay homage to that Renaissance master, who had a sort of cult following among certain artists. Looking back on that time, I would say the trajectories of our separate lives not only crossed but recrossed a few more times, becoming intertwined in profound ways. Lani and I spent three days with Bendt in Florence, going to the Uffizi and to churches together, discussing what we saw, and having lunches at Trattoria da Benvenuto behind the Uffizi.

Bendt showed us lithographs he had in an exhibition at the Palazzo Strozzi. His work was reminiscent of Giorgio Morandi's still life etchings and yet more intriguing in the nature of his choice of subject, and finer in his touch of the cross-hatching tones. In his paintings, etchings, and drawings Morandi gave simple everyday objects new meaning by their placement in compositions that were about clusters and voids, and how objects might touch and how sometimes their tops lined up in an unlikely precision, or how they might keep to themselves as though in defiance. But because Morandi's works were made quickly, they can lack a more contemplative quality that was something I found in Bendt's lithographs, in which a slow building of tones produced a very different result from what a more spontaneous technique would make. I sensed that a more thoughtful mind directed Bendt's hand as he set down each line in the delicate crosshatching of his black and white tonally elaborate images. In my favorite of those lithographs, a loaf of French bread stands alone vertically with a dried flower on top that I believe is the flower of a persimmon tree that leaves a stiffer version of itself as a persimmon grows behind it. The dried flower at the top of the bread is mysterious and strange in its unlikely placement and in its role as a character in a narrative, which is starkly simple and also suggestive of elusive meanings, whatever they might be. It was an allusion to the Metaphysical figuration of De Chirico and a fine example of how the image of simple objects can become poetry.

At the end of our days of sharing ideas and discussing what we saw together, Lani told Bendt that he had to go to Assisi to see the Basilica of San Francesco, where I had taken her for her first time just before the day of our almost meeting each other in Arezzo. We then went our separate ways, and Lani and I were back in Washington and Bendt was back in Copenhagen. And by mischance we lost touch with each other. Lani and I never received the book Bendt sent to us of the work of his teacher, Palle Nielson, and not receiving Bendt's gift, of course, we hadn't written back to thank him. We had sent him a book of an American primitive painting collection I found in the National Gallery book store, the best book I could come up with that was about something American. But because Bendt hadn't heard from us he didn't write to us. Or maybe, like with the book he sent to us, the book we sent to him was lost somewhere in the mail.

* * *

In the summer of 1975, to celebrate my divorce from Toni, Lani and I flew to Mérida and traveled by bus to San Cristóbal de las Casas in Chiapas, in the south of Mexico, and from there we went on to the Mayan villages in Guatemala for a few weeks of wandering before I had to be back in Washington to begin teaching again. It was a spontaneous decision based on seeing photographs of Guatemala in a *National Geographic* article. The Mayan women were beautiful and all wore clothing they made for themselves with very colorful weaving and embroidery in patterns unique to their separate villages. Lani bought a few of these beautiful *huipiles* (blouses) from the women who made them, and she wore them there. In the evening she wore a thick woolen sort of poncho that had a cluster of brightly colored braids of wool on the front and back that she bought in San Cristóbal de las Casas. And in one of the Guatemalan villages, where the men also still wore hand-made clothing, I was able to find a woolen jacket that was barely large enough for me, and I wore that to keep warm in the cool evenings. Lani braided colorful ribbons in her hair the way the indigenous women did. We were dressed like misfit Mexican-Guatemalan people, taller and unable to speak either Spanish or any of the indigenous languages. Nevertheless those beautiful and gentle people seemed never to treat us as unwelcome tourists.

We traveled by bus, and from the bus windows I saw small boys walking to the fields with their own small hoes over their shoulders, the same as the larger ones their fathers had as they walked together. We saw children with bundles of whatever it was they were carrying to the market with their mothers or fathers. The men carried heavy loads on their backs on wooden racks that had belt-like straps that went across their foreheads to take the weight, leaving their hands free. Where we traveled in Guatemala, the earth was dark and rich and beautiful and the people seemed to live in harmony with the world that surrounded them. Work and life were one and the same, and their work had a purpose that seemed to be uncomplicated and in balance with their lives. It was beautiful to be among people who didn't know the urgency that is so characteristic of life in the US.

We traveled with two large baskets inside net bags made of sisal hemp, the same as those used by the local people we traveled with, all of them atop the buses we rode from one mountain village to another. I decorated our two net bags with red pompoms made for girl's braids so we could distinguish ours from the others. We ate avocados and papayas, which we could peel in order not to get sick, eating from the open air markets rather than in restaurants. We spent nights in rooms that cost the equivalent of one dollar and often had no window, but instead would have a door that opened onto a courtyard with flowering bushes and hummingbirds. When we were ready to sleep, we turned off the one light bulb that hung from the ceiling and closed the door. I liked being in a place where the excesses of modern civilization were hardly known.

On our return to Mérida, to fly back to Florida, we stayed again in a beautiful hotel where our room was large and light and beautifully tiled. And in that room we ate our last meals of papayas and avocados sitting on the bed almost naked because, unlike the Guatemalan mountain villages, Mérida was hot. And in that colonial style elegance we bathed and washed our hair for the first time in a few weeks.

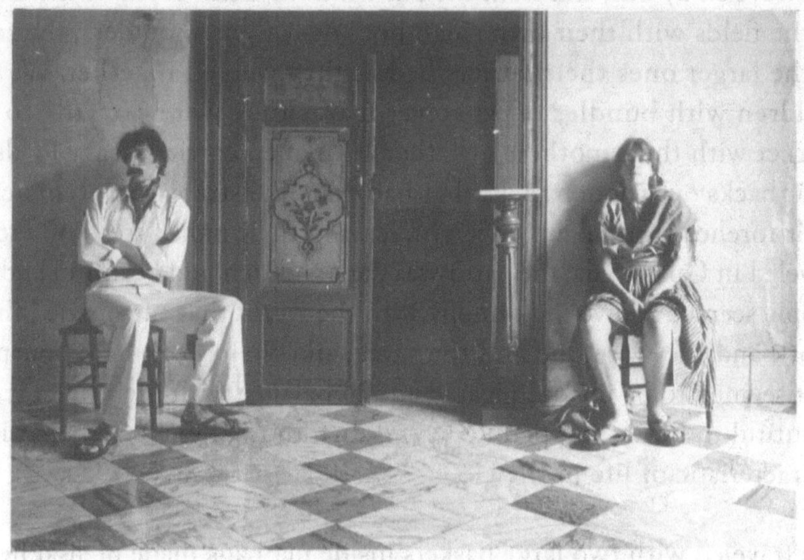

Mérida, 1975

* * *

When we began to plan our second trip to Italy, it involved another couple. My dancer friend, Cindy Beres, and Lani's musician friend, Linn Barnes, were living with us temporarily in our Connecticut Avenue apartment. We concocted a plan that would enable the four of us to travel Europe as a traveling troupe of street performers. Linn would play his lute and Cindy would dance. Lani was going to perform in some way with Cindy and I thought I would learn a few magic tricks. Lani and I each painted a backdrop for our little performing troupe. After all, we were the painters and Cindy and Linn were the performers. We thought to buy a used car, maybe an old deux chevaux, that would look right for our vision of an itinerant circus act and didn't have to hold up longer than the summer, and the backdrops could be unrolled and hung from the roof of the car to the ground, making a stage of the space in front of it on which we could perform. We thought we might paint the car as well, or put a name on it, something about a traveling circus.

If the traveling circus had worked, it would have been fun, reminiscent of Zampanò's motorcycle van rolling into towns in Fellini's *La Strada*, and like the little circus troupe we had seen in Bergman's *The Seventh Seal*. It would have given Cindy and Linn the money they needed for day-to-day expenses. But, unfortunately, in trying to save money we had booked seats through a charter flight organization. The backdrops were almost finished when our plans were thwarted as Educational Flights disappeared and we lost the cost of our four tickets. Lani and I went anyway, booking Icelandair flights for ourselves, leaving behind the backdrops, costumes, magic tricks, and Cindy and Linn.

On our return I stretched up my backdrop and finished it as a proper painting and it was shown and sold at Forum Gallery. And Lani stretched and finished hers and it was shown in Gallery K in Washington. Mine had two seated female performers in leotards with a very large ball between them, like the one in Picasso's 1905 painting, *Young Acrobat on a Ball*. Lani's was of a street corner somewhat like Balthus's two street paintings and also like some aspects of De Chirico's early paintings. She painted a house of cards and a mannequin and a toy car in the street.

Again in Italy, we were thinking to visit lots of hill towns we hadn't yet known and the museums and churches we already knew and loved. Again from Luxembourg I put out my sign for ITALIE and we ended up in a truck from Provence into Italy. This time the Italian truck driver looked like a small Anthony Quinn with a very large mustache. Soon after crossing into Italy, he unhitched his trailer in a parking lot and drove with the skill and daring of a race car driver. He, who told us he was infamous there in Liguria, would flirt with Lani when I fell asleep in the truck. But he was just being playful. He left us at a hotel in Imperia, where we stayed the night.

This time, once in Italy, we realized what we really wanted was to stay in one place and paint for a while. Looking at paintings without being able to paint is more exhausting and less meaningful than when we are also able to paint. There's a limit to how much one can absorb while traveling. And we chose to settle for a while in Arezzo so that we could paint in close proximity to Piero della Francesca's most important fresco cycle, *The Legend of the True Cross*. We found a room on the Corso Italia a block from the church with the Piero frescoes and we stayed six weeks. We bought little portable easels and canvas and stretchers and paints and brushes. We found two sturdy cardboard boxes on the street to use as palette tables, and a couple of discarded metal ice cream signs that bent over the boxes, printed side down, served nicely as palettes. We moved the bed to the end of the room farthest from the large window that overlooked Corso Italia and painted side by side there for those weeks. Lani worked from a still life she set up that had a beautiful polychrome wooden angel she bought in the monthly antique fair and hand painted wooden balls that she bought in Siena, patterned in the various colors of the Palio contrade. I painted one of my female figures. We would stop in at the church of San Francesco to visit the Piero frescoes at different times of day to see them in different kinds of light.

Our days in Arezzo were magical. I would go down from our pensione room, which was both bedroom and studio, and cross the Corso Italia to buy a loaf of bread, still warm, from the little bakery in the shadows of the church where Piero della Francesca painted his wonderful frescoes. We would eat yogurt and fruit and bread in our room and stop in a bar for a cappuccino before our morning visit to the church to stand in silence before the Pieros. Sometimes we would draw in our sketchbooks to better understand how the frescoes were organized, making simple line drawings plotting the positions and relationships in the *Battle between Heraclius and Chosroes,* and in the tranquil images above and opposite each other in the little chapel behind the main altar of the church. The battle scene was filled with knights on horseback and warriors on the ground, one nearly naked, others in Roman and medieval armor, or in fanciful oriental costumes, all pressed in a chaotic density in which the closest thing to an architectural framework that might provide a structural context to the battle's compositional complexity is an arched canopy over a field throne, with a large cross and a column on top of which stands a black rooster. Large banners bearing the insignia of various leaders dominate the upper portion of the fresco in the calm of a blue sky. In the fray below, straight lines in opposing diagonals are the lances and flagpoles, the swords and horns and the reins and bridles of horses. The structural order in this most action-packed vision of a heated conflict eluded us completely. I was fascinated by how this visual cacophony is in my mind more like the music of five hundred years after Piero's time, and the fragmentation of forms made by so much overlapping was close to the kind of abstraction of Cubist painting. On the other hand, in the fresco called the *Finding and Recognition of the True Cross,* Piero created serene groupings of figures perfectly integrated in the landscape on the left side, and in front of the facade of a church and other city buildings on the right side. The large crosses play an important role in the compositional structure in both halves of the fresco. And that scene was totally comprehensible in composition.

The Fiera Antiquaria di Arezzo is the best of Italy's monthly antique markets, and we were there for two during our stay that summer. It takes place the first Sunday of every month and the Saturday before, the Saturday sometimes being the last day of the preceding month. It fills Piazza San Francesco and Piazza Grande and the connecting and surrounding streets and smaller piazzas in the heart of the Centro Storico. As beautiful a backdrop for an antique market as you will ever find. We got to know two young Russian Jewish émigrés who came up from Civitavecchia, the port city near Rome that was the first stopping place of Russian Jewish refugees, the same way Brighton Beach and Coney Island in Brooklyn were to generations of Russian Jews arriving in America. Simone and Leone, as they called themselves here in Italy, were selling the strings of Russian coral beads we had seen other Russians selling at the Sunday Porta Portese market in Rome. When Russian Jews were allowed to leave the USSR in the seventies, they couldn't take money with them so they carried out quantities of those very beautiful coral necklaces. We would talk to Simone and Leone standing each with his strings of coral hanging from one arm in Piazza Grande, among Sicilian and Neapolitan vendors with their array of furniture and sculptures and very large ceramic pots and other things. When it was time to go for lunch we went together. It was sweet and funny that in their imperfect Italian both Simone and Leone would say, "Odessa andiamo mangiare" instead of "adesso andiamo a mangiare." Maybe when they said "Odessa" instead of "adesso" they were playing with us. Odessa is the Black Sea port city from which most of the Russian Jews left when heading to Italy or New York. It was where Bella Fishko, the founder and director of Forum Gallery, had come from as a child, and the name I knew from Sergei Eisenstein's *Battleship Potemkin,* the film from which Francis Bacon borrowed the scream of the screaming woman for his screaming Popes, that were also based on a Velasquez portrait of Pope Innocent X. A month later when we saw Simone and Leone, they had an old Mercedes, and from in the trunk of the Mercedes they showed us a full length mink coat. Simone was waiting for his visa to continue on to the US, and he hoped we would have some idea what such a mink coat might sell for in America. When Lani put it on it went down to her ankles. It was beautiful, but we had no idea what such a coat might be worth. Needless to say, Lani was never a mink coat kind of lady.

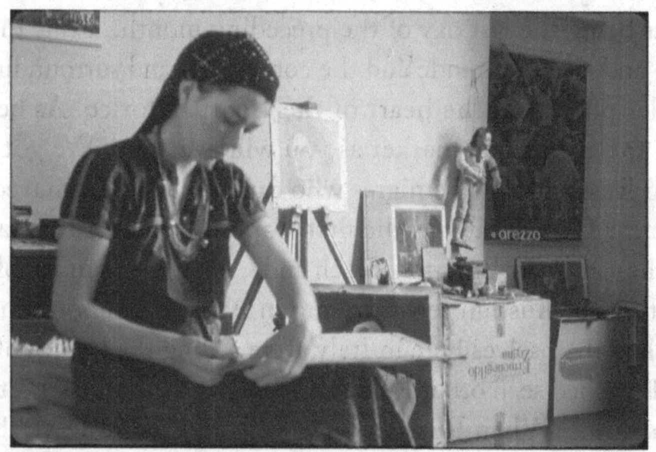
Our Arezzo hotel room studio, 1977

* * *

In Florence we would go to the Uffizi and stay the longest in the first rooms that had the magnificent altarpieces painted by Cimabue, Duccio, and Giotto in egg tempera on very large wood panels, strongly influenced by Byzantine painting, having symmetrical compositions and gold leaf backgrounds and a hierarchy in scale in which the Madonna and Christ Child are much larger than the saints and angels on both sides of them in the same space. Those breathtakingly beautiful paintings were made to calm one's inner soul and inspire gentle thoughts in ways that the paintings from a few years later, in the High Renaissance, were less able to do because, by then, a striving for a kind of realism replaced the more elegant and poetic and imaginative painting of a generation earlier.

In another room, standing in front of Paolo Uccello's *Battle of San Romano,* we decided to go to see all three Uccello Battle of San Romano paintings before returning to Washington. To see all three was a spontaneous decision and a wonderful pilgrimage that provided a framework for our wanderings. Both Lani and I loved Uccello's battle paintings, whose pale pink and blue and white horses are more like carousel horses than the horses in any other Renaissance paintings. The paintings were made to hang together as a triptych, but now the others are in the Louvre in Paris and the National Gallery in London.

Paolo Uccello depicted this battle between condottieri like theater more than like the ugly reality of an actual battle. What he made was lyrical and poetic. We don't see the crashing and clashing of a heated battle, but a deliberately staged drama in which the armor of the knights is elegant, like the abstract shapes of something painted by Arshile Gorky in the early 20th century. In the London painting, instead of a random haphazard scattering of broken lances and pieces of armor lying about on the ground under a raging battle, the broken lances and pieces of armor are positioned to form the receding lines of perspective on a stage floor on which the knights are seen as choreographed actors whose roles might be accompanied by chamber music rather than by the clanking and bashing sounds of an actual conflict.

During this battle in 1432 between Florence and Siena, my history teacher at the Overseas School of Rome told me, none of the condottieri had been killed. I never knew if that was true but I liked the possibility that a battle could be won or lost without giving up lives. I think of Paolo Uccello as someone kind and generous who sees the world in gentle ways. And I don't have that response to the painters of the High Renaissance, as great as they were. The best paintings are more than a depiction of events or personalities. They are personal, about the artist as much as about the subject of the painting. They could not be otherwise. A personal obsession makes for a particular kind of vision that separates the painters who interest me most from others.

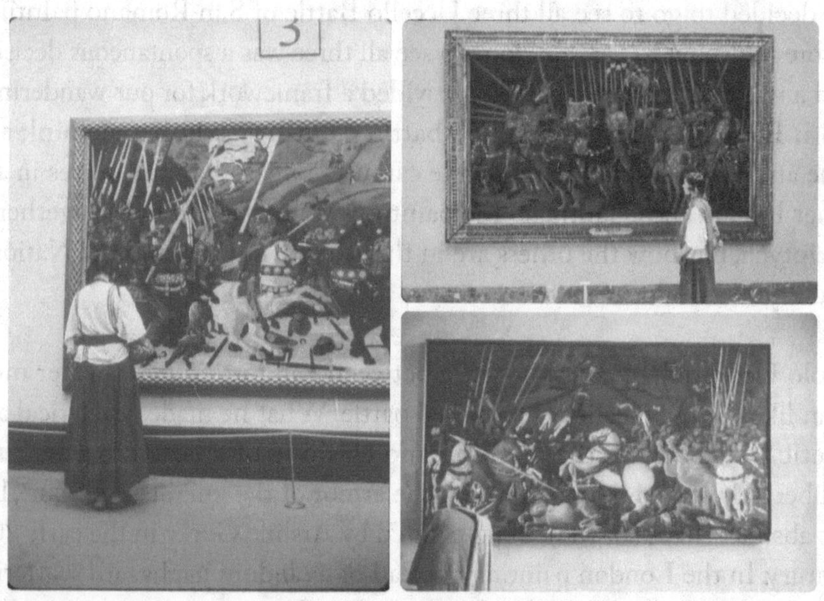

Lani during our Paolo Uccello pilgrimage in London, Paris, Florence, 1977

17

ANNE IN THE 1970s

That my brother and I may not have been brought into this world by choice I would not have understood as a child. Years later, realizing that my beautiful and charming mother was not a happy woman softened the suffering I attributed to her neglecting me much of the time. She, too, had a hard life, only for her it was easier than it was for me to compensate, to cope with hardship and appear to others to be a happy person in complete control of her life. And yes, there were moments when Anne was a tender and loving mother. I shouldn't pretend that was not so. It was just that a boy needs more than occasional reassurance that he is loved and not just tolerated. By the time I was old enough to argue and to have my own voice, my mother's critical nature and her bitterness toward everything she saw as unfair and working against her had outweighed the tenderness she might have shown toward me. But I was becoming whole and more able to separate myself from being a wounded child. Our conversations as two adults then brought another source of pain. Some things she told me would have been better left unsaid. For instance, she told me that she had had two abortions, which some years later in our fights she more than once elaborated on, saying that had she known how Peter and I were going to turn out she would have aborted us too. What did I say to her to elicit so cruel and damning a response? I have no memory of what treachery I was author to then. It was my adolescent rebellion period, the transition between being a child and a young adult. We all go through it. She left home when she was sixteen, I didn't leave home, except for the partial years in boarding school and they were not of my choosing. Then there was the full year in Greece and Italy when we lived together in close quarters when I was seventeen. Certainly that year wouldn't have been a model for compatibility. Both of us were stubborn and argumentative by nature.

She was beautiful and had the charm and ease with people that I never had. I saw myself as shy and invisible and as something yet to announce itself in such a way as to be noticed and not yet having anything worthy of noticing. I had to hope that would change in time. My inability to make conversation, my shyness, my everything a nothingness took years to overcome. It only added to my misery when my mother told me that, in my life, I had not known pain and suffering. In our year in Rome together for my last year of high school she illustrated that statement by telling me about her Italian lover who had survived in a Nazi concentration camp by having sex with the woman commandant. (Anne told me this long before Lina Wertmüller made *Seven Beauties*, a film that has a scene very similar to Anne's Italian lover's wartime experience.) I believed that one man's pain is as real as another man's pain. It's a human condition, not to be qualified. I understood that what she was saying was true in the way she intended, and I believed she was trying to be helpful, somehow. Anne's was an interesting case of survival.

Anne's letters fall into two groups. In one she describes people she meets and places she visits while traveling. Those are her nice letters. They can be amusing, and sometimes somewhat disrespectful or patronizing. This is a passage from a letter she wrote while on the Italian ocean liner SS Raffaello August 4th, 1973 that she sent a few copies of to friends:

> … The dining room is pure commedia dell'arte. The maitre in a flash of intuitive brilliance (when I asked for a tavola senza bambini), seated me in a quiet corner, with four gentlemen: one Sicilian, the size of a mosquito, without a word of English but exquisitely mannered, and a government official; another, a great fat Italo-American who works for the City of N.Y. in some responsible engineering capacity, who feels compelled to test and

compete with the Sicilian for status. One beautiful young black, out of Juilliard School of Theatre, well educated and good for conversation. And, of all things one tall and lanky type with a classic Greek beard whose costume was so colorful, but somehow un-tasteful, that he baffled me. He is a Yugoslav, with hardly any English, who, traveling in tandem with a now American-Yugoslav, also a fashion plate, is subjecting me to a courtship in Croatian. This is all played against a background of sheer hysteria, because the dining room staff is Sicilian. By about the third day, despite myself, I noted, I find it all fun. Excellent therapy, a sea voyage on an Italian Liner. The Yugoslavs have the stamina of mountaineers and dance through the night.

Letters of the other kind, sent exclusively to me, were often confused and at times incoherent outbursts blaming me for everything that had caused her suffering. I recently reread some of the many letters she wrote to me in the '70s, some of which were the nice letters like the one I quoted from above, and some were the other kind, complaining about bills she had to pay and her lack of money. Those had an undertone of suggesting that I should be doing more for her than I was doing. And many of those letters, directly or indirectly, criticized me for the way I lived my life with regard to how I tried to find gallery representation and various other things she believed I was incapable of doing intelligently. Still others were about how, back in the years when she was with my father, she helped him to get public relations clients he would then lose because he was inept at handling things she instinctively understood and was good at, and how he repeatedly failed in his position as a public relations consultant for businesses and would flee when being sued by those businesses. In one letter she referred to my father as "a congenital alcoholic, pimping, gambling, stealing and blackmailing his way through life." I had heard all of that for years, except for the word "pimping", sometimes embellished with stories and supposed factual references to specific events. And I know that in what she spoke and wrote there was probably truth as well as untruth mixed with her anger and hurt.

In 1974 Anne returned to the States from several months abroad and, because at the time she had no place of her own, she briefly lived with me and Lani in our small Washington apartment. We moved our bed into the tiny dining alcove attached to the kitchen to give Anne the privacy of the only bedroom. And once again she was with us long enough that conversations turned into disagreements easily, and often quite amazingly pointless arguments ensued.

After what may have been a few weeks living together in those close quarters, one day while Lani and Anne were alone and I was off teaching, Anne was pacing back and forth behind Lani while Lani was painting. And hoping for support in her criticisms, my mother started another conversation about her disappointments concerning her younger son, that being me. Eventually, Anne's questions and remarks incited responses that Anne didn't like. Lani had spoken her mind for the first time with my mother and thereupon lost Anne's complete admiration and approval, leading to a heightening of tensions between us that quickly became intolerable. And she moved out, but not without first a fair share of blaming and shaming clearly intended to hurt us. Before my mother left, in days when we were barely able to speak to one another, we sometimes resorted to writing notes. Though chiding and provocative, the notes I wrote to her were expressive of how hopeless I felt the situation had become.

Among the many letters from my mother that were filled with accusations of all kinds of things, this is page seven of an eleven-page letter postmarked April 22, 1975, sent after she left us to return to New York:

> ... It is obvious why anyone would resort to amnesia after a childhood of peeing in bed, and, a catatonic boyhood and youth: it is a useful protective device, like a bandaid, but it doesn't cure a deep disturbance. To forget what is unflattering, inadequate in oneself is a "normal" device — up to a point. You carry it farther:
>
> For example, of your reactions to your father: If your "no expectations" were rational, you'd have had the normal guts to

tell Arthur Travis that your father never looked at you when you were in his presence; never contributed a cent to your support. etc.; never wanted to see you since you were eight years old... never even wrote you a postcard when you were on the critical list in the hospital (your 18th? or 19th? year) although Peter told him of it. etc. I dare you to tell me you want to consider your father's role in your life. All you want is to blame me...

Amnesia, when so acute as yours, like a broken bone, is also an illness. A mental break-down. Healthy minds have the power of memory. Loss of memory is only normal in old age. Senility. I take the old-age-deterring pills to strengthen my memory.... Again, I've never reproached you for your cowardly attitude toward your father... I believe you cannot yet achieve anything healthier. Meaning stronger. I asked you about this, recently, to learn whether you are still so fear-ridden on the subject. Your answer was not re-assuring. Ergo, amnesia, applied to your father.

I could continue with a long list of your monstrously destructive little speeches, delivered to me in kindness, since your 17th year. But, unless there was a tape recording to prove you made them, it would be futile.

As is amply demonstrated, painters and performing musicians can function professionally in such states of mental un-health as you enjoy.

And it goes on like that. Anne failed to understand that I could not have clear memories of my mostly absent father from when I was three or four or five-years-old. No, I didn't remember if my father looked at me when I was in his presence or didn't look at me. How many men can remember such a thing from early childhood? It wasn't me who chose that man to marry and father her children. Why should I have been held accountable for what he did or didn't do, and if my mother wasn't suggesting that I should, why was it so bloody important that I should remember what kind of man he was? Why did my mother not understand that I might have wanted to believe my father was a good man? At least a little, sometimes? Would that not be reasonable and forgivable? I can see now, looking back on how she was before Alzheimer's softened the sharp edges to her personality, that my mother's behavior quite well fit the accepted definition of narcissistic personality disorder.

A couple of years later Anne was seeing a psychologist in New York and together they asked me if I would like to be there for one of their meetings, which I agreed to. The psychologist sent me this letter following that session:

ALFRED ADLER MENTAL HYGIENE CLINIC

OF THE INDIVIDUAL PSYCHOLOGY ASSOCIATION NEW YORK, INC. (IPA)

37 WEST 65TH STREET, NEW YORK, N.Y. 10023

(212) 874-2427

November 15, 1977

Dear Allan:

Your offer to come back for another session with your mother and me was most appreciated. However I feel that there is little that we can work on together at this time.

After giving a great deal of thought to your relationship and discussing it with a consultant in Family Therapy the following is our conclusion:

You and your mother seem to know instinctively that for you to become closer at this time would not be good for either of you. It seems to me that a loving relationship with your mother might threaten your marriage and your own autonomy. And if your mother should give up her battling ways, the thing that she fears most, over dependency, might well result.

I think you should make no attempts to discontinue your defensive-offensive stance. See your mother whenever you can. She will appreciate this although she will pretend not to. Don't walk on eggs either in writing or when you meet her. In fact if you provoke her a little it will make it easier for her to argue with you, and, strange as it may seem, this will be good.

Sorry the typing is so bad but you should see my handwriting!

Sincerely yours,

(signed in pen) Bee Ludlow

Dr. Ludlow's letter was typed on clinic stationary that had the names of Alexandra Adler, M.D. Medical Director, followed by the names of an Executive Director, an Assistant Director, and 14 Board members listed in the left margin. It was typed on an older typewriter with its ribbon losing ink and some letter keys filling in. Hence the apology for her typing. Anne didn't know about the letter and I don't know how long she was seeing Dr. Ludlow. I had gone up to New York only the one time to meet with them at the clinic. I remember I talked some in that meeting, and I cried, but I don't remember more than that.

* * *

On the 20th of October 2016, I woke from a dream in the early morning in which I was talking to my mother about her funeral. Dreams do that sort of thing. My mother had been dead sixteen years and not since the 1970s did she look the way I saw her in the dream. But it all seemed very real to me. She said I should invite Matteo Renzi to this funeral for her that she and I were talking about. "The prime minister of Italy?" "Yes." "Why, do you know him?" "Yes." It was clear in this dream that my mother moved in circles that I didn't understand or know anything about. She said "Tell him

I have been in the woods in Paris and New York," as though that meant something and Renzi would be impressed by that. She told me she was going to Venice, and to NY.

I think my dream might have been trying to tell me that I didn't know my mother for the woman she was when she was with other people, when she was not living in our mother/son condition.

Many of the letters my mother sent to me were carbon copies of letters she wrote to one or more of her friends. On those letters she would add bits by hand in the margins and between paragraphs in red or blue or green ink. Those were the letters that chronicled a few days of her travels in Paris or Rome describing dinners with people she would meet, or in India where she would be entertained by a maharajah. Maharajahs after the mid 20th century were descendants of and claimants to the legacy of the former royalty, whose lavish palaces are all over India. Fatehsinghrao Gaekwad, the Maharajah of Baroda, apparently was a friend of my mother. He held the title His Highness, The Maharajah of Baroda. Among the various photographs and letters my mother still had at the end of her life, I have three very short letters the Maharajah of Baroda sent to my mother telling her when and where he would be staying briefly in New York on business and hoping to see her. I expect they barely knew each other but enjoyed what friendship they had. I never understood what my mother could say to anyone like a maharajah that would enthrall him in the ways she suggested. She didn't tell me much about those occasions, or if she did, I have forgotten. I might have wanted to disbelieve, or to forget, the things she would say that would suggest how disappointed she was in me.

Clearly my mother made an impression on people. Whether a good impression or a bad impression, she was noticed anywhere she went and people wondered who she was. A long time ago, when Lennart Anderson was a visiting artist at American University and stayed with us, in a conversation Lani described my mother as a strikingly beautiful woman who wore a black eyepatch. And his first response was, "*She* was your mother? I always wondered who she was." And Elsie Russell once told me her father, Alfred

Russell, having seen Anne at The Club and at gallery openings throughout the years, had called my mother "The Art Bitch".

Of course, I knew my mother without her makeup and her jewelry, the other side of her, her private side. Because my mother never had much money, she didn't own many dresses. What clothes she had were carefully chosen; some she designed and sewed herself. And she didn't have a lot of jewelry, but what she wore at openings and places where artists like Lennart Anderson and Alfred Russell would have seen her, stood out. They would see something of her that maybe could be called a style that added to her allure. She had a small Shiva sculpture she had bought in India and had a jeweler friend dip in gold, that she wore hanging from a gold chain so that it would be nestled in her cleavage, attracting the attention of anyone she encountered.

Anne Winter managed to recreate not only who her parents were, but also who she was, able to appear self-confident and in complete control of most any situation she encountered. But all the while, in private, she was the person I knew to be troubled and bitter and complaining about how her life had been. With those two rather distinct personalities, my mother would navigate her way through life being admired by some and disdained by others. With some people it was curiosity, and with some, I think, there was an antagonistic rivalry based on nothing more than that my mother stood out in a crowd. Her closest friends accepted her for the complex person she was. And maybe the worst of her bitter and vindictive side was known only to me and my brother. And, of course, our father.

I see in letters my mother wrote to me while I was in graduate school and the years that followed that she was trying to control how I lived my life, as if to relive her own life better through me. I don't think she would have understood it that way or admitted that to me if she had. She seemed to believe her frequent criticisms and what she thought to be sage advice were given to me solely for my own benefit. I don't know why she could not have realized how futile it was to expect me to be the way she wanted me to be, given how unlike her I was. Maybe she was unable to believe that I didn't want to become the successful artist she thought I could be if that depended on manipulating people and working the scene in ways she was capable of, and I was not. In truth, I don't know if my mother was trying to live her own life through mine, and at this point that doesn't matter. She lived as she did, I survived, and she is gone.

I think the saddest aspect of my mother's life was that she seemed unable to accept the possibility that any man she might meet could love her, or that she might allow herself to love another man after her disastrous marriage to my father. I think it possible that my mother's love for me took the place of any other internally felt love in her life. When she gave up on my brother early on, believing him to be as hopelessly good-for-nothing as our father, her repeated utterances to that effect added to the underlying condition Peter suffered from throughout his life, and that left me as the only object of her love. And with that there was the possibility that I, more than anybody else in her life, could cause her deep pain. She more than once told me that was so. And that could not do other than make our relationship one of hurt and disappointment. She put on me the weight of responsibility for the continual cause and effect forever complicating our relationship.

* * *

When I was about thirty-two my father reappeared on the edges of my life. Along with Randy's then wife Paula, and their daughter Paulette, my father moved back to Washington to be where Paula's elderly mother, whose name was Pauline, had a little house in Georgetown. The infrequent times I saw Randy in that period he was old and broken. The father I vaguely remembered, who I thought of as looking like Clark Gable because he wore the same thin mustache and a 1940s suit and hat, was not like the white-haired, bent-over man he had become. During the years between 1950 and the 1970s, I had known only the bitter hatred my mother had for the father I didn't know, and that overshadowed the possibility that I might discover that there was ever anything like a father's love in my life. In the visits I made to spend a little time with my father in Washington, during which I didn't relax enough to really get to know the man, I was interested to discover that he and I had a similar sense of humor and we both had some of the same small barely noticeable mannerisms. I could almost see myself in him. My father seemed to be a nice enough person. This was not a man whose heart was evil and dark. My guess was that he did his best to care for the family he stayed with, whose names, Pauline, Paula, and Paulette, strangely indicated a diminution of sorts, and I wasn't wanting to hold him entirely responsible for having abandoned his two sons because it was clear enough to me that, were I to be married to someone as critical and demanding as my mother, I would have left, though I would not have wanted to disappear from my children's lives. I believed the situation was that Anne didn't allow Randy to have more than the one weekend with me and Peter two years after their separation. I could only see the older man I knew to be my father the way I see people I meet for the first time. In a sense, he was simply what I saw him to be, but he was also more than that because I knew he had once been my father. I was curious about him but also not wanting to ask a question that could open a floodgate that I knew would reduce me to a helplessly sobbing boy-man caught up in a kaleidoscope of mental images and feelings, whether imagined or real, in his mind or mine. Nor did I want to heap blame and anguish on my father, not knowing how he had internalized all that was connected to his marriage to my mother and to his two estranged sons. I think I was not acting in a cowardly way, as my mother had put it, so much as being kind to both of us for letting sleeping dogs lie.

This resurfacing of Randy in Washington in the 1970s was in a period when Anne and I were not getting along well, to put it absurdly lightly, and Anne didn't know that my father had returned to Washington. Telling her would have provoked another reproachful tirade, serving no purpose.

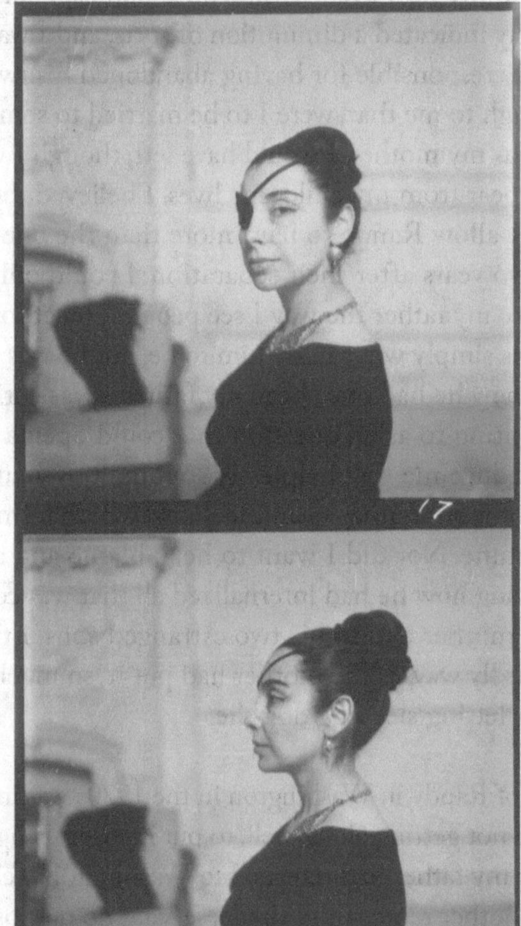

Anne, circa 1960

18

MARYLAND

In 1975, after our trip to Guatemala, Lani and I were common-law
married and living together in a larger apartment on Connecticut Avenue
in Washington, D.C. Three years later, after I was given tenure at American
University, we began to look for a place to buy. We considered a one room
studio apartment condominium that had a very large window and good
north light and was near American University. But I knew we wouldn't
be able to live in a building that had elevator music. I asked the woman
from the condominium office who was showing us the apartment if that
had to be there, and she looked at me with disbelief, and said "Yes. Why
would you not like that?" Musac inflicted on anyone having to be a captive
listener has always disturbed me. That's putting it politely. In my opinion
musac must be the epitome of purposefully designed bad taste, believed
by some to have merits.

We looked at townhouses in Northern Virginia and Maryland but we
couldn't find anything affordable within a short commuting distance to the
university and we ended up with a small farmhouse on a piece of land in
Hughesville, in Southern Maryland. A large cement block tractor garage
was the deciding factor in choosing the property because, with a little work,
it could become a good studio.

We hired out some of the renovations and a lot we did ourselves on both the
house and the studio. And then we filled the house with antique furniture

bought for very little that we restored and some pieces that I made. I enjoyed the physical work of building and became quite good at it, learning as I went along. Not far from us there was a barn filled with Victorian doors and newel posts and corbels taken from demolished houses to be resold for restorations. I bought various things from there and incorporated them in our renovations. I made two couch benches from interior doors. For each I cut one door in half lengthwise, the two parts becoming the front and the seat, and another door, uncut and turned on its side became the back, and I attached newel posts to the four corners. And I cut a large exterior front door into four sections, each with ornate panels, that became the front of a corner cupboard I built into our dining room.

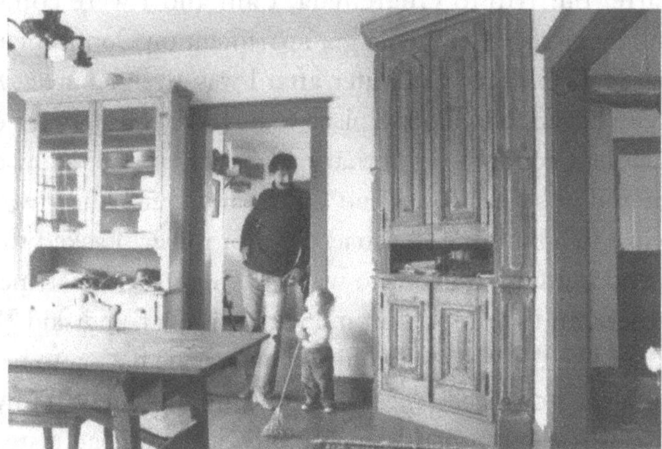

Hughesville, circa 1981

We bought our house in mid-winter and had no idea that we were going to be surrounded by tobacco fields and the spraying of toxic pesticides to kill the tobacco worm and toxic chemicals to slow the flowering of the plants so the leaves would grow larger. It didn't occur to us to ask what was grown in the fields we were looking at under a dusting of snow on all four sides of our one and a half acres. But there we were, so we made our own house and studio, and our acre and a half of ground on which we had our garden and a few animals into a peaceful and beautiful refuge that served us well.

Lani and I were not happy being surrounded by tobacco fields. To me the smoking of cigarettes never made any sense at all. The idea of choosing to breathe toxic smoke seemed completely crazy, and to pay money to do that, even after knowing full well that it can destroy one's health, I thought was an evil that society ought not to have embraced. But smoking was made to look glamorous in the Hollywood films, whose beautiful actors almost always smoked cigarettes, looking very erudite, or suave, eyes slightly squinting as they inhaled, a thin wisp of smoke trailing upward as the hand holding a cigarette moved slowly down.

Not too far away there was a weekend antique/junk market. My wanderlust could be satisfied in small measure close to home, making the best of what I had. There was country music playing on a loudspeaker which I grew accustomed to and almost came to enjoy for how it made being in the market more of a total experience, so unlike places where I would ordinarily find myself. And a few miles beyond the market there was an Amish community, which began in 1939 when several Amish families settled in Southern Maryland in search of farmland more affordable than in Pennsylvania. The Amish live without electricity and travel in horse drawn buggies and dress in their own mostly black and white Amish made clothing, which was different from how people dressed anywhere else nearby. Everything about the Amish seemed to be more considered than how it was with most other people in our culture, and there was a dignity about them that I admired. I saw how the word community to the Amish has a deeper meaning than what I had ever known, or been able to conceive of. In their world money is not the reason for, or the answer to, everything, the way it is in the world I was born into, where most things are complicated and fast moving and glitzy.

Living in a rural area, beyond commuter distance from the university and museums and places we knew well, we felt a little like aliens. Our neighbor, then in his seventies, might have been in Washington only a few times in his life and probably had never been in the National Gallery or any other art museum. In the living room of his house he had a picture of a deer standing in a landscape, not painted, but some sort of a machine woven velvet tapestry. I wondered what it would be like to know so little of the world beyond the place where a man was born and worked all his life, as it had been in the case of Carl, whose father had with his own hands built the house we bought, one small field away from the house that Carl built for himself when he had a family of his own.

Once when I was waiting for our car to be fixed at the mechanic's shop, one of the two mechanics asked me what kind of paintings I made. And I answered, without thinking, that I paint nude women. And his reply was "Aw… That ain't half bad." And that was fair enough. I think he was playing with me. Rural Southern Maryland.

* * *

Common-law marriage was recognized in the District of Columbia and nine states that didn't include Maryland. Therefore it seemed right that we should be properly married, and Lani and I were married in the courthouse in La Plata, Maryland on December 11, 1978. And on March 12, 1979 Tobias Alexander Feltus was born in George Washington University Hospital in Washington. He was born healthy and beautiful, wide awake and curious about everything. His birth was the happiest event of my life and it was the same for Lani, who was the most loving and caring mother imaginable. I was teaching and painting and Lani returned to painting just days after Tobias was born, and little Tobias lived with us in our studio while we painted.

When Tobias was six months old, we brought Anne down from New York to visit us in our little Hughesville house to see her first grandchild. Anne was still writing. She was working on a spy novel that she kept revising because it dealt with political situations that would keep changing. She told me the latest working title of her book was *Love Hate, Hate Love*, which she said was a reflection on my inner conflict, or on both hers and mine, in our very troubled relationship. She was in one of her states of unwillingness to communicate and she didn't elaborate on it at all. She evidently thought the title was self-explanatory. *Love Hate, Hate Love* stays in my mind like the title of that chapter in our impossible mother and son condition.

That weekend I had been very consciously watching my own behavior to see if it was possible for me not to instigate a fight with her. I wanted to know that it was not always my fault that our time together so often ended in anger or tears. In the car, taking her to the city, we were arguing. At one point, whether it was real or one of her acts designed to make a point and to hurt me, she started to open the car door while we were moving in traffic as if to jump out in order to end the conversation or to get away from me. A bit shaken by that, I drove her to where she asked to be let off. The next time we spoke, she told me that I had been "shrieking I hate you," and I knew I absolutely had not done that. Our relationship was surely one of love and pain. And maybe we were equally responsible for inflicting pain and maybe I should have grown enough to better handle what was inside me that I didn't understand and that would easily lead to behavior I was disposed to have and later regret. Looking back on those years I see that Lani helped me to pull myself together, to become whole, to be happy.

Our second son was born with Edwards syndrome (Trisomy 18) which is like Down syndrome (Trisomy 21) but more severe than Down syndrome. Trisomy 18 is a genetic disorder caused by the presence of a third copy of the 18th chromosome. Trisomy 21 has a third copy of the 21st chromosome. Very few babies with Trisomy 18 live more than a week or two if they survive birth, and our second son wouldn't have survived his birth had it not been by Caesarean section that was done because the doctor saw that there was a problem with the heartbeat of the baby and he thought the baby might not survive the trauma of a full labor birth.

The moment the baby was lifted out of Lani she could see in my eyes a terrible pain, and she was scared. And I was too helpless in my distress to be able to say anything. And what could I have said? It was a tiny moment, though it seemed a long time, and one that I can't revisit in my mind or speak of without being stopped again and blinded by tears, as I was then. I saw that our baby boy was crippled, with one leg unbent that had a twisted foot, and his hands were formed badly and his little face was in pain. At that moment the doctor could only say that the baby had a syndrome, and I didn't know what that meant. A little later we were told by doctors that he was a Trisomy 18 infant, and they never survive long. His poor little heart wouldn't keep him alive. He couldn't eat. He could only suffer in silence.

I thought about how this poor little boy would never even see what was outside those neon lit rooms. The hospital was not a place to feel pain of that sort. It was all white uniforms and chrome bed frames and white curtains and glass. There wasn't anything of our lives; no art, no music, no warmth except for the two broken hearted people Lani and I were, and a few friends, awkward in their not knowing what to say, who came to comfort us. Lani gave all her love to this sweet dying baby boy, and that was all he ever had in his tiny life. That and the immense pain he suffered.

We named our second son Justin Alan Feltus. I held him, looked at his tormented little face, and I wept. Nothing in my life has ever been that terribly, painfully sad. I thought Justin's sweet little face looked like my grandmother's face more than any other in my family, and that made my pain deeper still. Justin only lived four days and he never left the hospital. I cried for the pain he suffered. I cried for the life he wouldn't have. I remember looking out the hospital window in my deep anguish and thinking poor little Justin would never even see a bird. That is how my mind summed up the terrible unfairness of his very short life.

Some people believe that every person is born with a destiny to be fulfilled, and if an infant only lives a few days his destiny would have been fulfilled in those few days. Such thinking might have helped a little to get us through the pain, but nothing truly helped other than that we had Tobias to live for, and we had to somehow carry on. Although the doctors we talked to said there could be an increased chance of having another child with the same syndrome, they didn't know of a case in which that had happened, which made no sense to us. We wanted to risk having another child to be a brother or sister for Tobias. And Joseph Nicholas Feltus was born in perfect health on July 23rd, 1982 in Sibley Hospital in Washington.

I don't know if I had spoken of it with Lani at the time, but I had a fear deep inside me that when Tobias would reach the age I was when my father left me, I would also leave my family. I thought it might be like a curse that I wouldn't be able to combat, ingrained from when I was a boy and beyond my ability to overcome. When that didn't happen, I was tremendously relieved. And then, when Joseph was six and I knew I was not about to abandon either of my sons, I was beyond that fear. Instead of acting in the ways that had been so harmful to me in my childhood, I was a loving father wanting to do all I could for my sons.

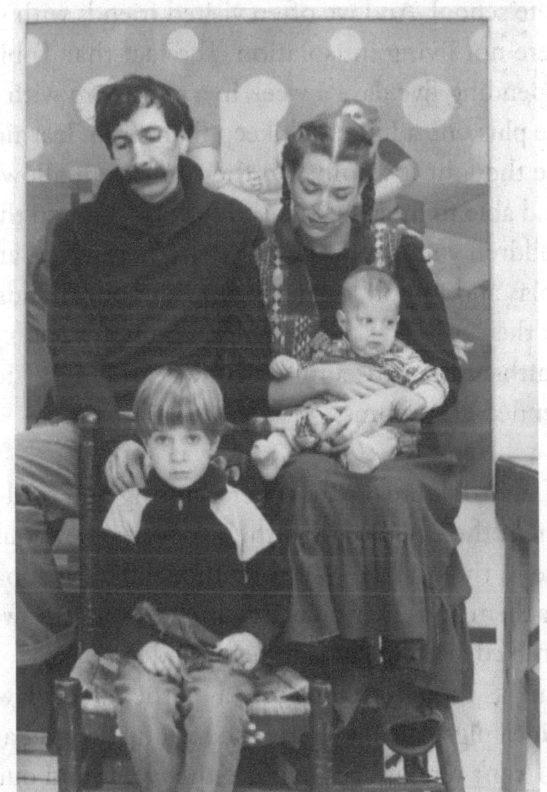

Family portrait, in front of Lani's painting *Balthazar's Room*, 1982

Bill Coperthwaite came to visit us in our Hughesville house and brought with him some back issues of *Growing Without Schooling* and introduced us to the writings of John Holt, whose beliefs about what he called unschooling, and homeschooling, made complete sense to us. Where we lived, the nearest schools were a Catholic school attached to a church and a public school almost opposite. The public school had one very good first grade teacher and one not good first grade teacher, friends of ours had told us. And there was no way one could choose which teacher one would be entrusting the wellbeing of one's child to. And so we decided to homeschool Tobias and Joseph. They studied Suzuki Violin with a good teacher we knew rather well as a friend. The violin lessons provided weekly contact with a few other kids, and they provided a traditional study framework more like that of a very good private school. And we often visited friends with young children so our boys were not living in isolation. The fact that Tobias and Joseph would not be spending five days a week in a classroom with other children of the same age plus one adult didn't keep them from learning to socialize, as many people thought it would. On the contrary, it allowed them to be interested in and able to interact beautifully with children their own age as well as with children younger and older than themselves, and with adults of any age. Tobias and Joseph learned from all of our friends whenever we visited them or they visited us. They were both interested in many kinds of things. The Smithsonian Museums and the art museums in Washington were their extended classrooms.

In our studio Lani took breaks from her painting and read to Tobias and Joseph throughout the day. They had their tricycles they could ride around the wood stove in the middle of our studio, and a cardboard playhouse that I made for them and their own art supplies, and they were happy. We had goats we milked and chickens for eggs and large cages of finches that kept reproducing as though to illustrate a mathematical law. And we had a cage with guinea pigs. We had garter snakes, turtles and a bullfrog. And we had things I can't remember anymore that we found outside and kept for shorter periods. We collected animal skulls and bones, and books of all kinds for Tobias and Joseph to look at long before they could read.

School in my own experience was a struggle between feeling inadequate and being disinterested, and that wasn't the best way to pass childhood years. I wanted to provide for my sons all the things that I would have liked to have had when I was a child, and I was glad to find that providing those things came by instinct, backed by thought and understanding. Lani and I were in complete agreement about educating our boys, and unschooling was the form of homeschooling we found ourselves doing. It was educating in the ways that made the most sense to us. At home, learning was not divided up into separate units according to a neat and orderly plan that didn't allow for crossovers between subjects separated by the ringing of a bell that effectively stopped thoughts in their tracks and had kids scrambling to their feet to go somewhere else. They weren't made to feel stupid when they didn't understand something as well as another kid understood it. They didn't know the torment of bullies and the misery of being an outsider where in-groups are ever present. They didn't have to walk long hallways lined in metal lockers painted beige or gray that, along with their cheap combination padlocks, made an ugly metallic clatter throughout the day. Their learning was directed by what interested them and we were there to enhance that the best ways we could.

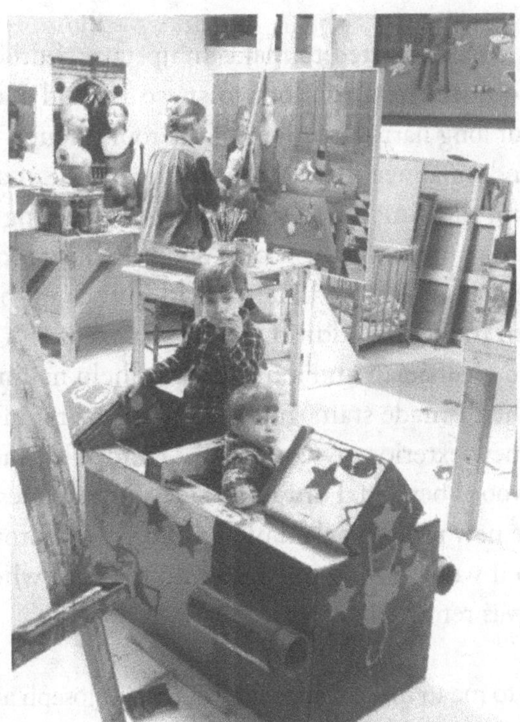

In the studio, 1984

***

I had never lived in an apartment or a house that my family or I owned prior to buying our little Hughesville farmhouse. In the rented apartments I lived in, anything built-in by the renter became the property of the landlord and the only changes one could make were repainting walls, if even that was permitted. So with owning our first property came the possibility that I could do with it whatever I wanted. The actual structure of our house could be changed to make it larger and more functional. And, of course, it could be more personal than any place I had ever lived in. At first Lani and I worked on repainting exterior and interior walls and repairing what needed to be repaired. We converted the tractor garage into a skylit studio, and a little later we had a screened porch on the house enlarged and closed in to make another bedroom. I took down a closet in the kitchen to open the space up. And we had a second bathroom added next to the kitchen, extending out beyond the house.

One Christmas break I started to make an upstairs bedroom in the attic. I put down a floor on the attic floor joists so I could stand on it while working. I cut out long narrow sections of the roof through which I erected 2 x 6 studs extending above the old roof to the height of a proper ceiling for the new room, allowing me to stand on the remaining part of the old roof while framing a new, higher roof. When the new roof was finished, I took down the rest of old roof that was within the new bedroom. And I was able to finish the whole addition by myself except for a few hours of work done by an electrician and a morning of help nailing plasterboard to the ceiling. Then I made stairs going up from the room below and put siding over the new exterior plywood walls. I added a window facing the studio and the woods beyond. For fun I made a secret access to the part of the attic that the new room blocked off. Its access was through a bookcase that I hinged so it would swing outward into the attic when the pin that kept it secured was removed.

It was important to me to make things for Tobias and Joseph and to encourage them to make things for themselves. For Tobias's second Christmas, I made a rocking horse out of scrap lumber from a construction site, using pieces of 2 x 4s and 2 x 6s that I cut roughly to shape and glued and doweled together. Then I carved and ground down and sanded and painted what became a rocking horse a bit like a Paolo Uccello horse from his *Battle of San Romano* paintings. It had a leather covered saddle and the mane and tail I made from horsehair taken from a Guatemalan horsehair rope. Because Tobias was with me in the studio where I was working on the horse, I had to devise a cover story so it could remain a surprise. I told him I was making it for *figlio mio*, which in Italian meant "for my son." Tobias accepted that as meaning it was for someone else because he didn't know the Italian meaning of figlio mio. That way I continued to work on the rocking horse without Tobias knowing it was for him.

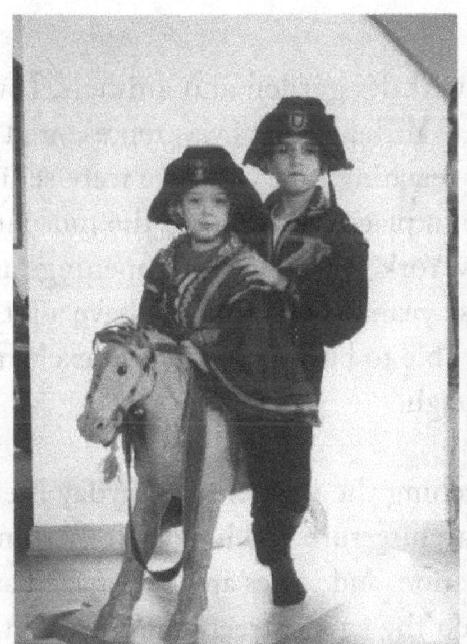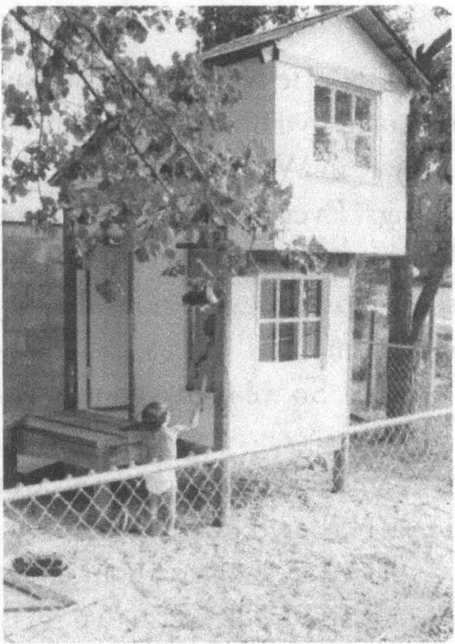

The rocking horse and the outside playhouse

I made an outside playhouse raised up off the ground on posts within the fenced yard attached to our studio so the boys could play outside within range of sight and sound while we painted. It had floor space big enough that the boys could sleep in it if they wanted to, and sliding glass windows and a door. We had a shed behind the studio large enough to house a couple of goats and their milking stand, and a place for hay bales and the indoor part of our chicken yard. Growing up in Midtown, Manhattan I didn't have animals in my childhood. I remember one summer when we were staying in the country for a few weeks, Peter and I each had a chicken. He called his Jack and I named mine Malelsky. None of us had any idea where the name Malelsky came from. I don't remember any other pets in my childhood except, later, when Anne was able to rent our studio apartment at 58 West 57th Street, Peter and I got ourselves a couple of chameleons to live in a terrarium on a windowsill. They weren't the true chameleons. They were like the small lizards we see here in Italy except they would change color from a brown to a green to match their surroundings.

* * *

In Hughesville we had our house with its garden and animals. I was represented by Forum Gallery in New York and Lani was represented by Gallery K in Washington. I had my teaching salary and we were selling paintings. Everything seemed to be in place. We went to the museums in Washington and we went to New York for my Gallery openings and to see important exhibitions. In those years when we didn't have a lot of money, Lani and I were occasionally able to barter paintings in exchange for services. So we managed well enough.

But we missed Italy. We missed watching the theater of everyday life in a piazza bordered by extraordinary architecture and how in Italy things are displayed in shops without affectation, and stores aren't oversized and imposing and unpleasant. We missed the small street markets and the larger weekly markets that might have the accompaniment of a musician's accordion. We missed the sense of history that is everywhere and always, and not something one has to go somewhere in hopes of finding. It was a longing for just being back in Italy that we often felt.

After a few years it got to a point when we couldn't hold off any longer, our desire to be in Italy was so strong. So in 1984 we made our first of two summer trips to Italy after Tobias and Joseph were born. Tobias was five and Joseph was two. We traveled by train between cities when Italian trains still had compartments that provided a kind of privacy the newer trains lack. We went to churches and museums and looked at a lot of art as we had always done, but having two small boys with us slowed our pace and we spent more time sitting in piazzas than we used to, and we sat in parks watching Tobias and Joseph play with other children in spite of not sharing a common language.

My brother and his girlfriend met us in Venice and from there we went together to Ferrara for Ferrara's annual Palio, which is the oldest in Italy, having been held continuously since 1279. Their evening procession coming out of a moated castle across a drawbridge into the torchlit piazza wearing Renaissance costumes was like being transported back in time seven hundred years. And the next day the race of donkeys was very entertaining because the two or three biggest donkeys, the ones I was sure had a totally unfair advantage over much smaller donkeys, turned around and refused to run, so one man would push and another would pull while much smaller donkeys would trot on past them. The horse race was not run that day because rain had made the track unsafe. Ferrara's Palio is gentle and unlike the much more famous Palio of Siena, where a former student of mine told us that he and his wife saw a horse impaled on a barricade in front of them at the tight curve in front of the Palazzo Pubblico. We went to Arezzo so Tobias and Joseph could see the processions and the *Sbandieratori* and the musicians that are part of the Giostra del Saracino that Lani and I knew from when we stayed in Arezzo a few years earlier. Sbandieratori are young men in costume who perform an elaborate flag waving, flag tossing event that is something between dance and acrobatics, and quite wonderful.

In Italian festivals, town people without makeup look much more convincing than Hollywood actors, who look like the actors they are, some of them dressed in painted plastic that can only pass for armor in a film because a soundtrack has replaced the soft thump of synthetic material with the sharp clinking of steel. We went to Sansepolcro to see their sbandieratori and the annual crossbow contest between Sansepolcro and Gubbio, and of course to visit the Piero della Francesca frescoes in Arezzo and in Sansepolcro.

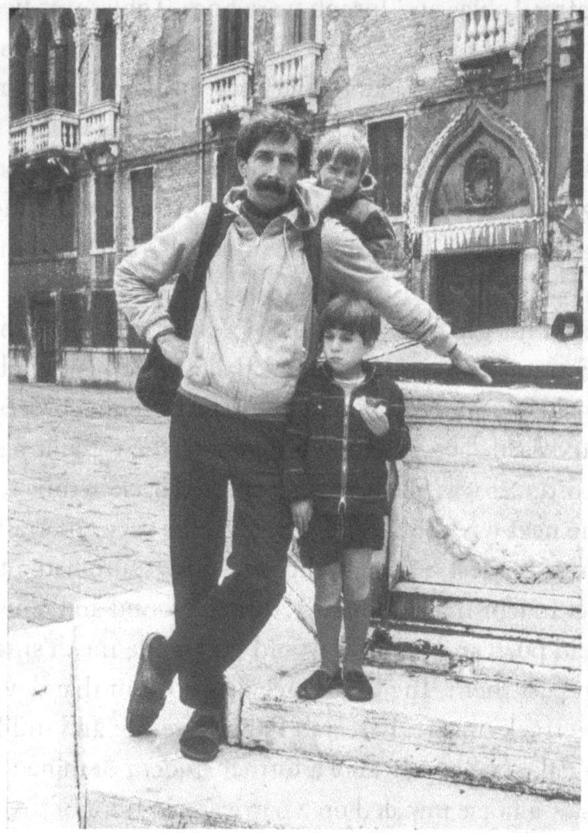

Venice, 1984

* * *

On our second trip to Italy with Tobias and Joseph, we had a rental car. And one day we drove to Umbertide to see if we could find William Bailey's house. All I had was a two-word address that Bill had given us when we visited him at the American Academy in Rome a few years earlier. It said only Migianella, Umbertide. Bill had no phone number because back then having a phone line installed in the hills was not likely to happen within years, and that was long before the emergence of cell phones. So I asked in a bar in the center of Umbertide if they knew what or where Migianella was, and they gave me directions to a zone of that name high above Umbertide. And we drove off in that direction and by chance encountered a man watering his lawn. It was not in the nature of Italians to water lawns, and this man turned out to be English. And he knew the Bailey's house and knew the Baileys weren't there. We talked for a few minutes while he watered his lawn. He told us he was in partnership with an Italian selling real estate in the area of Umbertide, and we decided to go with him to look at a few properties, thinking it would be nice to have a home base from which to day trip on subsequent Italian visits. That year Lani and I had sold a few paintings and the dollar was particularly strong against the lira. We thought if we could find a house that needed work and cost ten thousand dollars or less, we might buy it. So we asked to be shown a few freestanding houses within our price range. And after seeing several properties we decided to buy a small tobacco drying tower with an attached tractor garage that was part of a little hamlet on a hilltop in the Niccone Valley, not far from Città di Castello and Umbertide. It could be converted into a living space and it was affordable, and the setting was beautiful. So we signed the first papers and arranged to buy it long distance after we would be back in Maryland. And we arranged to have necessary renovations done while I was teaching in Washington.

19

GIVING UP TEACHING

In 1984 I gave up my tenured position at American University.

The decision came rather suddenly near the end of the spring semester. The reasons were several. I had long believed I would quit full time teaching as soon as I thought I could support our family on the sales of my paintings alone, and sales were good then. I also had a commission to make two large paintings for the lobby of the Montana Building on Broadway and 87th Street in New York. I figured I would have to take a leave of absence from teaching to make those paintings. Apart from that, the rotating chairmanship of the Art Department at American University was clearly going to be handed down to younger faculty members, and the three painters who had been chairman wanted to keep the position among painters. By 1984 one of the three had died and another was about to resign over the first heated dispute between Art Department faculty members in my twelve years teaching at the school. I knew if I were to become chairman, I would not have much time for my painting, and I submitted my resignation.

With my decision to give up full time teaching, Lani and I were faced with an interesting dilemma. If I were to no longer work in Washington, there would be no reason at all to spend a lifetime on an acre and a half surrounded by tobacco fields in Southern Maryland. For the first time in our lives we could actually choose where we wanted to live. So where might we like to live? We first thought we might want to move near the sea. We were familiar with Bill Coperthwaite's land on the northern coast of Maine and Bill had always seen me as someone he would want to share his remote piece of undeveloped land with as part of a community of like-minded people interested in simple living with traditional hand tools and enlightened ideas about education and raising children. But Lani and I didn't want to be as isolated from the world of artists and museums as that would be. We thought it would be better to live closer to Boston and to look at houses in or near coastal towns where the population might be made up of people more like ourselves who moved there from big cities.

We didn't have to make any such decisions right away because we were well set up for me to make the two commissioned paintings for the Montana Building. And after a while we found ourselves thinking if we could live anywhere, which was the case so long as we were able to get our paintings to the galleries that represented us, we could even live in Europe. And living in Europe had been a dream we both had since we were young. We thought about France and we thought about Italy, but Italy was the country we had known best and the country whose paintings meant the most to us. We understood that to live in Italy we would be more or less removed from the art scene, which might not be the best career decision we could make, but to live and work in Italy seemed right.

* * *

By this time my father had left Washington and was living in Bloomington, Indiana where his wife's family was from, and then after both his wife and her mother died and his daughter Paulette was in university, he went back to New Orleans. Sometime later, I got a phone call from a doctor who explained that my father had been hospitalized after an attempted suicide and was at that moment on his way to Washington to ask his old friend, Congressman Claude Pepper, to help him find a place to live. And a couple of days later Randy phoned me from a motel on the edge of Washington to ask me if I would cover the motel costs until Pepper's office arranged for a place where he could live. I didn't want to pay for a motel for what could be a long time, so I brought Randy home to stay with us while he was waiting to hear from the congressman. A few days later Randy was talking to a young woman who managed the Edes House in Georgetown in Washington where several George Washington University students lived along with one or two elderly persons. My father chose a basement room that had small windows high on one wall and water pipes running along beneath the ceiling. It wasn't a charming room but it was adequate for an old man who wanted to be left alone and little more. The basement room was bigger and more isolated than the upstairs room the woman showed him first. He stayed some months there and we visited him a couple of times. One day the woman phoned me to say that my father had walked out of the elevator and into the dining room wearing his pajamas and being quite drunk and disruptive. He had been getting whiskey delivered from a local liquor store.

Months later Edes House was up for sale and Randy had been transferred to another house in Washington. And later that year I was informed that my father had died. He was seventy-eight years old, lonely and in poor health. I regretted not having gotten to know my father better, which I suppose could have been possible during the period when we were in touch after his return to Washington.

My mother's total distrust and hatred of him had predisposed me not to accept him openly. She would have seen my spending time with him, or, if it should happen, actually caring for him in any way, as a gross mistake and an unforgivable betrayal. And that made it impossible for me to relate to the man who had been my father.

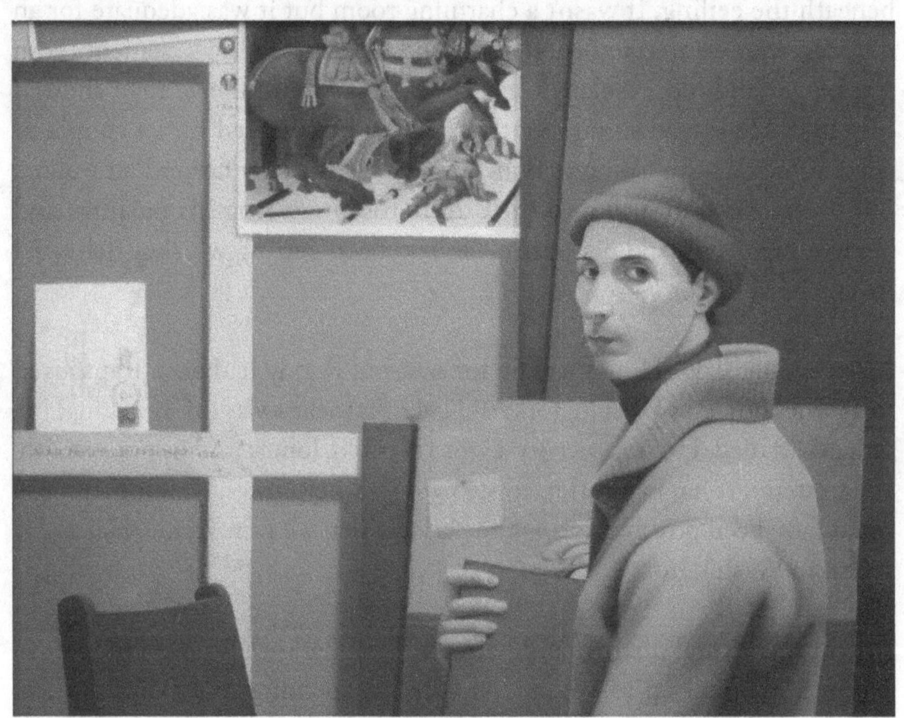

Self Portrait, 1986

20

ASSISI 1987

In September of 1987 we traveled once again to Italy, this time planning to spend at least a full year in our reconstructed tobacco drying tower, maybe to make a permanent move. We were rather unaware of the complications settling abroad would present and we were taking two children with us while not knowing how things would turn out. Our boys were eight and five years old. But we were optimistic and we were happy to be embarking on a dream we shared. We could figure things out as we went along. We thought if we made a permanent move, Tobias and Joseph would benefit from growing up bilingual and knowing the world outside of the US better. We had been homeschooling them already in Southern Maryland, and this could be like one ongoing school trip. It was what I would have loved as a kid.

I put cement blocks under the axles of our car and put a little oil in the cylinders and disconnected the battery cables as our mechanic had suggested. We moved most of our belongings to the studio and we found homes for our animals. We welcomed a family that would rent our house for a year.

* * *

Thirteen years after we had lost touch with Bendt, he saw an ad in an art magazine for an exhibition of my paintings at Forum Gallery and, having no way to know if Lani and I were still together and where we might be living, he sent two letters, one addressed to me and one to Lani, to

Forum Gallery. Bendt's letters were the most beautiful letters I had ever received, quoting passages of Rilke and telling us wonderful interesting things about his life in the years we hadn't been in touch. He wrote to Lani that it was because in 1974 she had recommended so strongly that he go to Assisi, she was in some ways responsible for his life. He loved Assisi and had returned again three years later, staying in a room in Casa Amica, a house belonging to a Danish man named Bendix. When later he met Bendix, they began a life together in a house in Denmark as well as the Assisi house.

I wrote to Bendt that we would be in Italy with our two boys in September and he responded saying we had to be their guests at Casa Amica since we would be arriving in Italy a few days before they were planning to be there. It was the end of the season for Danish paying guests and they would have the whole house to themselves. We spent a couple of wonderful weeks with Bendt and Bendix in Assisi.

Mostly we stayed in Assisi having days of conversation that lasted late into the night, with grappa and chocolates, while Tobias and Joseph slept upstairs. One of those days we all went to San Sepolcro to revisit Piero's *Resurrection* and his *Madonna della Miseracordia* altarpiece in the Museo Civico. We had a wonderful lunch in the restaurant of the Albergo Fiorentino, where Lani and I had eaten on previous trips and where Bendt told us that when he was there thirteen years earlier, the owner sat him under the framed reproduction of the face of Piero's Resurrection Christ because he, like we, saw Bendt's mouth very much like a Piero mouth. This jovial hotel and restaurant owner who prided himself on the quality of his excellent cuisine waited on tables speaking to his guests in their own languages of the specialties of the day. And he entertained Tobias and Joseph with some amusing tricks like passing a dish of pasta up and around in the air, momentarily upside down and then back right side up before setting it down in front of them. This man told us how, as a child, he had survived the war with all its deprivations to grow up passionate about cooking and eating well. There could hardly be a more perfect day than that.

Bendt and Bendix let us stay through the winter in Casa Amica. There were still no windows and no doors, no electricity or water in our converted tobacco drying tower. And we found out that the work done for us in our absence had been done illegally, in spite of my having made it very clear that I wanted everything to be done with the proper permits. Apart from that, seeing our little tobacco drying tower again, we knew it was not what we wanted. Not only was it soon going to be entirely too small for us, but at that point we thought we would be happier if we could find a house near Assisi. We were then thinking about a longer stay than the year or year and a half we initially planned. And in the months that followed, a longer stay gradually came to mean a permanent move.

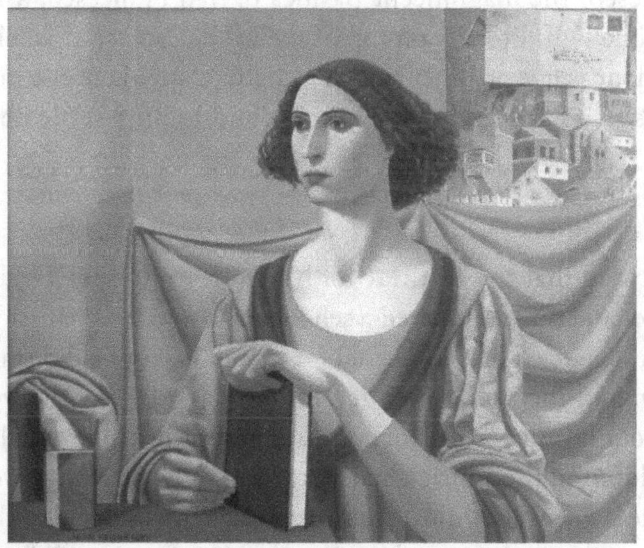

Arezzo, 1988

* * *

Assisi and nearby Spello were built of a very hard pink and cream-colored limestone that I have not seen elsewhere. These small cities also had their own building standards of measure, as can be seen on a carved stone on the bell tower next to the Temple of Minerva in Assisi. The temple of Minerva was 1st century BC Roman, whose original facade still stands. But behind those fat columns and their pediment is the 16th century church of Santa Maria Sopra Minerva, which was restyled in the 17th century to be the Baroque church it is today, one of the very few Baroque intrusions within the otherwise medieval architecture of Assisi.

Apart from its color, Assisi's uniqueness has to do with it being the birthplace and final resting place of Saint Francis, and for that, Assisi has exceptional art and history. The stories about Francis's compassion for the poor and for the unfortunate lepers, and his deep devotion to God and his mission to restore the true faith to a church that had become corrupt are the narrative of a fresco cycle in the Upper Church of the Basilica of San Francesco. The magnificent Basilica of San Francesco, which is two churches, one built literally on top of the other, each completely frescoed ceiling to floor, is like no other church in Italy, or anywhere else in the world. And it was that basilica that brought me and Lani to settle near Assisi.

***

Tobias decided that the best way for him to learn to speak Italian was to go to school and thus he entered a school classroom for the first time in his life. And Joseph tried nursery school for four days, but he didn't understand any Italian and the noise level in a foreign language with two teachers speaking loudly and waving their arms about trying to keep a large room full of children in their little chairs, drawing only what they were told to draw, made no sense to him. After three days it was decided that Joseph would not continue. I stopped by the school to pay a small insurance fee and one of the two teachers told me it would be a big mistake to take Joseph out of *asilo* because he wouldn't be prepared to enter elementary school and he might forever be behind in his classes. She said, "I can tell by his drawings." Had she cited anything other than his drawing ability, we might have questioned our decision. Instead of a house with a family and a sun shining, the same as the other children had drawn, Joseph drew his version of a spaceship. And that unintended little instance of rebellion was interpreted by the teachers as an inability to draw. At home Joseph was drawing people with six fingers on each hand, laughing as he gave them an extra finger.

I would walk down from Casa Amica to Piazza del Comune and Tobias would walk up from his school at the lower end of Assisi to where we would meet at the fountain. And we would walk together from there up the narrow medieval streets, passing the beautiful facade of San Rufino and on through the arch in the city walls and down the last narrow street again to Casa Amica where Lani would have lunch ready.

Piazza del Comune and the adjoining streets were being repaved in those months. Large new stones were laid over a thick asphalt membrane that would keep water from seeping into the excavations of the Roman Forum beneath the piazza. The stacks of paving stones that were delivered to fill the whole piazza itself fit together perfectly, but all the bordering stones had to be cut one at a time to fit the odd angles where they met the buildings. In medieval towns, and especially those towns that had begun in Roman, or even earlier Etruscan times, nothing is likely to have parallel sides or right angles, which is part of the reason why these towns are so beautiful. The oddly shaped stones to be fitted for the borders of the paving were cut on a large, heavy stone cutting table saw sitting next to the fountain. And from the mouth of one of the three lions of the fountain, water flowed day and night through a transparent red plastic tube to the saw and the drain below. In order to cut stone, such saws operate with running water to cool their diamond blade and keep the dust from rising into the air. I was intrigued by the simplicity and the ingenuity of the work taking place in so beautiful a piazza, and I loved that one of the lions of the fountain supplied the saw with its water that flowed, whether or not the saw was being used.

After Tobias's two months in the Assisi school, it was clear that he was not flourishing. Although he was doing well in his schoolwork and often his classmates would gather around his desk to watch him draw, some of the children were unkind, calling him names because he didn't speak Italian. The obvious solution was to return to homeschooling. The boys were with us wherever we went, and their lives were like one long, seamless field trip.

Early one morning, after a dusting of snow had quieted the already quiet upper end of Assisi, I passed a man standing in the street looking at something he held in his hands. I stopped to see what it was and saw he was holding a white dove. He looked up at me and told me the dove had been on a windowsill there overnight, and he had taken it in his hands because it was cold. Then he held his hands out toward me and asked if I wanted it. He knew I lived around the corner in Casa Amica and knew I had two boys. Remembering that Bendt had an old birdcage in the house, I said yes, and took the dove in my hands and thanked the man.

There was a flour mill in part of what was once the Roman amphitheater very close to Casa Amica. Assisi's anfiteatro is an arrangement of medieval houses that occupy the same precise oval form of the Roman anfiteatro that once stood there. Only a few sections of Roman wall are still visible, incorporated into the structure of a few of the houses. The mill sold a mix of seeds for doves and pigeons, so that is where I bought food for the dove we named Pace, which in Italian is pronounced *pahtcheh*, and means peace.

Once Lani and I realized that the small tobacco drying tower house was not going to work for us, we began to look for another solution. We understood that any affordable house within Assisi would have been tiny and it wouldn't have had even a little patch of garden. And having grown up as I did in Midtown Manhattan, I wanted our boys to continue to have the things cities don't have. I wanted them to have fresh air and land and animals and plants. On a four kilometer walk up to the Eremo delle Carceri on Mt. Subasio and back down again to Casa Amica, in the fog, with me carrying Joseph most of the way, we made the decision that we would try to find a country house in the hills not too far from Assisi.

We found a stone farmhouse with an adjacent barn that could be made into a good studio, twenty minutes drive from Assisi. The house had not been lived in for two or three years, apart from country mice, small country rats, and owls living in the pigeon holes facing the valley. We then sold the tobacco drying tower back to the realtors, who already had a buyer willing to pay for it including the partial renovations. We sold it without having spent even one day in it.

While waiting for the building permits to be approved, we were camping in our new ruin in conditions I can barely believe we endured. But we were younger then. And we were happy. It was a dream Lani and I had always had, and like a dream one has in the night, this dream we were living wasn't exactly grounded in reality. It certainly had its challenges and we sometimes had doubts about what we were doing. Friends thought we were courageous, and maybe we were more courageous than foolhardy, living day to day, not looking back and not knowing what lay ahead. We were living on trust, having to believe things would work out.

We took with us our white dove, who was a symbol of hope and peace in our life in that period of transition that had its moments of desperation and doubt. Given the ruinous state of the house we had to live in before reconstruction could begin, we decided to let Pace fly from room to room. I put a piece of tree limb high up in the kitchen downstairs, and attached a tray under it, and I put another in a corner of our bedroom/studio upstairs. Pace was usually in one or the other of those rooms keeping us company. He liked to sit on the upper edge of the plywood makeshift easel from where his droppings would add thin white vertical marks to my painting. I tied a nylon string between the tops of the easel legs that extended a couple of inches above both sides of the plywood, and for a while Pace was then flying to the easel and teetering with his little feet trying to gain stability on a thin string before flying up to the branch I had attached to the wall. It was very Chaplinesque.

The bureaucracy moves even more slowly here than elsewhere and it was months before our renovations could begin. We got some chickens and a pair of geese and kept warm by the old wood burning kitchen stove that came with the house. We slept on things resembling very thin futons that barely padded the rough wood platforms raised a few inches off the cold busted up brick floor. And Lani and I painted under a piece of plate glass I set into the roof as a temporary skylight.

We started to create garden beds, terracing the sloping land next to the house, making stone walls with what stones were lying about and those that had come loose from the banks of mountain roads after rain had eroded what held them in place, leaving them at the roadside. We planted roses, cypress trees, and fruit trees. And ten years later we planted 21 young olive trees of a variety that could withstand the coldest winters at our high altitude.

When the reconstruction started, I made an outhouse using three old doors for walls, leaving the front open because it sat high above the road, hidden from view by the bank and trees next to the road just below our garden, and was too far from houses to be noticed at all. It was a throne with a fantastic view. Long after I dismantled the outhouse, friends who paint landscapes painted that same view, looking across to the tiny neighboring hilltop village and beyond, to where, nestled between distant hills, softer in color, Perugia sits beneath a sky constantly changing.

When we bought the house, all of the electric wires and water pipes were exposed on the surface of inside walls. A cold-water pipe came through a wall and passed freestanding over the kitchen door and down to a faucet above a sink. The weight of a hand turning the faucet moved the full length of pipe, so the first thing I did when we started to live in the house was anchor that pipe to the wall so it wouldn't break when the faucet was used. Fortunately the previous owners had brought in acquedotto water that came to us through underground pipes from Nocera Umbra, the same water Assisi has. So we had water and a roof over our heads. The wiring was a kind I have not seen anywhere since then, that had a flat plastic strip between the two thin insulated copper wires intended for lamps and nothing more. Only lamps had been using the electricity in the early life of our house. The wires were held to the walls by little hardened nails tapped through the flat of the wire casing into the cement and plaster of inside walls.

When the renovations finally began, our nice quiet life became one of living in the middle of a great mess of demolition and rebuilding, with huge piles of rubble and stacks of wood beams and roof tiles and scaffolding, cement bags and sand piles, and with the churning noise of a cement mixer and the banging of masonry hammers morning till evening.

We had our renovations done according to the traditional methods used in country houses whereby roof and *solaio* (upper floor) have large wood beams spanning wall to wall, onto which smaller wood beams are placed in the opposing direction. Then hand made bricks are positioned on the smaller beams. We used old handmade bricks that came from our house and barn, and additional ones the builders purchased from other houses undergoing renovations that weren't reusing the original bricks. Typically, in older Italian houses like ours, there were no basements, and ground level rooms were used to house cows. In our house, where now we have our living and dining rooms, there was a cement floor that gently sloped toward the doorway for drainage. And there was a *mangiatoia* (feeding trough) of stone along the length of one wall.

Working with the *muratori*, or stone masons, I learned that adding lime helps to make a mortar that doesn't slide off the trowel before it is flipped to where it is wanted and to brush the cement between stones with a wire brush when it is set to the right firmness. Brushing gives cement the best texture for exposed stone walls. I learned to spray new cement with water on hot days to slow the drying so it can cure properly without crumbling. Being at home I could brush and wet down the cement the *muratori* left at the end of their workday. I watched them use a clear plastic tube with water in it, stretched out across the ground, both ends held up, to determine the level positioning of a floor or a wall. The height of the water at the ends of the tube will be level, one to the other. Much of what I observed were ancient methods of building still being used.

What I didn't learn from the muratori was to pace myself and to take breaks in addition to a lunch break. I didn't want physical work to keep me from the studio more than a minimum number of days. The workers always arrived punctually at seven in the morning and worked till lunch with a short break to eat a snack mid-morning. After lunch the head of the group would take a nap in his truck and the youngest of them sat in the wheelbarrow, tipped so the handles were on the ground next to his feet. It was the same makeshift chair our friend Bill Coperthwaite used to sit in when working outside at our house in Maryland. It's actually quite a comfortable chair design. After the *muratori* ate their sandwiches, they sat quietly looking out across the valley until one of them would start the cement mixer turning and the men would work again until it was time to rinse the wet cement off tools and leave.

Because the ends of some of our beams had rotted over the years, our initial renovations included the complete demolition of two thirds of the roof and *solaio* of the house, and the full roof and *solaio* of the barn. The old windows and outer doors all had to be replaced. In renovating an older house in Italy, doors and windows are made to exact measurements by a carpenter because none will match anything like a standard size. In fact, no two are likely to be exactly the same in measurement within a single house.

In the period of our massive renovations, a friend told me a story about building codes. The strict regulations requiring permissions to do any structural work on an Italian house accounts for the unspoiled beauty of Italian towns and cities. Though there are exceptions that may have predated the strict building codes, or may have been allowed by virtue of bribing the authorities, in general within the historic centers of any Italian town or city there are few structures that are modern, or that are out of keeping with local architecture. In recent decades almost no changes can be made to existing building facades. In this story, the owner of a house in the *centro storico* (historic center) of Perugia had his *muratore* doing some interior renovations and he wanted to have a window added to the facade where there was no window. So he went to the office that grants permissions for work on houses and asked if he could have a window put in on that wall, showing them a photo of the house. The official said, "Absolutely not." He went home and told his builder the verdict. The builder said to the owner, "Ci penso io", (leave it to me). And behind his parked truck, or maybe it was behind a scaffolding already in place with a covering to keep the building dust contained, he removed stones, making an opening in the wall, and made the sides look like those of a window opening. He uncovered and photographed the wall with that opening, and took the photo to the same office asking for permission to fill in the window. And he was told "Absolutely not." So he made a window there.

I like to read the changes that have been made in stone walls. In towns like Assisi, where most of the building facades are exposed stone, all the changes remain visible. These would be mostly medieval houses in which, for whatever reason, starting centuries ago, windows and doors were moved or changed in shape or closed off with stone. Virtually every facade shows those changes. Working with our *muratori* and then working later on my own with stone and brick and cement has made me more appreciative of how these walls were made, and I have become more sensitive to the materials and the traces of the hands that worked to make and remake them over many hundreds of years.

Our initial phase of reconstruction took about nine months, with a team of between two and five men working at a time, depending on what they were doing. They did all the demolition and rebuilding with stone, brick, and cement, and it was left to me to prepare the large and small wood beams and *architravi* and the thousands of old handmade bricks that would be used for ceilings and floors. The bricks required scraping and wire brushing and rinsing to ready them for the workers. It was days and days working on a long table of wood planks on iron sawhorses under one of our big oak trees, where I had a view of the rolling hills and valleys between us and Perugia.

Work started on the *fienile*, a hayloft above two rooms, of which one had been for pigs and one for farm equipment. The hayloft that would be our studio had no windows to close in the floor-to-roof openings spanning most of both side walls. Adding windows had to wait until all the construction on the house and studio was finished and approved, because the authorities could deny permission to put windows where none had existed before. Windows would be added later and then be legalized under a *condono edilizio*, which is an amnesty for building done without permits. While the house was being worked on, I slept on a little folding bed in the room under the hayloft, which became a laundry room, tool room, and storage room. Tobias and Joseph slept with Lani in a borrowed camper van that we managed to get to a level spot in a field above the house, out of the way of the workers. We ate meals in the open-air hayloft that would become our studio, which had a small sink with cold water. We were essentially picnicking outdoors under a roof. For a bathroom we had the laundry sink with its very small mirror and the temporary outhouse.

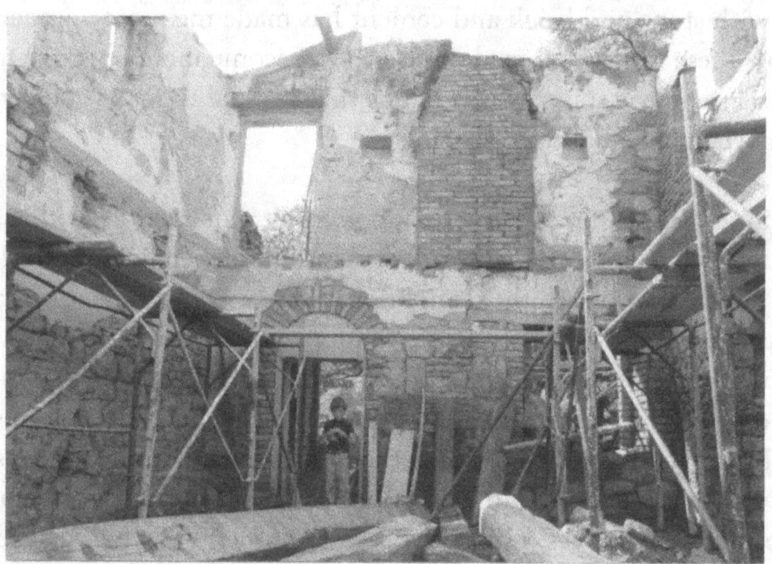

Joseph with a cat, standing in the living room entrance, circa 1989

21

INDIA

While we were living in the ruin of our house, and then in the midst of the complete chaos of its reconstruction, I went through a short-lived period of opening myself up to the possibility of a belief in God, which for me was very unlikely. It came about as a result of Lani's spiritual searching, and of our being in the spiritual center that Assisi has been since Roman times, and it had also to do with new friends who were on one or another kind of spiritual path and, like ourselves, had settled near Assisi. But more than all that, it had to do with our friend Valeria having introduced Lani to the story of her Indian spiritual master, Meher Baba. Meher Baba claimed to be the Avatar, or God in human form, and the same who in earlier incarnations had been Zoroaster, Rama, Krishna, Buddha, and Jesus.

Valeria was planning to return to India, and Lani asked if she could go with her. I felt that I owed it to Lani to take care of Tobias and Joseph by myself while she would be in India because I had just been on my own in Maryland for a few weeks emptying our Hughesville house and studio and arranging for the property to be listed for sale. So Lani and Valeria went off to India together. And in Lani's first days in India she saw how life and death and poverty and joy were all accepted for what they were in ways she had never before seen anywhere. And soon after arriving at the Pilgrim Center in Meherabad, she found herself spending time with the teenage Down Syndrome daughter of a pilgrim. And the experience of getting to know that girl and her mother, and seeing how that child brought a kind of joy to everyone whose life she touched, engendered in Lani a deeper healing of the pain she had been suffering that was about our son, Justin.

A few months later, Valeria organized a small gathering in Assisi of followers of Meher Baba that included Bhau Kalchuri, who had been one of Meher Baba's disciples, chosen by Baba to be his night watchman, staying awake while Baba slept. Then, after Meher Baba died in 1969, Bhau was involved in the administration and operations of the Avatar Meher Baba Trust, which ran the Pilgrim Center and a free school for village children, as well as free health clinics. And he wrote books that included a twenty volume 6,472-page biography of Meher Baba based on diaries kept by Baba's followers. Because Assisi was one of the places that Meher Baba had visited when he was a young man in the 1930s, Assisi was an occasional place of pilgrimage among Meher Baba devotees. Valeria also invited a few American musician friends who were followers of Meher Baba.

While Bhau and the others were in Assisi, Lani and our boys stayed in a little hotel in town to be part of the discussions and the music that carried on into the evenings. I went back and forth to be with them in the evenings and to be with my bricks during the days. At home I was alone with my wandering thoughts while my hands were busy scraping and wire brushing bricks endlessly, repetitively, day after long day in the shade of an ancient oak tree in hot mid-July. And then, there, something unexpected started to happen to me. A desperate sense of sadness and loneliness had overcome me and I could think about nothing but how much I loved Lani, and how incredibly sweet and good she was. I had already been in love with Lani and appreciated her sweet and kind nature through the years we had been together, which did have its ups and downs the way marriages have, but this was different. This was tumultuous, and something I hadn't asked for. I thought maybe it had been given to me, so to speak, by Bhau. Or possibly it was even Baba's doing, requested of Baba by Bhau. I did feel I had something of a deep and unspoken connection with this beautiful man, Bhau Kalchuri, who was telling us stories about Meher Baba. I felt that the change in me was not something to do with understanding the teachings of Baba, which I knew next to nothing about. If what I was experiencing was in any way related to the idea of God, or the stories Bhau was telling us, it was not about accepting a spiritual dogma. All I knew was that I was experiencing powerfully disturbing and also exciting things at the same time that Bhau was present in my thoughts. It seemed it could have been coincidence, but also possibly not. I welcomed it, or encouraged it, because it felt very real to me.

I was feeling a pain that I must have longed for unknowingly, that was the pain of love, or being in love. The kind of pain that songs are written about and romances are written about, that I may never before have understood in any real sense. It was a pain that brought with it a fear that I could lose Lani because I was living through something torrential and I didn't know if I was in control of anything. It was that fear and that sense of being out of control that I wasn't able to deal with.

* * *

In December of 1990 when our *muratori* had only a couple of weeks left to finish the last of their work on the outside of the house and I was cold and thoroughly exhausted and wanting a break from hard physical work, we booked flights to India. And on our way to India we spent a night in Rome with friends. Daniel Serwer was the Economic Minister for the American Embassy, and his wife Jackie was a curator at the Smithsonian National Museum of American Art before and after their time in Rome. They were living in a large beautifully furnished floor of a palazzo near the Villa Borghese. And there, when about to take my first hot shower in more than a year, I saw myself naked in the full-length mirror of their guest bathroom. The only mirror we had at home was barely large enough to let me see my face. What I saw in the full-length mirror was once again the skinny, sinewy, person I had last seen myself as when Lani and I were in Mexico after our four weeks wandering the hill towns of Guatemala on a diet of avocados and papayas.

From Rome we flew to Bombay, now Mumbai, and from there, though I don't remember exactly how it came about, we took a small minivan with two drivers to Pune. The drive seemed quite perilous as we went over passes where the driver would toss coins in the little shrines as we drove by, apparently to insure a safe journey. From Pune we made our way to Meher Baba's Pilgrim Center, a beautiful complex designed and built like a medieval Italian monastery with two courtyards, one on either side of the dining room.

We stayed six weeks over Christmas and the start of the New Year and it was gloriously warm. The Pilgrim Center provided good and abundant meals and we were given a bucket of hot water on alternate days for bathing. And that, after months of living in the middle of a worksite, without hot water, was an absolute luxury.

I stayed in a large communal room with Tobias and Joseph, and Lani stayed among the women on the other side of the courtyard. There Lani met a very nice, beautiful German woman from Paris who was at Meherabad with her Down syndrome daughter, Laura, who was very ill in those first days of our stay. Lani spent a lot of time helping Dagmar and being with Laura. To Lani, it seemed more than coincidental that, during both of her trips to Meherabad, she was confronted in a very personal way with a Down syndrome child. Once again Lani was made to think about our son Justin, and about how those two Down syndrome children were loved and accepted for the extraordinary young people they were. Laura was about our Joseph's age, about seven, and she spoke German and French and English and was doing children's gymnastics when they were at home in Paris. I remember how the palms of Laura's hands were callused and how she looked stronger than any other little girl I had known. And I remember her as having a smile that could break my heart.

Every morning when we walked up the hill to the Samadhi, to Meher Baba's tomb for morning prayers, there would be a new tomb cloth on the marble cover of the tomb, on which pilgrims would place garlands of marigolds and red roses. On January 5th, our son Justin's birthday, the tomb cloth was exceptionally beautiful, having intricate patterns of small blue and pink beads, and it was more beautifully covered and surrounded by garlands of red roses than I had seen on other days. Because we hadn't mentioned Justin's birthday to anyone who might have been responsible for preparing the tomb that morning, it was hard for us not to believe that in some unexplainable way the tomb of Meher Baba was meant to be more special that day because it was Justin's birthday. Lani felt all her time in India over both trips had been a gift to show her that she could be with her pain in a less upsetting way letting go of some of the darkness that she had been carrying for eight years. And it was a help to me as well, though I know that Lani suffered in a far deeper way than I after the birth and then the death of our son, Justin.

I liked most of what I could understand of what I heard or read about Meher Baba's teachings. I liked that we were driven to a restaurant one evening in God's 1947 Chevrolet sedan with Bhau Kalchuri, who for many years had been God's night watchman. I liked that we saw films and photographs of Meher Baba throughout his life. They were actual film footage and photographs of God himself, if I wanted to accept such beliefs, not of a Hollywood actor unconvincingly playing a Biblical role. I thought in the many photographs of Baba that he looked like many different people at different times in his life. In one I saw my father's face in his, and much later a face totally different than that of his early years, when he was very beautiful. He was, in a sense, every man and at the same time no man at all. I liked the abundance of garlands of fresh red roses laid on Baba's tomb every day, and the music lovingly played and sung for him in front of the open door to his mausoleum, and how completely humble and sincere he and his devotees all seemed to have been. But ultimately I couldn't believe Meher Baba was God. It just didn't make sense to me, and I was soon back to my inability to believe in God, but with a more gentle respect for those who do believe in God.

***

India was interesting and exciting in the same ways Mexico had been when I was little and again when I was in Mexico and Guatemala with Lani. I liked being in those places for how they were unlike the places I came from.

I saw life in India as being honest and direct and lived without pretense. Everything was decorated and everything was celebrated. And time had a different kind of pace; it was slowed, and experienced without a sense of urgency. I saw India as a place of beautiful chaos, so filled with life and so much about living in the present that it can bring us to question the meaning of our own existence and the way lives are lived in the West. I'll give you a little idea what that means. An Indian truck is manufactured and sold as a cab, with its driver's seat and steering wheel and gear shift and pedals in place, with its engine and with wheels all attached to a bare chassis, and nothing more. I saw one being driven like that, naked and strange like a man driving something I could only know in dreams. The truck is then finished by carpenters, who make and mount wooden doors and sides to complete the structure. And then all of it is elaborately covered in hand painted patterns and decorations. On the back of every truck are the painted words HORN OK PLEASE to say please use your horn to alert the driver of that truck that you intend to overtake his truck. And that is because most roads in India are very narrow, and anything can be on them. So the honking of horns can be noisy. A truck often has people riding on top of the cab as well as in the open back, and a bicycle might have a whole family riding on it, or it might be ridden by one person carrying some animal, or something large extending out on both sides to the width of a car. In a town a cow can be standing still next to parked cars and moving cars and people crossing the street. Because cows are sacred animals, they are not interfered with by anyone. We saw cows whose horns were painted orange. I saw elephants that were painted. And anything painted had been painted in bright colors and with great skill and patience. I saw houses with scaffoldings of bamboo poles, and brick walls whose bricks looked like loaves of whole grain bread, with rounded edges and fibrous surfaces. They looked ancient, and it wasn't easily apparent whether what I saw were new houses being built or old ones being demolished. I was seeing the hand-made face of India. It felt honest and unpretentious and unchanged by the technology one takes for granted, unquestioned, in the US and Europe. Being surrounded by all that beautiful chaos was very different from the calm and the order I seem to need in my life, and for that it fascinated me.

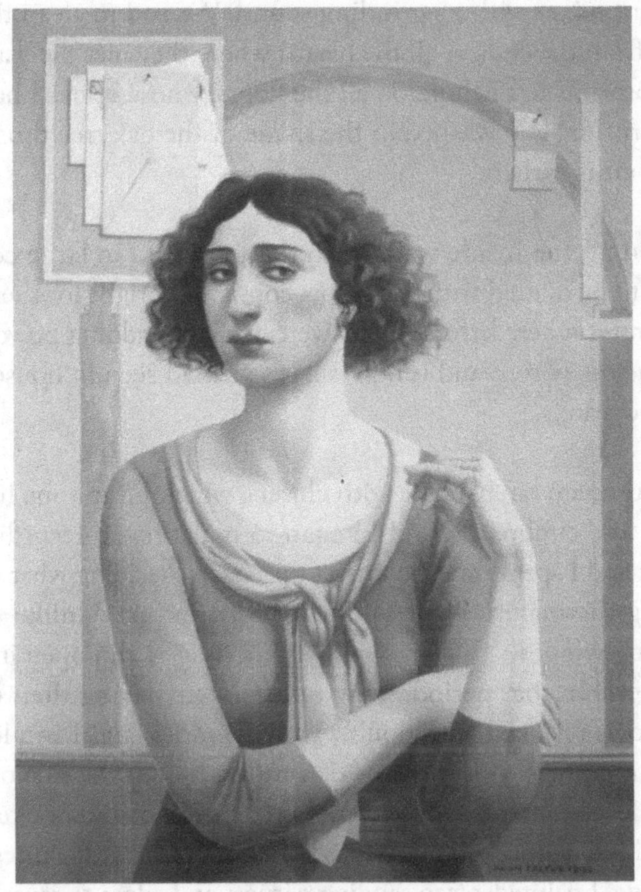

Archangel, 1992

* * *

In our first years in the house we had a bare minimum of anything. We had come to Italy with no more than what our suitcases could hold and added to that our makeshift temporary beds and some pots and pans and dishes, knives, forks and spoons, rubber boots and work gloves and an old car. That was it.

We returned from India to find the same mess of a construction site we had left five weeks earlier, minus the workers and their scaffolding and their cement mixer with its grinding sound. We had to clean the residue of cement from the ends of all the beams where they met the wall, and the cement footprints left behind on all the floors, whose bricks I had scraped and wire brushed and washed in the shade of the oak tree those hot July days six months earlier.

We painted all the inside walls with tempera sold in large containers, which had to be diluted with water to a consistency right for the very large brushes common here before rollers were available, adding powdered tints to make the dusty rose and yellow ochres we had seen in houses painted in past generations.

In Italy houses are rarely made with closets, which means one has to have wardrobes and cupboards, and I began to make those according to our needs. Lani and I spent time looking at the spaces, deciding what we needed and finding the materials for cabinets and furniture. Unlike American double-hung windows, Italian windows are hinged and open inward like cabinet doors. In that period many houses were having their old single pane windows replaced with double pane windows and I would find the old ones, sometimes with their inside shutters, left at the side of the road at trash collection points. Those were perfect cabinet and bookcase fronts that I could build around. I made wardrobes using discarded interior doors. What I made, I painted, often sanding corners and edges to reveal the color of the wood or an under-layer of paint below the new paint. Lastly I used furniture wax with added color to tie together the old and the new and to hide the patching inherent in everything I made.

I seem always to be making and remaking what we live with. I made our beds. I made three couches for the living room that could be guest beds if needed. One of them I changed after many years so its back could be swung easily across from one side to the other. When I had almost finished converting the couch to a two directional one, I remembered where I had seen the idea before. It was the benches on trains I rode when I was a kid traveling between New York and the New England boarding schools; they had backs that could be swung across from one side to the other so passengers could sit facing each other if they chose to. I cut and welded iron to make a pivot mechanism to support the back and hold it firmly in either fixed position. When we watch television and films, the couch faces the TV in its cabinet, and when we have company it faces the other couches and the window. Trial and error with a measure of patience usually resulted in yielding a good solution for whatever I set my mind to making.

Our life at home in the hills behind Assisi settled down and became one of painting and spending time with painter friends. Rather an idyllic life. The work we were doing within our house and studio and the land surrounding continued, as things were slowly becoming more beautiful and more personal. Over the years I made furniture and cabinets for every space we have, and our walls have become full with the things we have collected.

22

WHILE THE MUSIC PLAYED

Periodically I would return to New York to carry paintings from Italy to Forum Gallery and to be there for my exhibition openings. I was interested in how the city changed between visits, and I enjoyed the vivid contrast between New York and Assisi. The dissimilarity of the enormous glass, steel, and cement towers compared to the low medieval pink stone buildings and quiet narrow streets of Assisi often caused me to feel like a displaced person while on those trips. I would stop to watch break-dancers in the square in front of FAO Schwarz, across the street from Forum Gallery, when the gallery was at 745 Fifth Avenue and FAO Schwarz was still there. And I liked the performers in subway stations and the drummers who played on sidewalks using plastic buckets and old refrigerator drawers as their drums.

When back in New York, I would hear language that sounded wrong to me because, in my absence, new forms of speech had insinuated themselves into common usage. I would hear a doubling of "is" when people would say "the thing is is that." And I would hear the word "like" carelessly replacing all kinds of more meaningful words and phrases. The question we instinctively ask when meeting someone became answered by "I'm good." I'm good may be as grammatically acceptable as "I'm well" or "I'm fine", but to my ear it sounds wrong. We accept what we hear being spoken if we stay in one place as long as it takes for something new to replace what was in common usage before. In language, what is no longer in common usage begins to sound awkward or pretentious. Whom is a word I almost never use in speaking, even when I am aware of it being the correct word. I remember a New Yorker cartoon of a young man standing in his graduation cap and gown holding the receiver of a payphone, and under the drawing it said "It is I." That fairly well says what I mean.

* * *

I carried paintings to New York in 1991 for the first one-person exhibition I had after we moved to Italy. I stayed in Arthur Cohen's New York studio while Arthur was still in Provincetown. The idea was that in six or eight weeks I would make one painting larger than those I brought from Assisi that I had painted at Casa Amica and then at our house before the interruption of our renovations, during the period when I didn't have a proper studio.

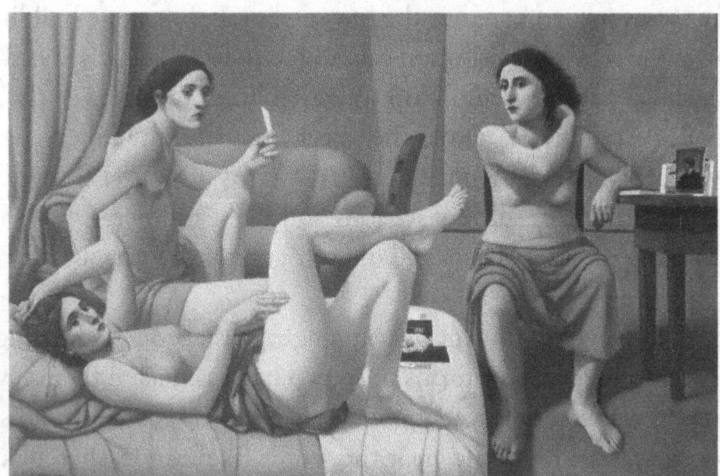

While the Music Played, 1991

Arthur was a painter I had known since I was a Cooper Union student. He is the one Tommy and I took breakfast to when he was painting Provincetown from Sal's canoe. The first time I remember seeing Arthur, he was high up on a ladder repainting the sign over the window of McSorley's tavern down the street from Cooper Union. And then I saw him at an art gallery opening, wearing a leather coat that went down almost to his ankles and somehow made his arms look unusually long as they hung at his sides. His strong features and very curly hair, along with the coat I thought I had seen in WW II films, had me thinking he looked Eastern European, and like a man who might not speak a word of English. But not only did Arthur speak perfect English, he spoke with a voice that was exceptionally rich and beautiful. When later I introduced him to my mother, the first thing she said to him was, "Do you sing?" Arthur would spontaneously speak in an amusing broken English of foreigners in accents of all kinds, and he would make sounds the way someone who worked with sound effects for radio shows might make. One time when he was in the back seat of a car I was driving in New York I heard a police car siren a few blocks away and coming nearer and nearer, only to realize the siren was Arthur. And he would make the sound of a dog whining after being kicked, and a train whistle that sounded exactly like that of the toy electric train Peter and I had. Arthur's sound effects were interspersed with the sounds around us for no apparent reason. They were just part of his behavior.

Arthur's studio sat alone on the roof of an apartment building on 108th Street near Broadway. At the foot of Arthur's small single bed, I painted next to an open door to the black tar-surfaced roof. That gave me good north light and ventilation. Those were the hottest days of July. The nearest building high enough to have windows facing that door was two streets away, so I sat in my underpants with the door wide open while I painted. The painting I made there was titled *While the Music Played*. I painted every day, going to the Metropolitan Museum Friday evenings when they stay open until 9:00. A pair of doves were often on the roof while I was painting with the door open. I thought of them as reminders of home, and a sign of good things to come as I listened to their cooing. It was hard for me to be without Lani for so long a time.

New York was sad in that period. It was at the height of the AIDS epidemic, and testing centers and information hotlines were being announced by the posters in English and Spanish above the windows of all the buses and subways, some in the form of cartoons with minimal text and others more informative. I saw emaciated young men sitting on sidewalks holding cardboard signs saying they had AIDS and needed contributions for food. Homeless people were begging in the subways and on the streets. I saw a man sleeping on a park bench on the median at the pedestrian crossing of Broadway near where I was staying, his head inside a cardboard box and the rest of his body uncovered with his large naked stomach exposed because his shirt was open. He looked incredibly vulnerable as people walked past inches from that bench all day. It was impossible to be in New York without seeing these signs of the hopelessness of fellow beings whose lives were so tragically beyond recovery. The doomsday appearance of those days was more evident than I remembered from any previous or subsequent stays in the city.

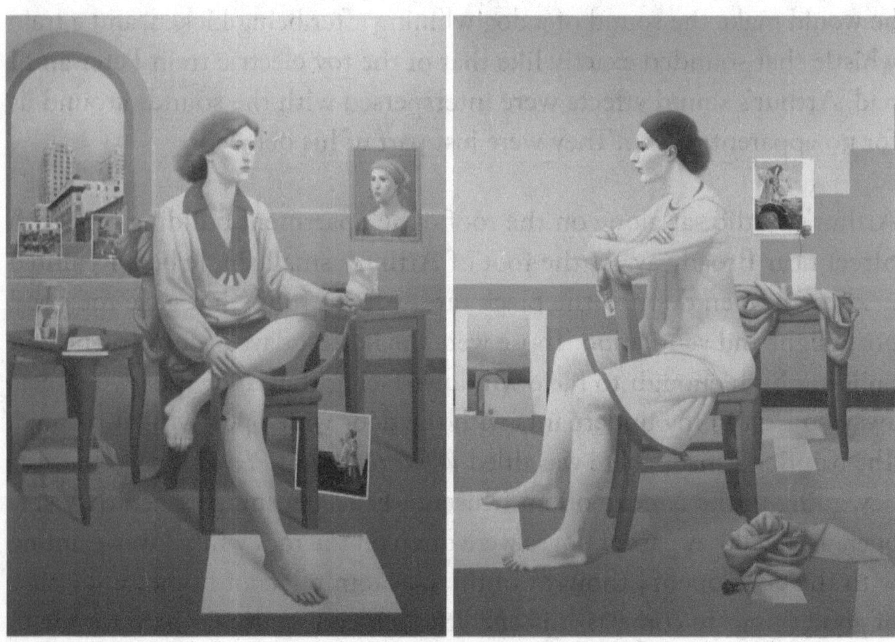

Untitled Montana Building Commission, 1986

But it was not only like that. One day while I was walking from Arthur's studio to the Metropolitan Museum, crossing Central Park, I was enjoying reliving old childhood memories of walking on the bridal path next to the reservoir, with the scent of horse manure and volcanic lava gravel lifted in the air by the warm sun. A jogger came up just to my left and glanced at me as he was passing. He slowed and asked, "Aren't you the painter Alan Feltus?" He had never met me but he recognized me from self-portraits he had seen at Forum Gallery. What are the chances of anything like that happening in the middle of Central Park, in the middle of Manhattan? And as he was walking next to me it got even more strangely coincidental. He asked me about the two paintings commissioned by the owner of the Montana Building. I told him they were no longer in the lobby of the Montana Building and I didn't know where they were. He then told me the paintings were temporarily being stored in his studio racks downtown. He was a friend of the widow of the owner of the Montana Building. At one of my later Forum Gallery openings, I met the woman who owned those paintings and she told me she was enjoying them in her home in Connecticut.

On my New York trips, I would write to Lani at least part of an air letter every day, dropping them in a mailbox every two or three days. That was my way of telling her what I was doing, and it helped to stave off loneliness. In my mind I could see her reading what I wrote and that helped me not to lose a sense of who I was.

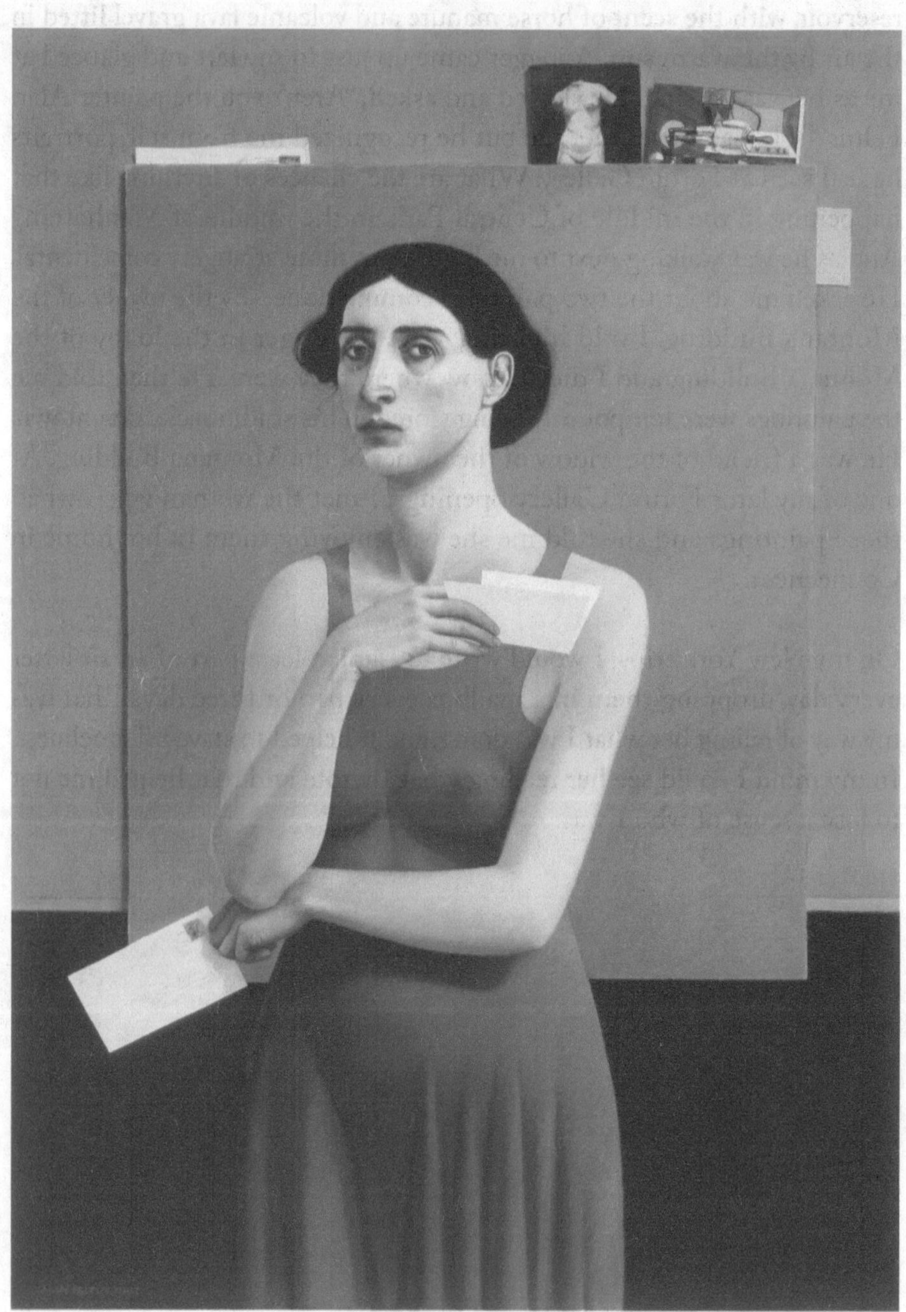

Motherself, 1993

23

MOTHERSELF

In 1993, I started a series of paintings about myself with my mother. It began while I was painting a single female figure while referring to myself in the mirror. I saw she was becoming more and more like me as a female figure, but younger and more beautiful. The painting could be both a woman and at the same time myself. I liked that it was looking somewhat like me as a woman, combining myself with my mother. Although usually I title my paintings after they are finished, this time was different. I decided to title it *Motherself*. Near the top of the painting I copied a postcard of Carlo Carrà's Metaphysical period painting titled *Mother and Son*. In the Carrà both the mother and her son are mannequins. As I was painting *Motherself*, I thought it might be interesting to see what would come of making several paintings that would be about myself with my mother. The theme was somewhat related to Gorky's mother and son paintings, but it was unlike those in that what I wanted to do was to see if I could better understand how I managed to survive the conflicted relationship I had with my mother. I was curious to see if my focus on this subject might result in anything like what psychotherapy could do.

The second painting of this series was much larger, and it depicts a young boy standing with two toys at his feet, his shirt front crumpled from anxiety, his arms in a somewhat protective attitude, and with a slightly furrowed brow. His mother lounges in her chemise, self-absorbed in her book of the *I Ching* and the three coins she tossed to find specific passages in the book that would address questions she had about her life. But what book she was reading in the painting was less important than that she was not interacting with the boy. She was focused on what she wanted to be doing, as though she were by herself. The toys on the floor represent the toys I made in that period of my childhood when we were living out of suitcases with few belongings of any kind to call our own and no money to spend on things like toys. I didn't paint the boy as skinny as I was throughout my childhood, and I gave him a face that was different from my childhood face. The mother figure was beautiful, but not in the same ways my mother had been. And I didn't paint her wearing a black eyepatch that would have identified her as Anne Winter to those who knew her, or knew anything about her. I wasn't interested in people knowing the painting was about me and my relationship with my mother. It was a painting. The other part was personal and private. I gave this painting the title *Once Upon a Time*.

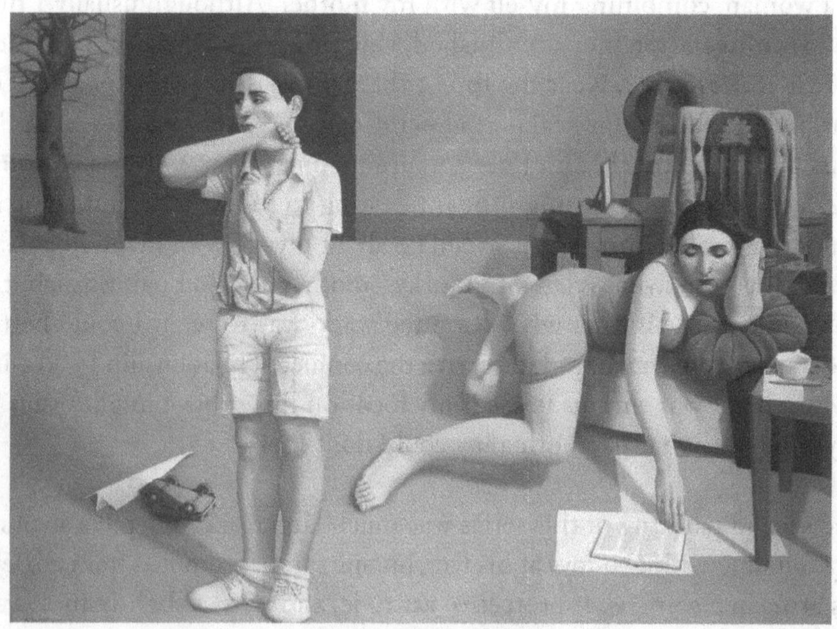

Once Upon a Time, 1993

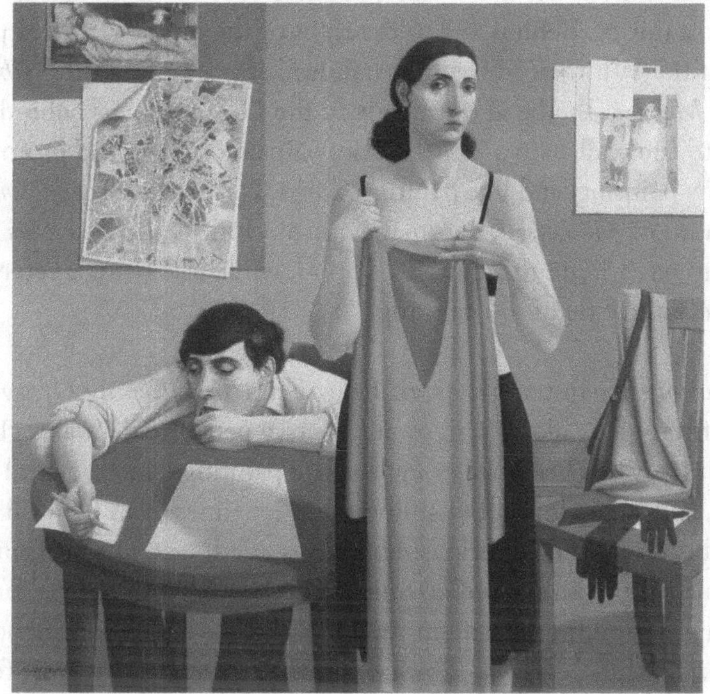

Seventeen and Forty-Three in Sixty, 1993

In the paintings that followed *Once Upon a Time,* I depicted myself as an adolescent boy during the time when my mother and I were living together in Rome, when my memories were clearer, and a time in which I was experiencing changes within myself. The one of these that I titled *Seventeen and Forty-Three in Sixty* has a nicely meaningful title while at the same time it would say nothing to anyone else who would see it. I liked the ambiguity the title would have in the absence of an explanation. It came to mind when I realized that in that year I was seventeen, my mother was forty-three, and the year was 1960, and adding her age to my age totaled sixty. On the wall behind the boy sitting at his table writing, I painted a map of Rome to suggest place and time. And above that I made a little copy of Titian's *Venus of Urbino,* whose sensual and erotically posed reclining female figure hinted at my desire for a romantic relationship. My, one might say, "seductive" mother stands in her black slip and bra, holding a

245

red dress in front of her and looking out at the viewer as though looking at herself in a mirror. Behind and to the right of the mother figure, I painted a copy of the Whitney Museum's Arshile Gorky painting titled *The Artist and His Mother*. The head of the boy in the Gorky copy is behind a note pinned to the wall to avoid the Gorky painting having too prominent a role in my painting, and like painting Carlo Carrà's *Mother and Son* in the background of *Motherself*, the small copy of Gorky's *Artist and his Mother* is there to pay tribute to an artist I admire, while also being a reference to the subject and title of my painting.

In *Mélancolie* I painted a copy of Rousseau's *The Sleeping Gypsy* on the table in front of me along with some papers, a pencil, and a water glass. *The Sleeping Gypsy* had been one of my favorite paintings since before I started to paint, and to me it is about stillness and loneliness. On the wall behind my head is Giorgio de Chirico's *Melancholy of a Beautiful Day*, from 1913, one of his early paintings of an empty piazza with a single person and a statue, and a building facade in forced perspective. The melancholy and loneliness in those early de Chirico paintings mirrored my own feelings. In my *Mélancolie*, my mother stands in her black bra and slip, with eyes closed as she adjusts her hair.

Awakenings and *La Nostalgia Del Figlio* refer more specifically to my adolescent awakenings of sexual desires in a time in my life when I was living with my mother in the most romantic and magical place I had ever known. These are paintings that have an undercurrent of tension between a seductive yet detached woman and the innocent longings of a young man.

Though embarking on this series of paintings about myself and my mother didn't prove to be very meaningful in ways I hoped they might have, it became useful to me with respect to how I regard narrative imagery in my painting. Many of the paintings that followed the seven paintings that made up the mother and son series have had one male and one female figure who might be lovers, or they might just be people in the same room space, unspecified. They were, and are, no longer intended to be paintings about myself.

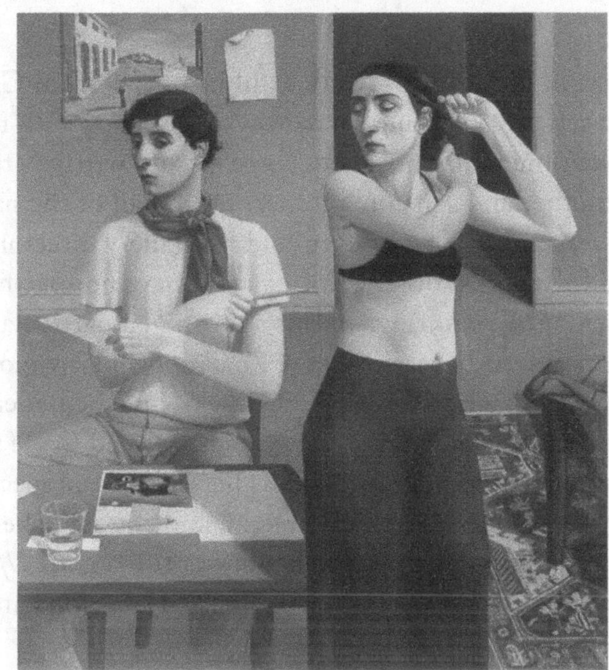

Mélancolie, 1993

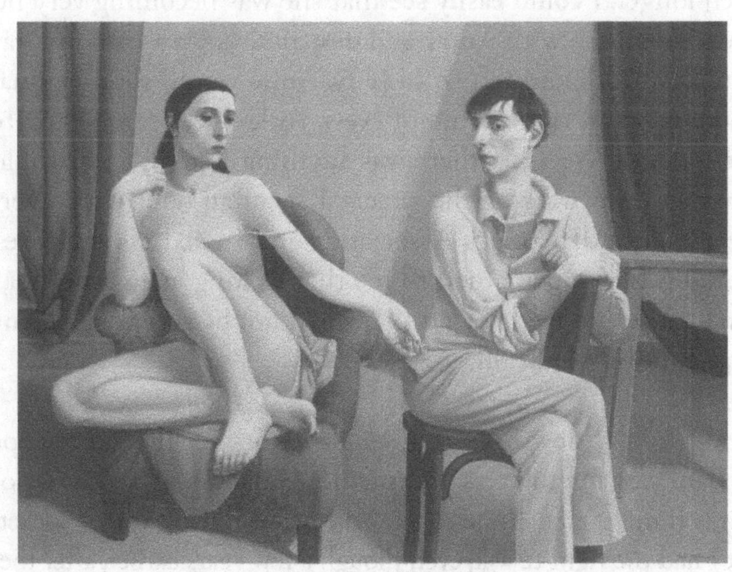

La Nostalgia del Figlio, 1993

* * *

In 1994 I was in New York for my exhibition at Forum Gallery that included the series of paintings about myself as a boy with my mother. When I took Anne to see my show, there was no written statement to explain the mother and son content that was in half of the paintings on view. I don't remember if I had even told the gallery director or anyone else that, unlike with my other paintings that have no specific narrative content, seven of the paintings in this show had a particular theme or narrative about my early years. I know I had not told my mother. Anne had recently been diagnosed with Alzheimer's, but she understood that it was my work on the walls and, strangely, she seemed to see the mother and son theme. Even without seeing it as herself and me specifically, she identified in some way with those images, and she said she didn't like them. She particularly didn't like the painting titled *Once Upon a Time,* the one that best depicted the mother being self-absorbed and ignoring the young boy.

It was clear to me that my mother would not be able to take care of herself for much longer. I could easily see that she was becoming very helpless and I was overcome with worry and despair. I knew I couldn't leave her alone in New York and return to Italy. Anne would soon be unable to live on her own in the middle of New York. I was terribly distressed because I couldn't see that there was anything I could do. I would start crying while I was walking the streets. I spent an hour with a very nice volunteer at the Alzheimer's Association and I cried in her office much of that hour. It was explained to me that as long as my mother could dress and bathe and feed herself she would not be accepted by a nursing home paid for by Medicaid.

Lani and the boys flew from Italy to New York for the gallery opening. When Lani saw my distress and the hopelessness of the situation, she said it was time to take Anne to live with us in Italy. It wasn't something I thought I had the right to ask, even though a few years earlier, after the NYU Hospital doctor had phoned me to inform me of my mother's dementia, we had a bathroom and central heating added to the space under Lani's studio, and connected the two separate rooms to make a small guest apartment that Anne could stay in if it were to become necessary. When we asked Anne if she would like to live with us in Italy, in her very small and faltering voice she said, "You would do that?"

Lani and the boys returned to Assisi and I canceled my return flight to Italy in order to renew Anne's passport, organize and pack her belongings, and book new flights for us. It is impossible to describe the process of managing innumerable suitcases and carry-on bags through two international airports with my mother unable to follow even the most elementary directions, much less help. She could stand and she could walk but I couldn't take my eyes off of her while struggling with multiple pushcarts and bags.

Anne would often be in the house during the day and we ate meals together as a family. She could wander around outside staying close enough to the house that we didn't worry about the infrequent passing of a car or that she might walk down the road and not find her way home. She would stop to look at a flower, and often she had something in her hand that she wanted me to explain. It might be a letter sent to her in New York by her friend in South Africa. She had a box with a few letters that she knew had some meaning to her, but she didn't know what those meanings were. Even holding a letter close to her face, she could barely read a word or two, and she would look up at me to be told what was written. She didn't seem to be troubled that what I read had little meaning to her. The only blessing about having Alzheimer's is that the person afflicted doesn't know she has lost her mind. Anne would stand in the kitchen waiting for a meal to be prepared, like a little bird waiting to be fed by its mother. Her presence was that of a child who hadn't yet learned to speak.

Anne was with us thirteen months, deteriorating gradually until she could no longer dress herself in any reasonably logical way, and wasn't able to bathe herself. One cold winter day she walked across to the house from her little apartment wearing only the down jacket we got for her that was barely long enough to hide her underpants, if she had underpants on.

Another day she walked outside wearing all three of her eyepatches on her head in a haphazard cluster over her missing right eye. Of course, all of those moments were painfully sad, but because in her state of mindlessness Anne didn't seem troubled by her inability to do simple things, we could also sometimes see a kind of humor in what she did. At times I have found laughter and crying to be almost one thing over which I have little control.

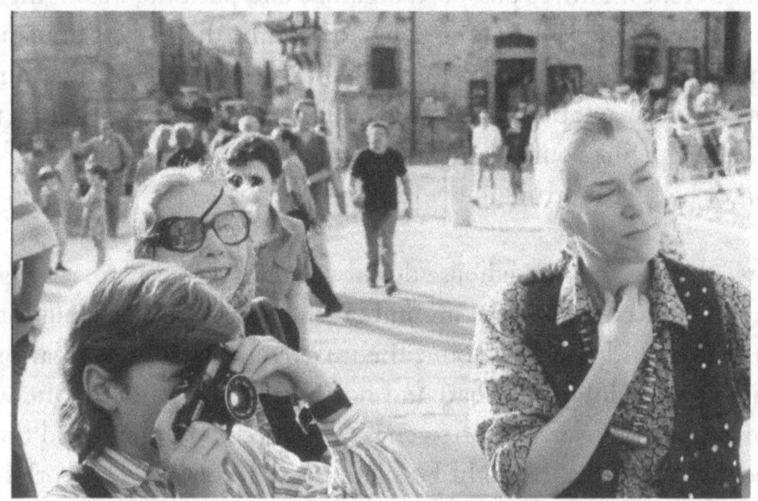

Anne, smiling at the camera, in Assisi (with Joseph and Lani), 1994

In New York, with the help of a registered nurse who interviewed me while looking at my mother because my mother was beyond understanding a question or answering anything in any way at all, Anne was placed in the Hebrew Home for the Aged in Riverdale. Smaller and more frail, her mind rolled backwards, skipping almost everything along the way, like a film run in reverse as though to become born again. The first time I visited Anne in the nursing home, I found her sitting, holding hands with a man who was watching the TV in his room down the hall and around the corner from her room. In his dementia, I think the man didn't know my mother was holding his hand. Whatever was flickering on the TV was all he could manage to be aware of. I stood and watched. Anne very slowly looked at me but she didn't recognize me. Only Alzheimer's patients lived on that floor in the nursing home that I remember as being a cross between *One Flew Over the Cuckoo's Nest* and *Awakenings*. It was a place where patients turned inward in gloomy silence or called out to no-one in words that had no meaning.

When I last saw my mother, I was in New York on another trip from Assisi and again I took the bus up to The Bronx and walked into the nursing home. I took the elevator to her floor and I found her sitting by herself in the dining room. I took my mother's delicate hand in mine and stood a minute looking down at her, poor creature that she had become, and her one eye very slowly turned up to look at me. No other signs of life to be seen. She no longer resembled a living person. She looked more like a poorly made Victorian wax doll. She had shrunken still more and what remained of her inhabited an empty shell of a body. After a while I left, feeling that deep, deep sadness I was so accustomed to.

Anne died in 1999. What I felt was like the emptiness I feel when I am too exhausted to think at all and I need to slip into sleep. Sleep for me can be a welcome exiting from reality, much like how waking from sleep can be a welcome realization that the frustrating series of situations my mind had been wrestling with moments before were only dreams. I had already suffered through the pain of grieving and crying uncontrollably that started those several years earlier. I will always feel that sadness about my mother, but it is a sadness I accept, one that is about love and about regrets, for as strained as our relationship had been, she was my mother.

* * *

My brother, Peter died in his sleep in 2012. As unlike as we were most of our lives, we were brothers and I miss him. It is interesting, however, that my slightly older brother who shared the same childhood environment had next to no knowledge about art and he had no real understanding of what I did. He was not a maker of things. For him a good day was sitting in his favorite cafe talking to any friends who might be there, or reading. He liked to discuss political ideas with anyone and often became insolent.

Fate reunited Peter and our father when Peter was eighteen, living on his own in New York. He had dropped out of high school and was sharing an apartment with roommates while I was with Anne in Greece at the start of our year in Europe together. While we were traveling in Greece without an itinerary of any kind, there was no way to reach us. Anne had given Peter the contact information of a lawyer friend should he need help. And when Anne and I got to Rome and she collected what correspondence was sent to her at the only address she had given anyone, there were telegrams from the lawyer in New York saying Peter was in hospital on the critical list with an appendix operation gone wrong. After no response from our mother, the lawyer had tracked down our father, who was back in New Orleans, and both Anne and Randy flew to New York and appeared at about the same time at Peter's bedside in the hospital. Randy told Peter that if he recovered, and if he wanted, he could go to live with him in New Orleans. After his recovery, Peter did join Randy in New Orleans. So from that point, Peter had very different experiences from my own. Randy enrolled Peter in some part time classes at Tulane University, Randy's alma mater, and that worked to erase Peter's high school drop-out status. Not long after Peter joined his father in New Orleans, Randy was hired as a public relations person for the new Hilton Hotel in Hong Kong and Peter went with him. Peter lived in Hong Kong for a few years before returning to the US to study philosophy and business at Berkeley. He lived in Oakland until his death.

24

EARTHQUAKE

On September 26th, 1997 a very strong earthquake struck Assisi at 11:42, after an earthquake in the night that itself had been the strongest we had ever felt. Two large parts of the ceiling vault in the Upper Church of the Basilica of San Francesco came crashing down, killing two engineers from the monuments office in Perugia and two Franciscan friars. The first news reports said the whole ceiling of the Upper Church had fallen, but that was because throughout the day of the earthquake, the air inside was so thick with a suspended dust no one could see what had fallen and what had not.

The tons of brick that crashed down on top of the four men just inside the entrance of the Upper Church had been moved out immediately and placed in a long mound extending halfway up the lawn and a corrugated metal roof was erected to protect it from the weather. When I heard volunteers had started working in front of the basilica to recover fresco fragments from the partially fallen ceiling, I wanted to be among them, for it was the Basilica of San Francesco that had lured us to settle here ten years earlier, and no other way I might be able to help in the aftermath of the earthquake made better sense to me. Tobias was eighteen years old, the youngest they allowed volunteers to be, so he and I joined the volunteers. For about a month I alternated between working a day or two at the basilica and a day or two in my studio.

The fragments recognized to be from faces were put in plastic trays on a layer of fine sand, placed next to actual size photos of the saints' heads. The rest were put in boxes of unsorted fragments grouped together according to color. And all the recovered fragments were temporarily sheltered inside a large L shaped tent next to where we worked until the entire mound of rubble had been sorted through. Most of the pieces of plaster that had a flat surface with color were hard to identify because they were small bits of whatever decorative border or image they would have been part of, but faces and hands were painted differently from clothing and surrounding colors, so it was easy enough to separate them from the rest.

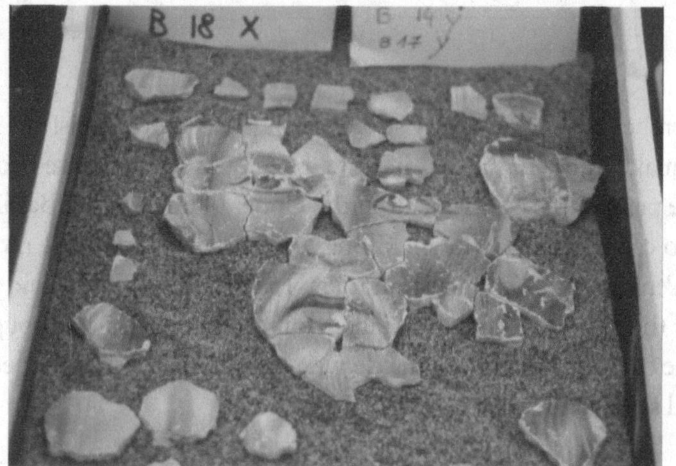

Fragments of the face of San Rufino, Basilica di San Francesco, Assisi, 1997

One of those many days while I was sitting quietly on my plastic box, paintbrush in hand to brush off the dust that obscured what might be color on any piece of rubble flat on one side, the man sitting close to me stopped working. His hands lay still on his lap. After a few minutes he turned to me and said he found Bruno's eyeglasses. Bruno was one of the two engineers from the monuments office killed beneath the ceiling vault that terrible morning just a few days earlier. Bruno was this man's closest friend. He sat and wept.

Along with other volunteers, Tobias and I watched the crane on the back of an enormous truck lift a slightly smaller truck with its own crane up and over the wall that separated the Sacro Convento from the piazza next to the entrance of the Lower Church. Men using ropes attached to the suspended truck guided it so it could be lowered to the ground on the other side without bumping into the wall. A large truck floating high above the wall was like something from a film, or something I might remember from a dream more than something real. When the suspended truck's tires touched ground, there was a cheering from the volunteers watching, and a small cloud of dust rose from our clapping hands.

One day toward evening a storm moved in and Tobias and I took shelter in the tent, looking at the pieces of saints' heads already found, when there was a great crack of thunder right above us. Lightning hit the iron cross on the peak of the basilica facade close to where we stood. We were there beautiful days and we were there stormy days, joyful days and painfully sad days. When I stayed home I was painting a self-portrait wearing the dust-covered yellow hooded sweatshirt onto which was pinned the name badge that identified me as a volunteer working at the basilica retrieving fresco fragments.

The recovered fresco fragments, though spotty and incomplete, are now back where they belong, on the reconstructed ceiling vault of the Upper Church of the basilica.

* * *

Standing in the dining room of our house at 11:42, it felt like we were on a boat in the open sea in the middle of a storm, the floor heaving with the movement of the earth, the few seconds seeming interminable. There was the muffled sound of the earthquake rolling toward us from the distance, and within the house, a rattling like one giant tray full of glasses and dishes shaking, some crashing to the floor, everything in movement. Pictures on the wall were all crooked. It seemed incredible that the house was intact when the movement stopped and we were left with only some cracks visible.

Our house and studio had been built on rock that aeons ago had fractured and become discontinuous within the subsoil. Without solid bedrock or clay that had never been exposed to the elements, the stability of a stone house depends on strong foundations, and ours were not what they needed to be. So a new team of *muratori*, working with an engineer adhering to exacting seismic codes, dug deep trenches around our house and new foundations of solid brick and reinforced concrete were made and tied into the existing walls under the house. Then the damaged sections of wall were remade. It was months of work, and unlike when we had our first renovations, this time I wasn't permitted to work alongside the builders. For that I was glad. In this second phase of restorations, we slept among boxes and stacked furniture in our studios.

An Italian government earthquake grant covered the reconstruction of our house following the earthquake. It was explained to me that those grants exist because the houses we own are part of the patrimony of Italy. We are the temporary caretakers of these houses for as long as we own them, and then new owners will be new caretakers. All the while the houses belong to Italy.

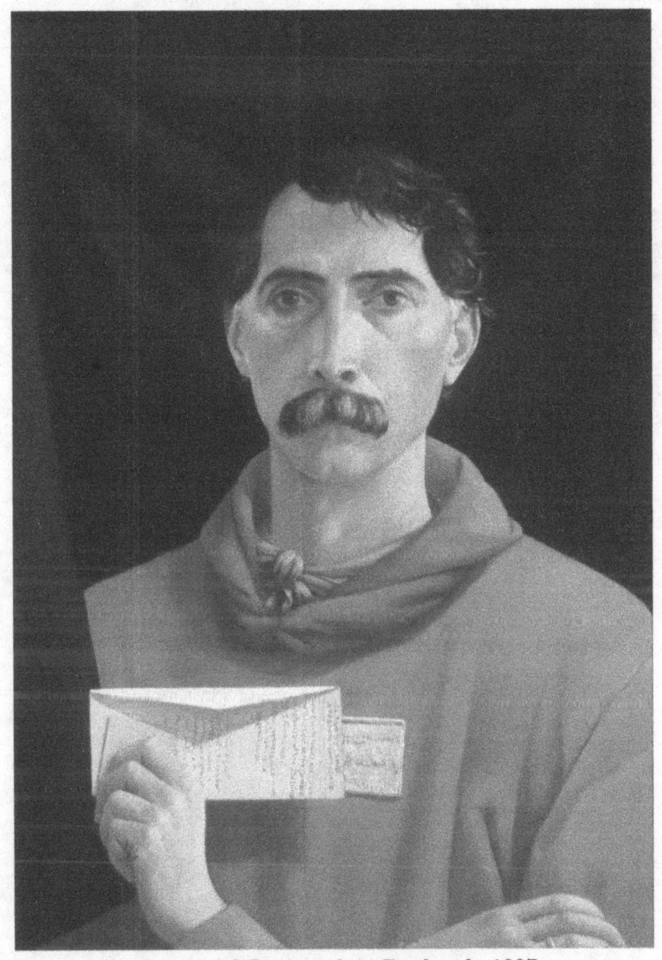

Autumn Self Portrait, Assisi Earthquake, 1997

25

LIFE IN THE STUDIO

Our intentions are informed by knowledge and desire, subject to the best of our abilities, and also by our limitations. I see my limitations as part of my identity as a painter. In the making of paintings, I have the confidence that I lack in many other things. These paintings are carefully rendered, to a degree realistic, while at the same time they are altogether invented images with all manner of visual distortions or unreality. For me it would be boring and almost pointless to render a fully formed study on a canvas.

Not working from models was a choice I made early on. As a young painter on a very small teaching salary, I couldn't afford to pay models to pose for me and I didn't want to ask friends to pose. But more than that, I liked my studio time uncomplicated by the presence of another person. I value the solitude of my painting time and I want to invent my figures as my paintings evolve within that solitude.

In any painting day I take breaks to look at books of various painters from different centuries and countries and books of photos of nude models, the best of those being vintage photos, Victorian period and into early 20th century. More than looking at images for a source, I refer to myself in the mirror. So I am my model, whether for a self-portrait or a painting of female or male figures. I look at a hand or a head, a torso. I have a fairly good sense of anatomy but not good enough to work entirely without referring to anything. The figures I find leafing through books of paintings and sculptures and the photos of models rarely have a figure in the position I need. So I turn to the mirror.

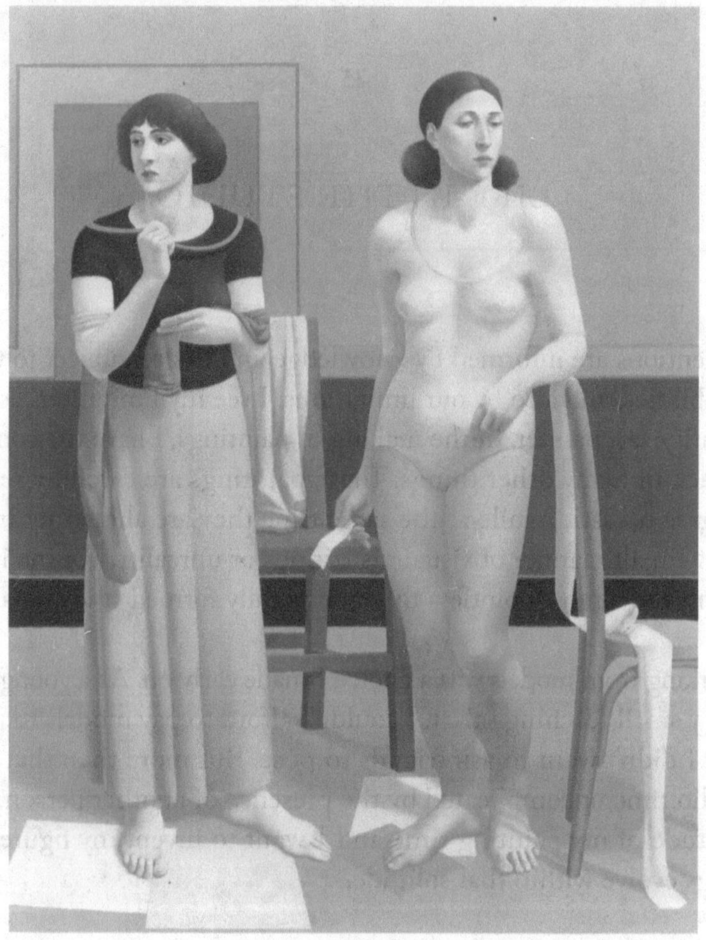

Two Women Standing, Greensleeves, 1982

I learn more from painters whose compositional structure is as apparent as the subject they paint, such as Piero della Francesca in the 15th century and Balthus in the 20th century. Another example of this, though more extreme, is Picasso's Cubist paintings in which the forms we see might suggest, without fully describing them, recognizable objects or figures relating to each other and to the vertical and horizontal edges of the canvas, becoming an image that is about compositional structure.

When making a painting, I am choreographing figures and objects. Every element is a considered part of the composition, so any line or color, any object or any space between objects, has been positioned, and then adjusted and adjusted again, and again, to work in a precise way with everything else. This holds true for the division between floor and wall, the shape of a cast shadow, the presence of a book or a teacup, and so on. If I paint a piece of drapery or a piece of paper on a chair, that will be there partly because it has a compositional purpose. It might serve to continue a visual line across the painting's surface, establishing a relationship between those several parts that line up in a particular way. A piece of paper painted in perspective becomes a tipped plane. Placed on the floor, such a shape can hold an otherwise ambiguous area of color down as a floor and thus define the space. We can create a whole complicated patterned floor drawn in perspective, or we can paint, in effect, one square of that checkered floor that will serve the same purpose.

Hilton Kramer wrote, "In the life of art there are no virgin births." I like that statement for its simplicity. I have always understood that art comes out of art, and the sources we look to will span many periods and cultures. The ways a painting in progress might be influenced by another artist can be as much unconscious as it might be deliberate. It's something basic to the process of painting. It is right that when we make a painting, in our minds we are in dialogue with various painters from the past. Each of us will have a unique compilation of remembered sensations. For me, the accumulated knowledge I have in my head is always there providing the basis for inventing figures and their environments.

I believe there is no progress in art. We might complicate things by introducing new materials and new techniques that make possible new modes of expression, but the art of recent centuries isn't better in quality than the best of what was made throughout history. And it isn't new. The depiction of a cow (or bull) from the Lascaux cave paintings dated something like

17,000 BC, particularly the red one with a black head, facing to the right, is unsurpassed in translating observed nature into an elegant and refined understanding of the essence of a particular animal. It is as sophisticated in terms of drawing as any cow in the history of art. 16th century Dutch painters like Aelbert Cuyp painted cows that are anatomically accurate and as descriptive as photographs of cows. And Picasso's much more abstracted bulls might, in their way, be as good as the 16th century Dutch cow, but I can't say any of those depictions of a cow are better than the one painted 19,000 years ago. When Picasso painted *Woman With a Fan* in 1905, what he did to spatially separate the forearm of his woman from her torso is precisely the same as what we see in the Lascaux cave painting to make clear that the legs on the far side of the cow come from behind the cow's body. In both cases a lightening of color behind what is in front interrupts the otherwise continuous contour surrounding the body.

A Cycladic sculpture head from about 2,500 BC and Constantin Brâncuși's elegant abstract sculptures are very similar. The Cycladic heads have no eyes, which is highly unlikely for any kind of depiction of a head in almost any culture. I have no idea why that was, or how a cave man could draw with the intelligence we see in the Lascaux paintings. Ancient Roman marble portrait heads from the 1st century BC to the end of the 1st century AD are remarkable in their realism, and are great portraits. The best of the wax encaustic Fayum portrait heads from the Coptic Egyptians, dated from about 160 AD, are as beautiful as any portrait painting of any period, anywhere. Yoruba terracotta and bronze heads from Ife, in West Africa in the 12-14th centuries are unsurpassed in realism and elegance, and they are surprisingly advanced compared to what was being made in Europe in the same period.

* * *

Over the centuries, in a long-standing tradition, painters from many countries have come to Italy because they find something they hadn't found elsewhere. For me, Italian painting throughout the centuries has always been of great interest. And for me, to be surrounded by the art and architecture of Italy is like, but far better than, living inside the Metropolitan Museum, which had been a fantasy of mine since I was a child. It did not surprise me when I recently read a passage Degas wrote in his notebook while in Assisi in 1858, after spending time in the Basilica of San Francesco, stating that he could be happy living in Assisi.

For landscape painters it can be the forms and the colors of an Italian landscape that belongs to Jean-Baptiste Camille Corot and to Giorgio Morandi. They find a quality of light which is subtly different from what they knew at home, that changes with the seasons and changes continually within any day. When Dan Gustin and Israel Hershberg taught together a few summers in Montecastello di Vibio, they went in search of the exact spots where Corot had painted in the late 1820s, comparing paintings in the book, *Corot in Italy,* with the landscape in and around Civita Castellana. In talking to me about the experience, Israel questioned the discrepancy between the numbers and positions of windows on a house both he and Corot had painted. Were the windows changed by generations of homeowners to become what Israel saw, or was it Corot's decision to alter what he observed to suit his needs in a painting? It was not the sort of question that most people would ask. It was one that I liked.

Our choice to live in Italy with all of the art and beauty meant leaving the support and company of friends and choosing a certain isolation from the world of contemporary art. There were times we felt isolated and lonely. Being part of a community of creative people who share interests is important. Over the years we have been fortunate that many people, many artists, have visited and become friends. We get together for lunches and dinners coupled with studio visits. Our studio visits and conversations feed all of us and keep our isolation from becoming a problem.

Entering my studio is entering my personal private world, the quiet refuge where I make my paintings. Reproductions of Rousseau's *Sleeping Gypsy* and Gorky's *The Artist and his Mother* hang on my studio walls, along with three taxidermy boar's heads and the partial musical instruments and old locks and hinges and tools that I find in the monthly antique markets. They hang next to photographs of Lani and anonymous vintage portrait photographs, most of which are still in their original frames. And I have art books and paintings and drawings. There is a palpable quiet that my paintings create when friends first enter my studio. Then conversations start that are about what I have been working on. Often there are two paintings in progress, maybe of the same size, one might be vertical and one horizontal, and one or two already finished paintings.

Typically when I start a new painting, I'll tentatively place first one figure, and then a second figure on a blank canvas. As I'm shifting them in position to work together, I might add a third. Or I might take out a figure that had been there. A head turns, eyes shift in the direction of their gaze, an arm changes its position. A book or a cup on a table will move. The table moves. A nude gets dressed or a dressed figure sheds her clothing. A chair turns to face the other direction. A wall moves back and a shadow divides it diagonally. Its color changes. A window becomes a landscape painting, or it is painted out. And it goes on like that. Decision-making will continue until I accept the way everything is working. This can take weeks or months, depending on the size of the canvas.

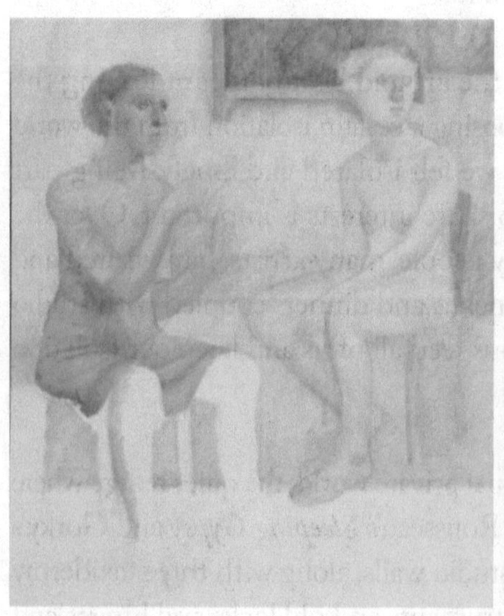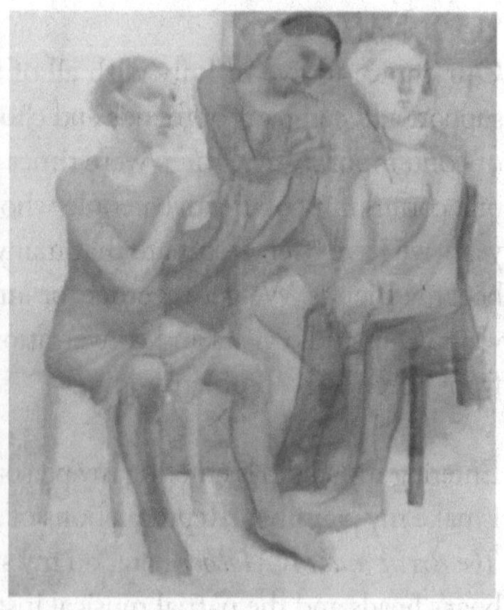

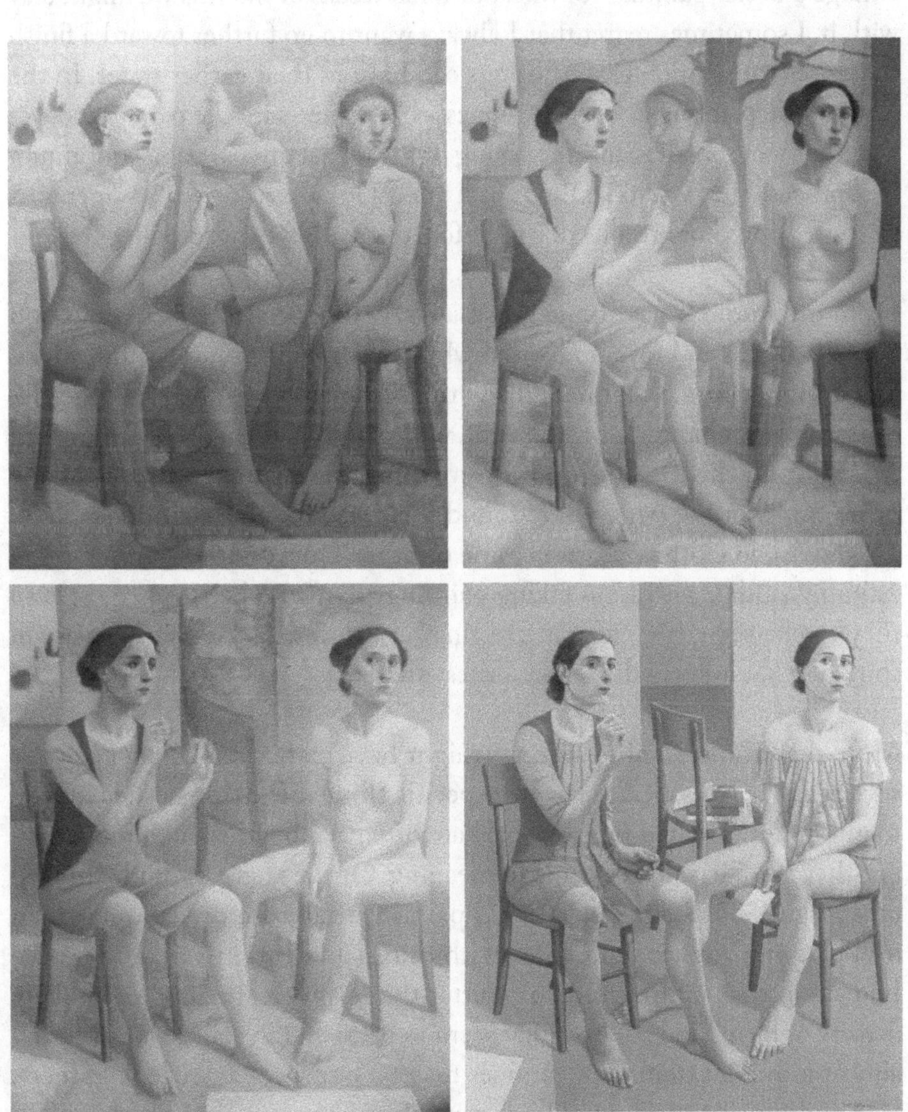

Progression of *Inner Voices*, 2006

Sometimes during studio visits with artist friends, someone will suggest that I leave a painting in the unfinished state that they see it in, though they make this suggestion with the knowledge that it would be an unlikely thing for me to do. I have briefly considered doing that, but we seem always to have to keep working to take an image through further changes, believing it will emerge a better painting for the additional weeks or months we might stay with it. I sometimes regret that I always want to go further toward a finish that loses the spontaneity paintings can have in their earlier states. In the way I work, paintings lose the openness that comes with the painterliness of faster moving brushes and the trying of ideas that are part of a continuum in a process that will take them past what looks exciting for its openness to something more resolved, which for me would be more right.

From my studio we continue into Lani's, with its collections of dolls and puppets, bones and toys, and with owl decoys standing on their thin sticks, and antique church mannequins with their glass eyes, and Japanese silk butterfly kites hanging on the wall, with parts of theater costumes, and corsets from the markets draped on seamstress mannequins, and many other things, all of which have found their way into her paintings as still life props and clothing at some time or other. Conversations unfold there as in my studio, with Lani taking paintings out from her storage racks so they can be seen. It's aways interesting how different our paintings are in spite of what aspects they more or less share.

More than mine, Lani's paintings might have stories. Or if not stories as such, they have associations with specific things. The things she chooses to put in her invented private world are often symbolic, though more than not they are fairly non-specific in meaning. Or they have multiple implied meanings. Compositionally, Lani's paintings can be more complex than mine, having a space more filled with things and patterns than the space I create in my paintings. It isn't clutter that Lani creates, but an unlikely density of forms and patterns that seem to press on the paintings' edges and almost move out from their confines to enter our space as we look at them. Her recent paintings are unlike anyone else's paintings I can think of. She will do things I cannot do with my imagery. She creates an unreality that is not like the dreams I have, nor like places or situations I would find in my imagination. And for those reasons I am fascinated to see where her paintings will go from beginning to end.

Lani can look like someone belonging to the world she creates in her studio, sometimes wearing the dresses she has made for herself from fabrics and costume fragments collected over a lifetime, reconfigured to become a mixture of parts from different ethnic cultures. She makes these dresses in a process that is like how she makes her collages and her paintings, and how she makes necklaces, even how she might make a meal.

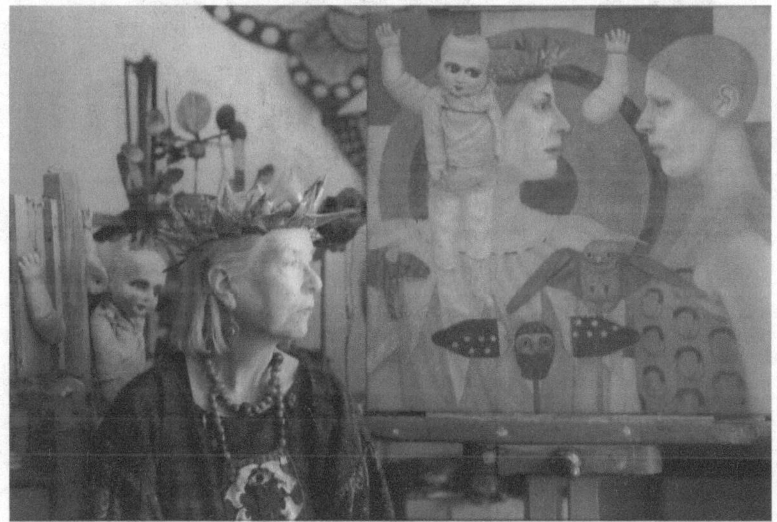

Lani in her studio, 2023

* * *

I found a stone bead on the ground in Mexico when I was six. It was drilled and barely carved with some geometric pattern to make it special, possibly some sort of talisman. That was probably the first little possession of this kind that I treasured. Peter and I owned very few things normal to childhood. In our years of no money and no home of our own, to have two or three small things of my own was a comfort. Somehow they grounded me. They were there, in my possession in a drawer or somewhere secret and not left behind when we moved from hotel to hotel or briefly to the apartment belonging to one of my mother's friends.

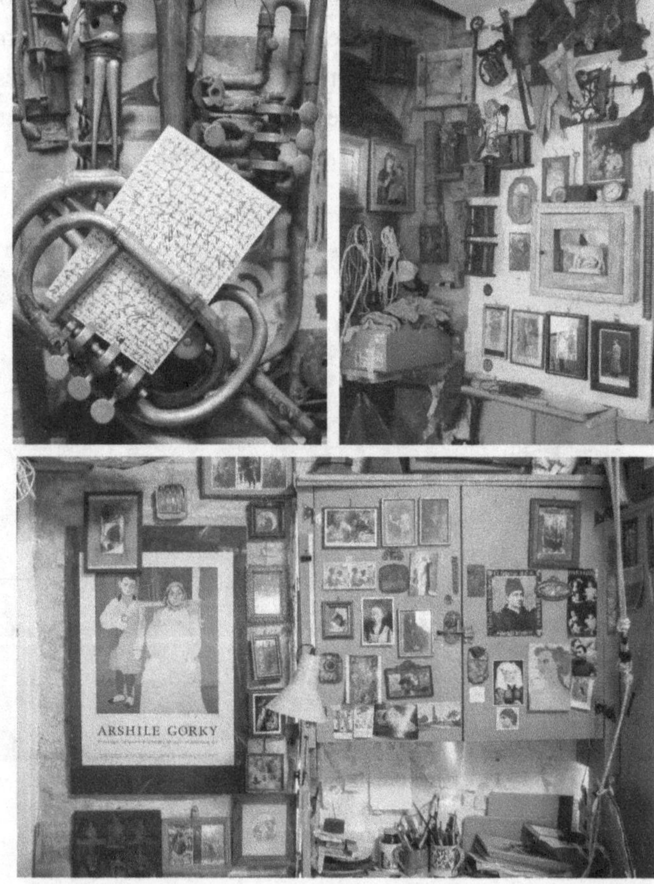

A postcard with writing in two opposing directions, and old parts of wind instruments and other collected objects in my studio. A view of my desk and the Whitney Museum poster of Arshile Gorky's *The Artist and His Mother*.

For me, collecting is about surrounding myself with things that I identify with, so they are, in a way, there to define or identify me to myself and to other people who enter my space. It would be reasonable to say, I live in an accumulation. For many people it may seem obsessive, a curiosity that Lani and I live among the many things we have collected. For me it is a wonderful obsession to collect and live surrounded by things so rich and lovely, or so peculiar and unlikely as what we find and bring home.

Wandering through an antique market is like a slowing down of time and being outside of the continuum that time ordinarily is about, being surrounded by things that are parts of all kinds of times and places, like being in the present while also being in flashbacks that slide freely through time. Rome's weekly Porta Portese market had wonderful things among a vast sea of uninteresting junk. There were little piles of silver plated brass ex-votos that in my Academy days cost very little. They were images of various separate parts of the body, such as a head, a pair of eyes, a breast, a hand, a foot or a leg, lungs, kidneys, a nose, an ear. Sometimes they were men in a suit or dressed in a uniform with a rifle, or women wearing an apron, infants in swaddling, or children, or animals like a cow or a pig. The most common and often the most ornate were hearts, because a heart represented any illness. In addition to their peculiar beauty, they have stories that resonate among themselves as they hang on our walls.

Now there are few votives in the markets and they are no longer cheap, so I buy paper things instead. Envelopes, postcards and photographs, often old family portraits. I find things that might seem insignificant to other people, but when I take time to think about what they are and what stories they might tell, they take on meanings, fictions I create.

Years ago in Italy, when a postcard was sent in the mail the cost of the stamp varied according to how much writing was on the card. So a simple greeting in a few words cost less to mail than one that was *tutto scritto* (all written). I found a few postcards in Italian street markets that had writing not only on the message half of the address side but also written on top of the photo on the other side. I even found a few postcards that have small handwriting in two opposing directions, vertical and horizontal, one on top of the other, on top of the photograph of the postcard, legible because their separate directions don't become one confused mess. All of the old postcards and envelopes have a very beautiful calligraphic handwriting, and the stamps from that late 1800 to early 1900 period were all single-color stamps that might have something like a man's head in profile looking to the right, and when the stamp was put on an envelope sideways the head would look up to the sky above. I liked that. An envelope with its calligraphy and a stamp that had no value to a stamp collector can be a wonderful little unselfconsciously made work of art I might buy for only 50 *centesimi*.

A tool fashioned by a *contadino* can also tell a story. I recognize in such objects a need to invent a tool or an object to serve a purpose, and the way it was made reveals a thinking process that makes sense to me. I have a rat trap made from an olive oil tin, with a grooved wood frame holding a sliding metal door of sufficient weight that it can drop down with a thud in a fraction of a second, trapping a mouse or a country rat that moved a hair trigger bait lever at the opposite end. It is a perfectly fine trap, made of things generally considered worthless clutter. Because I, too, am a maker of things, such objects tell me their stories, and each has its kind of beauty, unique unto itself.

Occasionally something happens in these markets that I think of as spontaneous theater. One such time was at the Pissignano market. A few months earlier in Pissignano I had bought a taxidermy crow. When I was a boy, long before I started to buy anything for myself that wasn't essential, I remember thinking it would be really nice to have a taxidermy raven above a door that would look down on me like Edgar Allan Poe's raven. And my mind would speak the word "Nevermore." This crow, with its link to my childhood memory, now perches high up on top of a cabinet in my studio, its glass eyes looking down at me as I paint.

A month or two later, when I was in Pissignano, I stopped to see what the man I had bought the crow from had in his collection of open boxes on the ground. Remembering that I had bought his crow, he told me that he had a stuffed penguin at home. Very rare, he said. Interesting, I thought. A penguin. Thinking later about the stuffed penguin, I was sorry I hadn't asked if he wanted to sell it. I guessed it would be way too expensive, if he did want to sell it, because penguins come from the Antarctic and indeed are rare in most of the world outside of natural history museums or zoos. But at the next two Pissignano markets, the man wasn't there to ask about his penguin.

The weather was nice for the March market and all the vendors were there, even the penguin man. He recognized me and called me over as I approached his area. He said he had brought the penguin. And he picked up an old cardboard box from beneath a table and set it on top and opened it and took out his penguin. It was about two feet tall, and nothing like the beautiful pure black and white of all the penguins I have in my mind, but a mottled brownish gray and a very disheveled looking thing. Disheveled isn't the right word. That word brings to mind something far less miserable than what this man was showing me, holding it up and explaining to me that its head needed to be glued back on, that's all. Very rare, he said again. The penguin's head was barely attached by a bit of brittle skin, and what I think was once sawdust was falling out of the neck into the penguin's dusty cardboard box.

The man was still holding his penguin, supporting its head with one hand so it wouldn't fall into the box, and he said forty euros, what do I think. I said it was rather ugly. He said yes. Just then another man who was walking by stopped to look at the penguin, still held above its dirty cardboard box. The vendor told that man forty euros, without having been asked anything. And he put it back in its box on top of a scattering of dirty sawdust the same color as the penguin. And I thanked the man for showing me his penguin and wandered on.

About ten minutes later I was looking at what was on another vendor's table quite a ways beyond. There was a figure of Jesus, about ten inches high, standing in the middle of whatever else was there that I don't remember. It was broken cleanly at the neck, hollow inside, white edges of porcelain above its white and blue gown. The head of the Jesus was next to this broken body on the table. Just then a voice said to me something in Italian like "another thing decapitated." And I saw he was the man who also didn't buy the miserable looking penguin.

Buying clothing from street markets and thrift shops is a carryover from the years when I couldn't afford new. There is also the challenge of finding a bargain or something especially beautiful. When I was an art school student I found a beautiful tweed jacket of a soft ochre color with a subtle pattern of vertical and horizontal lines in pale blue. I loved that jacket. Probably it was an English gentleman's tweed sports coat. But it was a bit too big for me. And I also had a dark gray Brooks Brothers suit that was a little too small for me, but was beautifully made and fine in its material. Because neither one was quite my size, I was undecided about whether I ought to try to lose a little weight so the suit would fit me better or to gain a little weight so the jacket would fit me better. I kept both the jacket and the suit for years although neither ever fit me well. I have always had a sense that fine clothes like those were special, however, when I wear ill-fitting second hand clothing I don't worry about wear and tear and I'm more comfortable in them. Sean Connery described himself as looking like an unmade bed in *The Russia House* when telling Michelle Pfeiffer how she would recognize him when they were to first meet. I sometimes think of myself as looking like an unmade bed.

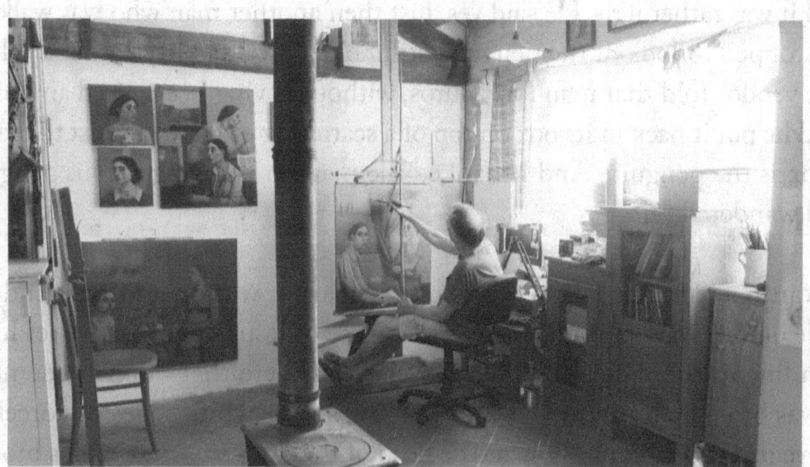
In the studio, 2023

26

LOOKING BACK

On January 24th, 2017 Lani and I flew from Rome to New York and stayed a month in the States. Forum Gallery was planning an inaugural opening of their new gallery space and I wanted to be there for the occasion. Also I wanted to return to where I spent my childhood and where I took Lani when we were first together, to revisit familiar places to see how they remained or how they are different from what I remembered. I thought a trip at this time might help me to find a way to bring closure to the memoir so that it would not continue on and on endlessly.

In the past, I would return to New York and very quickly Italy would fade away, as though I hadn't just come from there. And then when I would fly back to Italy at the end of a few weeks in New York, soon New York would fade the same way. This time I didn't feel that. It was and it was not the place I knew well, where I could feel completely at home. I could only feel the familiarity of the city if I didn't look up, or if I wasn't looking out toward far uptown or downtown, because it was mostly what I was seeing above the store fronts and entry ways of buildings that had become shockingly unfamiliar. On side streets between much larger buildings there still might be a few brownstone houses like the one I lived in on 56th Street as a little boy, but they are so outnumbered and dwarfed by the new buildings that they seem to be doomed to demolition in this outburst of competing billionaire egos erecting towers in a 21st century version of what Italian cities and hill towns once had, of which San Gimignano is the best example, where rival families had once built 72 towers. Of those only 14 remain today.

The Metropolitan Museum itself has remained more or less as I remember it. Over the years it has been added onto here and there and the additions have made it an even greater museum than it had been when I was a boy. Ten years ago the skylighted hall that had been the cafeteria was renovated and given over to the Greek and Roman sculptures and the cafeteria was moved to a well-hidden location in the lower level. There used to be a grand piano in the cafeteria in the spot where now stands a big headless bronze male nude figure.

We went to the Metropolitan Museum to look again at things that have been particularly important to me. One was Charles Despiau's *Little Peasant Girl*, which I remembered for how subtly the planes of her cheeks moved from under her eyes down to the form of her mouth. I could almost see how the sculptor's thumbs would have followed and formed that change with his other fingers gently holding the sides of her face, a gesture that speaks of love. I still think of her face when I paint my female heads more than fifty years after first standing in front of her in the museum. She was very beautiful and I wanted to see her again but she wasn't on view. Museums rotate much of their extensive collections.

There are two pieces of European armor made for jousting that have parts connecting the back of the helmet to the backplate with a nicely curved narrow piece of iron attached by fairly large wing nuts that I thought were very interesting for something made that long ago. I like how form and function can work together to make things like armor so extraordinary. Armor and musical instruments, in particular, are beautiful precisely because their forms are more logical and utilitarian than are things made or decorated solely to be visually pleasing.

There's a Spanish courtyard to the left of the grand staircase, identified as a patio from the Castle of Vélez Blanco, that visitors seem to walk past without entering. It's a favorite part of the museum for me. Unlike most of the rest of the museum, where what is displayed on walls and pedestals is what we are there to see, it is the tranquility of this courtyard itself that I like. And then I walk through the large hall of medieval art and on into the Robert Lehman Collection, where I always stop to see Balthus's 1955 *Figure in Front of a Mantel*. The Met and MoMA both have great Balthus paintings that I know well and visit whenever I can.

Upstairs I wanted to look again at Aelbert Cuyp's *Equestrian Portrait of Cornelis and Michael Pompe Van Meerdervoort with Tutor and Coachman*, ca. 1653. When I first came upon that painting years ago I was immediately stopped by it. I loved it for the way the horizontal riding crop held by the man sitting on his horse and the vertical crop of the boy in blue on his smaller horse framed the boy's torso and head, separating them and singling the boy out in stillness as the detail in this group portrait to take particular notice of. The boy turns his head fully to look out at the viewer in a way few figures in group portraits do. When I've seen that in Renaissance paintings, it is when the painter has added his own self-portrait to a painting. It will have the effect of spoiling the sense that the people in a painting are unaware of the viewer. We cease to be invisible to the painted characters. The person depicted as looking out at the viewer breaks the barrier of that pictorial world by looking at us looking at them, and strangely that makes them part of our world of today more than it makes us part of their world.

We wandered through rooms of Rembrandt paintings to find a painting my mother showed me when I was little. It is Rembrandt's *The Standard Bearer (Floris Soop)*, 1654. My mother saw the flagpole combined with the plume of the hat next to the man's head as a mop the man was carrying. And I still see it that way and look back to a nice moment with my mother from my childhood. In the same room, on the opposite wall is Rembrandt's painting, *Aristotle with a Bust of Homer*, 1653, that I remember seeing in my art student years when it was publicized as a recent acquisition, making it the focus of a lot of attention and having it roped off to keep people from getting too close, while equally beautiful Rembrandts in the same rooms had no ropes to keep people back. The rope later came down. On this visit I was aware of seeing how Rembrandt's portraits had a warm inner glow that Franz Hals' portraits lacked. I saw at least two Hals paintings there of smiling boys, and thought again about how a smile in a painting never works for me unless it's only a hint of a smile. A painting wants to be more than a reflection of reality in the outside world.

We looked again at Jules Bastien-Lepage's large painting of Joan of Arc, of 1879, which had been a favorite painting of mine since I was an art student. She, dressed as a peasant, stands serene and beautiful in her garden at the moment when three ghostly saints behind her speak to her of leading the French in battle against the English invaders in the Hundred Years War. That makes the painting an annunciation painting of sorts, and one that I remember played with my emotions as few paintings have done, in that it aroused amorous feelings for a woman who existed in a painting. A kind of Pygmalion thing.

We went on to look again at three favorite paintings in the Italian rooms. Two of them are panels from a cassone, or chest, painted in about 1475. One is called *Scene from a Novella* and the other is called *The Chess Players*, those titles having been made up by the museum curators to identify untitled paintings. In fact, it was unknown even who had painted them. They are now said to be by Liberale da Verona. Years ago when I first saw them, they were attributed to Francesco di Giorgio Martini, and some years later, if I remember right, to another Sienese painter. Such is the way of curators and art historians, who reattribute works in a guessing game, or maybe upon discovering some long lost written document that sheds new light where light was dim. It is part of their métier. In a case like this, the painting stays the same but what image I might have in mind of the painter who made it has changed, and I am informed that I was wrong in what I thought was true. It is like encountering someone somewhere who looks at me blankly as I say, "Oh I thought you were someone else, my mistake." I even forget some of my own paintings completely if I haven't seen them in many years, only recognizing them as mine because they could not be by anybody else. In the same room at the Met with the two paintings by Liberale da Verona is a long time favorite painting of mine and Lani's, Fra Filippo Lippi's *Portrait of a Woman with a Man at a Casement*, ca. 1440, that I wrote about earlier. These three paintings are among the ones that we will visit at least once during any trip to New York.

I was grateful to have Lani with me those days going to museums because her interest in certain objects and paintings is both like my own and different. She stopped to look at a small Cycladic figure in the Greek and Roman collection that I had passed, and then we were looking at it together, seeing how its arms crossed over its abdomen and a fold of flesh indicating the weight of the stomach was there. Those more distinctive, almost realist aspects to that particular sculpture were unlikely, given the degree to which Cycladic sculptures are similarly abstracted. We were seeing the same things differently and learning from watching the other just looking at things, without the need for words.

Unlike the Metropolitan Museum, which is the same as I found it on previous trips back to New York, the Museum of Modern Art had already changed for the worse in the extensive renovations that ended in 2004, that about doubled its size and made it into something like an echo chamber for the hugely increased museum visitor traffic chatter and the sound of whatever irritating video installation they have continually playing. For me MoMA had lost the character it used to have as an extraordinary collection properly displayed that could be visited in quiet. I was there again, it turned out, for not much more reason than to have that impression confirmed. More or less. But I do like to spend time with Rousseau's *The Sleeping Gypsy* and other paintings that I have loved most of my life.

The new skyscrapers, popping up like some unchecked plague of weeds that threatens the survival of infinitely more beautiful buildings in New York are cold and hard and they don't offer the possibility of being part of an interaction on a human scale, although they, too, must have human stories related to their existence. There would be stories about the lives of construction workers and the like, but those will be untold stories. There would be the stories of the lives of the men whose fortunes paid for the skyscrapers, but those wouldn't interest me. To me the new buildings look like science fiction and Star Wars Space Odyssey futuristic nightmarish horrors imposed on a population when probably few people want them. It may be that a younger generation that grew up with new technologies will identify with the cold reflective surfaces of the new towers and the faster moving, continually changing way of things today more easily than what my generation is likely to prefer. I don't know. But I believe what is warm and vulnerable and personal is more attractive, and the lives of people are more interesting and more worthy of respect than this, which doesn't look related to lives of people at all.

The changes I saw in the city of my childhood are gargantuan. The unwelcome intrusions of these glass and steel skyscrapers that I am amazed by and saddened by have to be accepted as fact since they aren't about to be taken away and replaced by buildings on a human scale with friendly attributes. I feel as though time has erased all traces of my existence in the city I grew up in. Not that I exist at all in the minds of most people. Few of us are remembered or have any part of ourselves preserved even in distortion. At best, something is held onto in the far reaches of collective memory in books or museums. A film might be made, or a mention made in a classroom somewhere at some time. And I shouldn't be concerned with any of that. Mostly what troubled me was the absence of things I cared about. And that was a revelation of sorts.

Initially, when trying to plan the trip, Lani and I considered renting a car to drive from New York to Provincetown to see Sal Del Deo again, stopping along the way to stay a night or two with other friends north of the city. Josephine had died not long before and Sal was in his house in the woods by himself, but with his son Romolo and Romolo's family living close by. But the trip was scheduled to coincide with the gallery's move, which put it at the least ideal time of year to meander by car from New York to Cape Cod. I regret that we were unable to see Sal and Provincetown once again. And I regret that we didn't make it to visit Emmet and Edith Gowin in Newtown, Pennsylvania. But we couldn't manage those visits.

We took the train from Grand Central Station to New Haven, where William Bailey and Sandra Stone met us and drove us to their house in

Branford. Outside the large windows of their enclosed porch is the sea, made calm by the facing but distant shores of Long Island, the way the last stretch of Cape Cod curls around to shelter waterfront properties in Provincetown from the open sea beyond the dunes on the back side of town. Their house reminded me of Edward Hopper's painting *Rooms by the Sea*, of 1951. It's a painting that has the sea right outside the open door of a room in a house, looking absolutely unlikely and unreal. All you see out the door is sea and sky. Coincidently, that Hopper is among paintings we saw in the Yale Art Gallery collection the following day.

Waking up and seeing the sea right outside their windows was so amazingly beautiful. Inside the house, wooden walls that were once the outside walls of the house surrounded by a porch, were painted pure white. The Baileys had small paintings and drawings and prints by various artists. Some by friends we hold in common. This was a place belonging to people who considered everything thoughtfully. Everything in the house was so right, so natural and peaceful and gentle, as it was with the homes of Sal and Josephine Del Deo, Bill Coperthwaite, Sari Dienes, Emmet and Edith Gowin, and a few others, all of whom I have known and loved and who live in complete harmony with their surroundings. And it may well be that I feel this profound kindredness with their way of life, their furniture, their collections of objects and art, because they have been the people who have had the deepest influence on me, in some cases going way back to my childhood. With the Baileys it hasn't been that far back because I first knew them in the 1970s and had previously only been in their Connecticut home once briefly, and then again now with Lani for an evening and an overnight. However I have known their Italian house for decades. I feel clearly how much a place can be so very important in how I see myself, how I am within myself, or who I am in an unthinking way.

Bailey's New Haven studio in the old Erector Set factory was substantially bigger than the average New York City loft. Bill was working on a large painting of a girl standing with a tree in a landscape. Or rather a girl together with a tree as one element in a serene landscape. There's a house on the left and a horizon line of hills behind. Together they have a subtle presence of being, and for me, that is magical and it is the subject of the painting. The girl standing under the tree holds a cell phone a little above her ear so that it is not easily recognized. Something small and red in color. A subtle allusion to the 21st century in an otherwise timeless setting.

While we were wandering through the recently renovated and expanded Yale University Art Gallery, enjoying its beautiful collections, snow began to fall. Bill also wanted to show us the studio where he painted many years ago that was now incorporated into the new museum, but that part of the museum was closed. The snow outside the windows was starting to look as though it would make driving somewhat dangerous, so we cut short our time in the museum and went out to find a restaurant for lunch and then to the train back to New York. New Haven didn't look familiar to me. It doesn't remember me the way the homes of old friends remember me.

We also visited Pamela Goldman in Connecticut. Pamela was the first person I met on the first day of attending Cooper Union way back in 1962 while we were filling out forms for the school. And from that day we remained good friends. After our shared foundation year, Pamela went on as a design student and I as a studio major. What I saw in their new house was largely unexpected. I didn't know that over those many years Pamela had been collecting the same kinds of bones and taxidermy and ceremonial masks and church mannequins that Lani and I have been collecting since we were first together. She keeps those things in a downstairs room. Upstairs, and through the rest of the house are the things they have been collecting together. On the very high walls of their living room is a sizable collection of beautifully framed Alphonse Mucha lithograph posters above large ornately carved pieces of antique furniture, which tell of a very different lifestyle from our own. On shelves where they have small bronze sculptures there is a collection of miniature rooms and figures, some made by Pamela and some made by people she has taken classes with, and some being older. Pamela's miniatures I suppose could be thought of as the art side of dollhouses, showing a kind of obsession artists and craftspersons have when making things for themselves. But what was most meaningful to me was seeing that over these many years Pamela and Jerry have been living with paintings and collages on their walls that were made by me and by Lani. What I hadn't fully appreciated was how my work had been part of the lives of friends like these over all the years during which I have had little contact with them. It means that, in a sense, these friends have been living with me every day, and because that has been so, their lives have been affected by me. That they had been living with our art all these years meant something much more tender and personal than how I had already been seeing our friendship in my mind.

One of my paintings they have is of a female head on a small canvas, from when I was a graduate student still under the influence of Gorky. And another is a self-portrait from some years later, both of which I had no memory of at all. And on another wall were three of my Cooper Union etchings that evidently I had given to Pamela when we were students together. I did remember the collage they bought when they gave me a little private showing of collages at their 86th Street apartment in New York when I was leaving Dayton on my way to Rome in 1970. I remembered they had the collage on which I glued feathers to the top of the head of a woman in an old portrait photograph, but I couldn't envision the collage itself. As with the two small paintings, I didn't have a photograph or a slide of it. Pamela also had bought a few of Lani's paintings from her New York exhibitions in different years.

It was Jerry's pied-à-terre studio apartment on 63rd Street that I stayed in four years ago when I was last in New York, and again this time with Lani. There are two paintings of mine on the walls of the 63rd Street apartment, one they bought at Forum Gallery many years ago when the gallery was still on Madison Avenue and 79th Street, and the other is a little head painted over a lithograph that I left in the apartment as a thank you gift on my last visit.

* * *

During our month in the US, I went back several times to the Metropolitan Museum between visits to friends out of the city. There was an exhibition at the Met of Max Beckmann paintings from 1920 to when he died in 1950. While looking at Beckmann's paintings, the paintings of Susan Yanero came to mind. Beckmann's are more harsh and overtly expressionist than Yanero's. Beckmann's can seem to shout, whereas Yanero's are strong and painterly but their strength is quiet. Both share a kind of composing that is not about real space and time. Both work with symbolism and allusions to mythological characters. And like Max Beckmann, Susan Yanero has painted circus and vaudeville performers. One part of a crowded Beckmann triptych about his childhood, titled *Beginning*, has a cat hanging upside down from a trapeze that seems as whimsical as Susan Yanero's cats can be. It looked as though Susan had painted it, and I think she had never seen it. Shortly after seeing the Max Beckmann exhibition at the Met, we were in Washington staying with Susan and her husband, Richard, for two nights.

I first saw Susan Yanero's paintings when she was a graduate student at American University, working on self-portraits that looked as if they could have been painted by Willem de Kooning in the late 1940s or Franz Kline in the mid 50s, if those two painters had painted their own versions of a female Rembrandt self-portrait. They were well beyond what one expected to see in the work of someone so young. She was in her twenties.

Following her self-portraits, Susan began a series of paintings about her West Virginia childhood memories of children playing together with a red wagon or beneath the broad curving ribbons of a maypole. What she painted was elegantly drawn and nearly abstract, being reduced to an essential geometry, and within that structure she could paint the gentle innocence of a child's face.

She then gradually moved into a world in which her cast of characters play out dramas on a stage that is both circus and life as she knows it. Looking at these paintings, it is clear that she internalizes her understanding of the paintings of past centuries in a direct and honest way, almost unconsciously. It is as though Duccio, Masaccio, and Paolo Uccello reside within her being and have become inseparable from herself. A little girl holding a cat, in her arms, or in other paintings holding a doll, is borrowed from a Madonna and Child in Renaissance paintings, reborn as a Susan Yanero child, maybe her own child self, among circus clowns and vaudeville characters, who are sometimes funny and sometimes sinister, existing as a metaphor.

On top of and within the layers of paint in her paintings are structures and figures that may be no more than thinly drawn lines alongside of strongly stated passages making the painting seem like something indistinct, the way memories and ideas behave in our dreams and our musings. The fainter marks are remnants of an earlier image if not the beginnings of something not yet fully stated, lending the painting a sense of time like that in medieval paintings.

Susan refers to her large recent paintings as her "black" paintings. They are about mysterious, ominous forces and the opposition between gentleness and danger. That, perhaps, makes her "black" paintings stronger than those that appear to be more playful, although these are also playful and her circus imagery is similarly engaging and about how she sees life.

I am reminded of Paul Klee's 1904 etching, titled *Two Men Meet Each Other Supposing the Other To Be of Higher Rank*. It's a wonderful image of two naked old men bowing down deeply to each other. What that etching has to do with Susan and me, in my mind, is that for years I have told Susan that she is incredibly talented and makes very strong and wonderful paintings, and she denies that and in turn says those things about me. In my estimation, Susan Yanero has always been my equal. She is driven by a spirit I wish I had. It is like being possessed. I believe her immersion into a world of paint and imagery is beyond anything like choices and desires.

What Susan has said about what she owes me as a teacher I accept as true. But I am convinced that what she already had within her was entirely hers. I helped her to believe in herself, and that would have been very important. Maybe the greatest purpose I can attribute to my own doings is to have affected positive change in various people whose paths have crossed mine. Our visits on that trip made a few of those cases more evident to me than I had been aware of. And it goes both ways. I have been so fortunate to have benefitted from knowing these several people in the same way they have benefitted from knowing me. Lives interweave, they entangle, or they bump up against one another and the bumping makes for change. We are never alone in our lives, and shouldn't assume anything is insignificant. We can ignore the way we might impact on others and they on us, and how our lives might have been shaped by interactions often in ways unknown to us, but that doesn't mean it hasn't been happening.

* * *

The last out-of-town visit we made before flying back to Italy was to spend some time with Alex Shundi and Elizabeth Seewald Hill. I don't think I have had a friendship with another man that has been as comfortably, or as naturally deep as how I think of mine with Shundi. Our friendship is very different from what I have had with my brother all our lives. But what happens between siblings is another thing, having all kinds of difficulties that come with the territory from day one. Part of what I experience with other men would be about the shyness that I have always had that will almost always keep me from feeling completely safe and secure in any relationship. I think it is different for me to be with women. Why is that? Maybe it is because with a woman I don't feel a competitive element that I may feel with a man. With a woman I might almost flirt, as though I am doing what nature has ingrained within any species, whereas with another man there could be an invisible wall between us and we don't easily let down our guard.

Alex is from Parma, in northern Italy. His father relocated the family to Connecticut when he was twelve, after which he has lived mostly in the States, sometimes in Italy. We share many things in our separate lives apart from having been together as graduate students at Yale. Both he and I are painters with strong Italian connections and both of us are fairly compulsive collectors. Their home and studios, once a church and then a grange hall, are now filled with things he has made or collected much the way my house is filled with things Lani and I have made or collected. And he has reshaped his house as I have reshaped mine. After reconnecting with Alex, I saw that in the years when we hadn't been in touch with each other, both of us had made toys for our children, almost as though he and I had worked side by side to make them. When I visit Shundi, I buy a Pinocchio figure and rework it to give to him. The first two I made into Pinocchio Kachina dolls, to be mixed culture figures to live among his many Kachina dolls in order to help maintain a reasonable balance in their home between Alex's adopted Native American roots by association, and his birthright Italian heritage.

Shundi's paintings are kaleidoscopic in their complexity of composition, often like labyrinthian game boards filled with personal and traditional symbolic meanings and references. They are intensely autobiographical the way Frida Kahlo's paintings are, and they are all encompassing. Some of them depict the Baptistry in Parma, with its tall bell tower twisting like a great pretzel above de Chirico shadows cast dark upon the stone paving, where there he is, little Sandrino, playing with his ball in Felliniesque nostalgia. Elizabeth's paintings are like Alex's in complexity and their inclusiveness of references to painters of the past, and like his, her paintings could be considered surreal in their imagery. Many of them are the visual equivalent of music. Elizabeth's unreality plays with juxtapositions involving time and context in which she will sometimes place herself. Alex also makes trains that often start with the old roller skates I remember from childhood onto which he builds train cars that are about artists and art movements and places he has known and about ideas that live in his mind and are the narratives of his paintings. He is prolific beyond belief, as though he doesn't sleep, as though possessed by some urgency and madness. And yet he is a relaxed and entertaining man who loves to tell stories and to cook abundant and elaborate feasts and to laugh. We visit each other when we can, and he and I have been writing fairly insane and silly emails back and forth for years, our shared commentary being escapes from seriousness that do us both good.

* * *

The public opening of the inaugural exhibition in the new space of Forum Gallery at 475 Park Avenue at 57th Street was canceled due to the many obstacles playing havoc with their schedule. In the end they had a private opening party for the gallery artists and their families while we were still in

New York. I was able to spend a little time with Bob and Cheryl Fishko and to introduce myself to some of the new gallery staff and other artists. It was good to see the elegant and well-designed new space. For the first time the gallery had its windows and door on the street level where it could be seen and entered without stairs or elevator.

A month after arriving in New York, we left 63rd Street on a SuperShuttle airport van, caught up in heavy traffic, with pedestrians thick at every corner while the driver had to head downtown, and then east a few blocks, and then uptown again and west again or east again because many streets are one way streets, making convoluted what should be simple in the rectilinear grid of Manhattan. And there were other passengers to be picked up before we could leave Manhattan for faster roads. I was tired of that aspect of the city. I'm tired when having to get to an airport with heavy bags. Then we crossed the East River and were driving through Long Island City, also in transformation with new buildings taking over, and through Queens past La Guardia Airport on roads still slow enough with local traffic that Lani and I worried we might not arrive at JFK with enough time for check-in and security and getting to our gate before the plane would leave. But we made it. Then there was the wait before boarding the plane, and then the hours of the flight with films to watch on tiny screens on the backs of the seats in front of us that were half reclining, reducing what little space was ours. I watched films in discomfort, only to know they aren't worth watching at home. A waste of time acceptable only because wasting time is all I can do on a transatlantic flight. I slept some, my head hanging forward or sideways, straining my neck while I was squeezed in a cramped seat with my restless legs jerking as though to try to get out of their confinement, surrounded by others having the same experience, less the restless leg bit.

And then we were in Rome waiting for the Sulga bus, and finally on our way heading toward Perugia. Once leaving the sprawl of the outskirts of Rome, nodding off in sleep, as I am prone to do even if I had a proper night's sleep, I opened my eyes and there were the sheep grazing in fields that I see there more than in Umbria where we live, and the beautiful big umbrella pines, the Italy I love returning to, for which I feel so grateful that this is the place I have made my home.

Our house and our hills behind Assisi are still there, unchanged, welcoming as though not aware that we had been away. I was glad for the work I have to do around the house, pruning rose bushes and wisteria and buddleia and fruit trees and olive trees and giving them fertilizer. Spring settling in after a cold wet winter.

I went to Pissignano for their March antique market but drizzle had discouraged half the vendors from being there and many tables that were set up were covered in plastic, so I came home having bought only two small photographs. But I liked being at the market again, nonetheless.

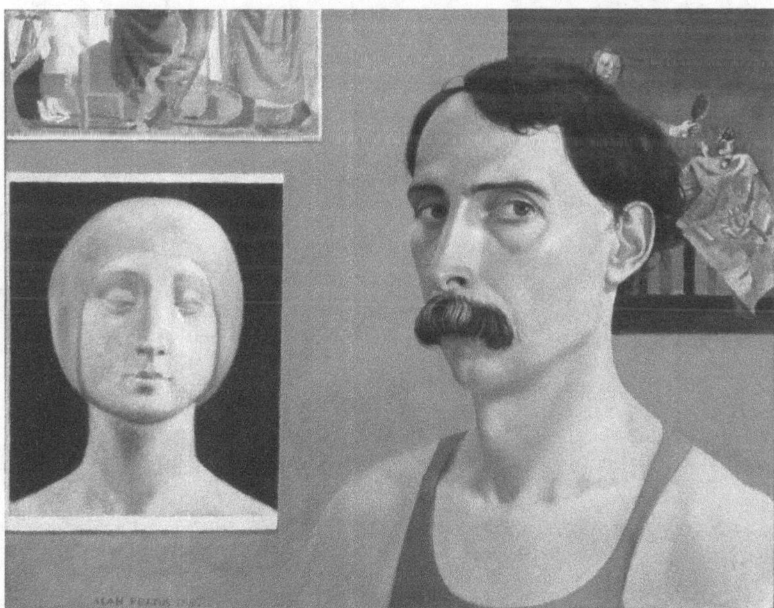

Spring Self-Portrait, 1997

POSTSCRIPT

At eighty years old, looking back on how my life played out, piecing together experiences and revisiting old memories, I can see that my life could have just as easily been a far less rich and interesting journey. Fate as well as the choices I have made have played all kinds of roles in my life. Any adult life will have regrets and any of us can question what might have happened had we done things differently for whatever reasons. Too much is beyond our control to be able to follow a plan without encountering unforeseen obstacles that impose changes of direction. It's not a question of whether we had the wisdom to do things differently. Life is altogether too complicated for that. I am happy with how things have fallen into place and what I have been able to do with my time. I am grateful for having found Lani when we were still young and for having been able to spend many years together. She has been right for me. I love that I still love Lani and would do anything I could do to make her and our two sons happy. She has been much more than a companion with whom I have shared my life and my dreams. I have called her Lanilove, and Lani and I have called each other Mougouch. That was Arshile Gorky's term of endearment for his wife. We have lived constant and nearly inseparable lives for more than fifty years, during which she has believed in me as a painter, teacher, husband, and father. We have traveled together, gone to museums and galleries together, worked side by side, and at times exhibited our work together. And though there are areas of common ground in our paintings, our work has always been distinctly separate, each of us having our own respective identity. As it should be.

And there are our two sons. From the moment of their birth Tobias and Joseph have enriched my life in ever so many ways. I was given the opportunity to provide unconditional love and understanding for my sons, freeing me from the fear I had that if I were to have children I might fail to give them what was missing in my own childhood. And in return, Tobias and Joseph continue to enhance the quality of my life with their abilities and accomplishments. The wonder (somehow *meraviglia* seems a more expressive word) of seeing Tobias and Joseph make amazing sculptures and paintings, photographs and films, and many other things, always with great competence, has given me incredible joy and satisfaction. Knowing them has been a gift beyond description, and I marvel in watching their stories unwind.

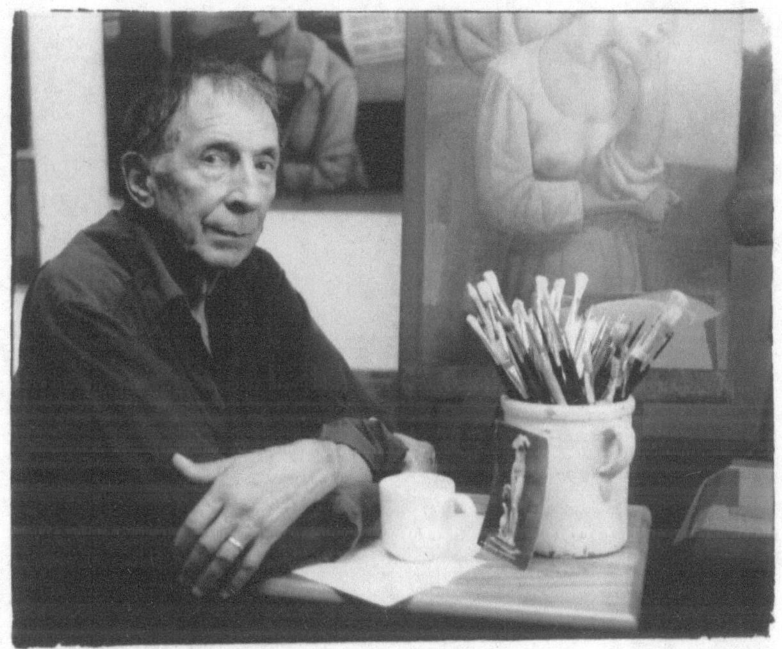

In my studio, 2023

PLATES

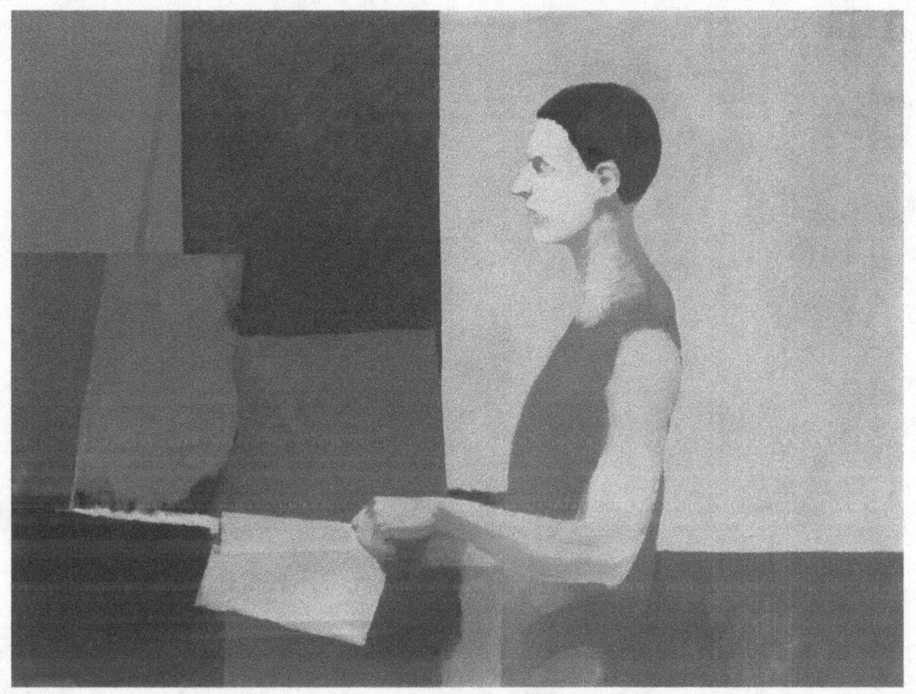

French Mime, 1967
oil on cotton, 44 x 58 inches (112 x 147 cm)

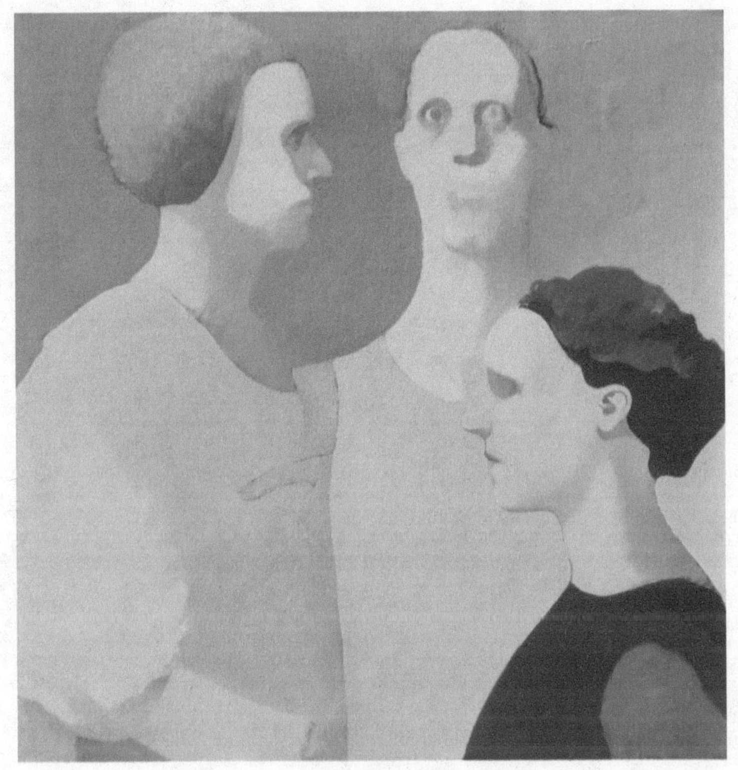

Three Figures, 1968
oil on linen, 32 x 30 inches (81 x 76 cm)

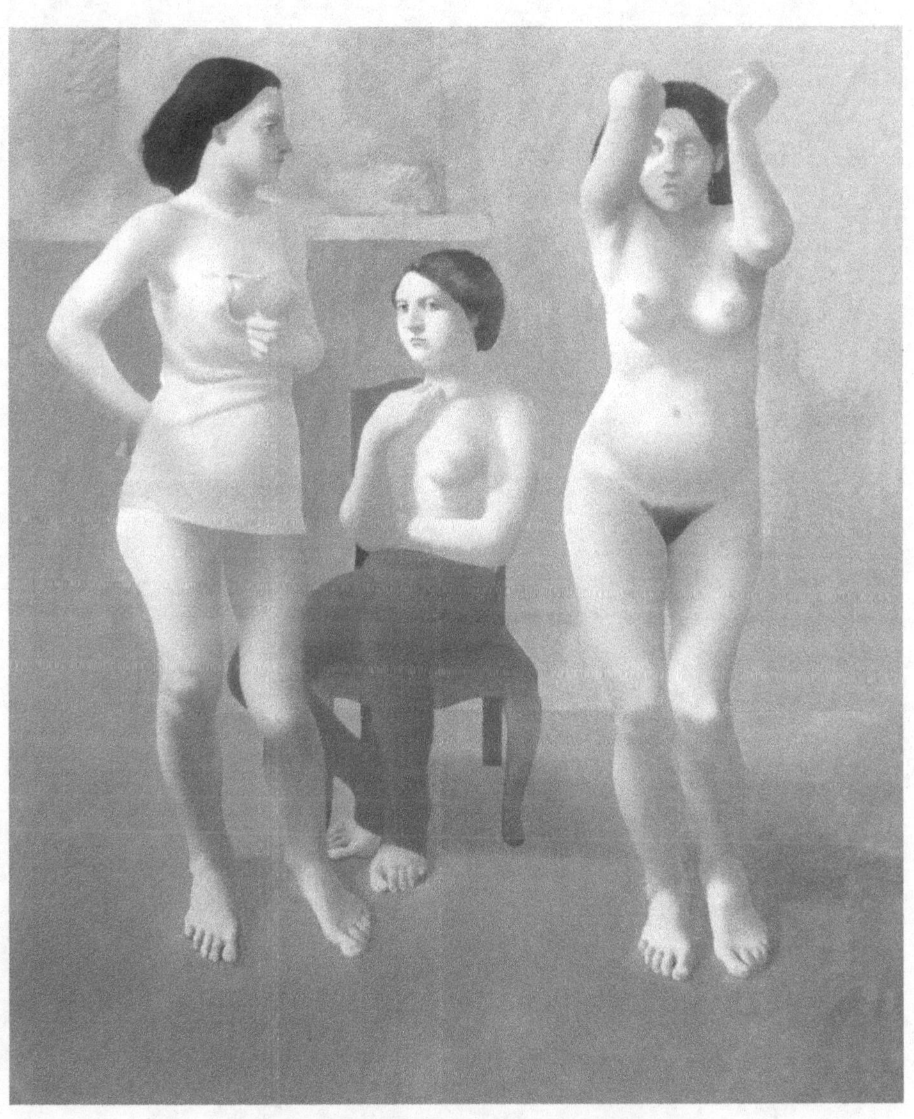

Three Women (One Seated Wearing Green Tights), 1973
oil on linen, 72 x 60 inches (183 x 152 cm)

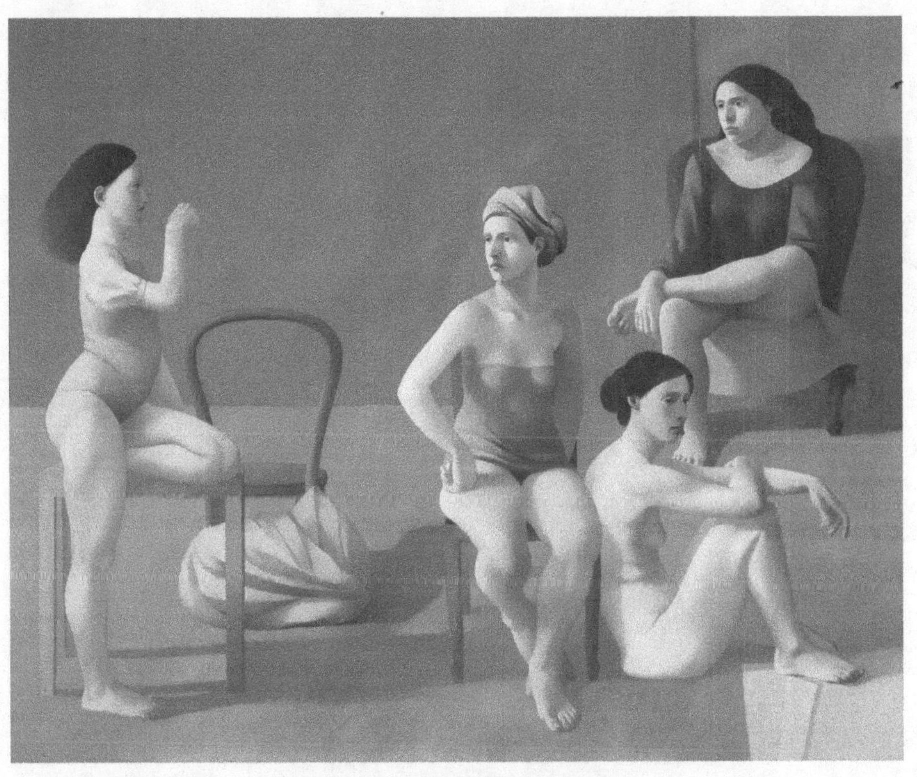

Annunciation: Four Women, 1975
Oil on linen, 58 ¼ in x 70 in (148 cm x 178 cm)

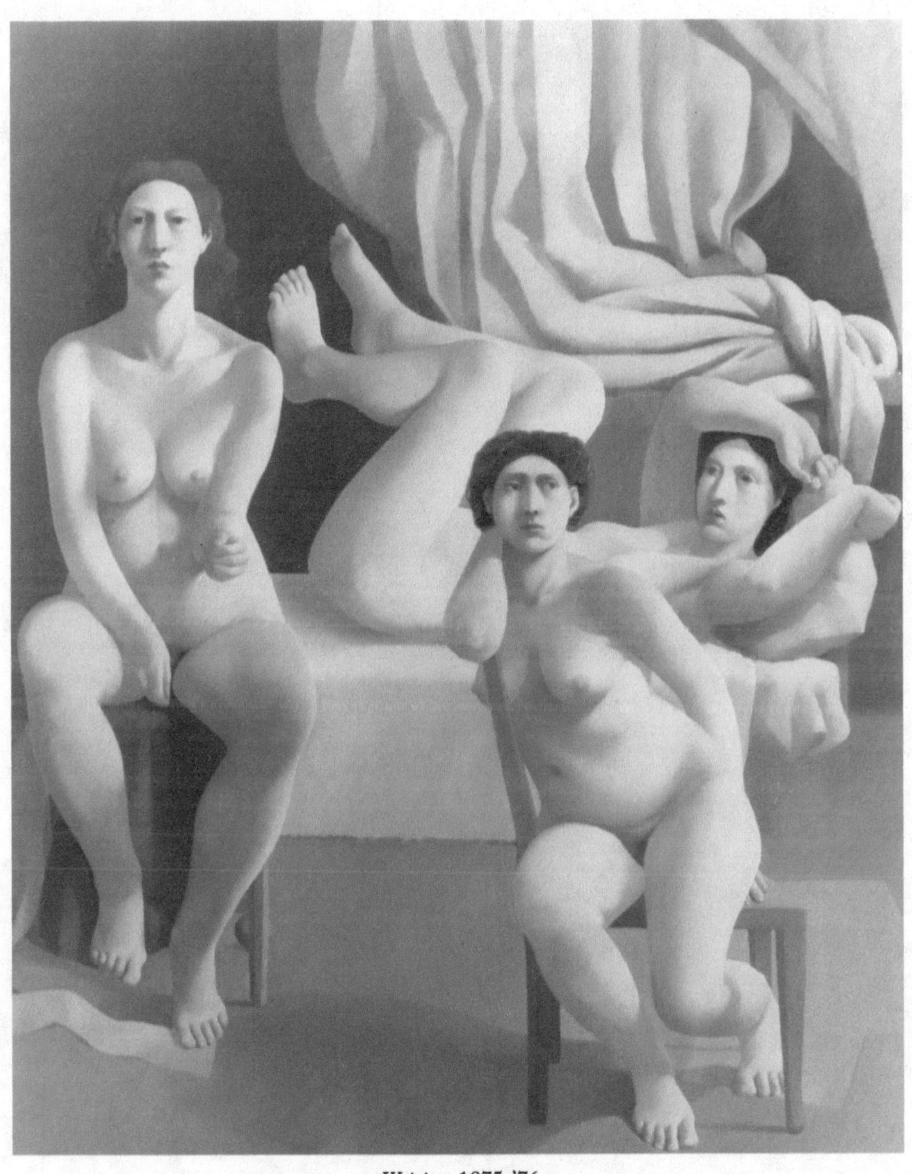

Waiting, 1975-'76
oil on linen, 70 x 56 inches (178 x 142 cm)

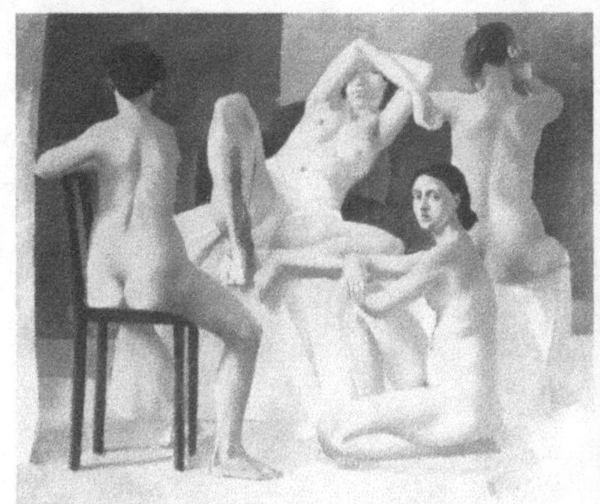
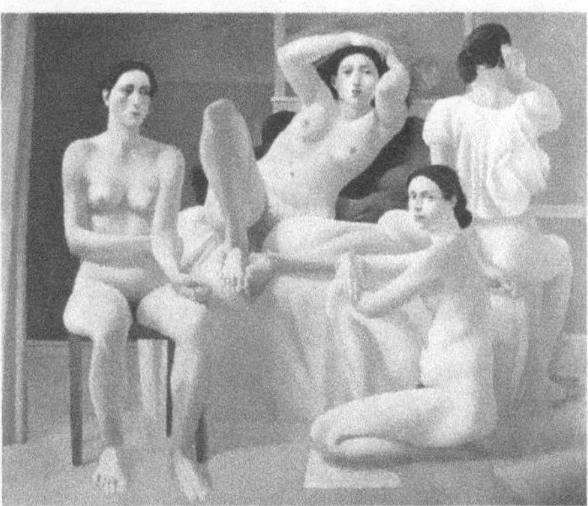
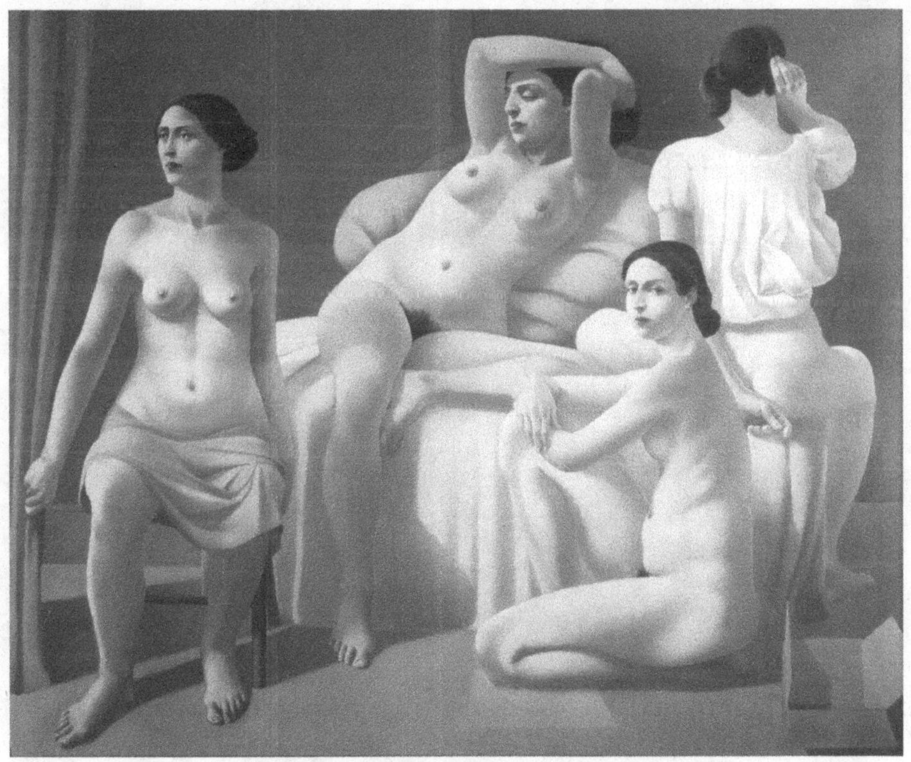

Four Women, 1978
with two earlier stages
oil on linen, 59 x 69 inches (150 x 175 cm)

305

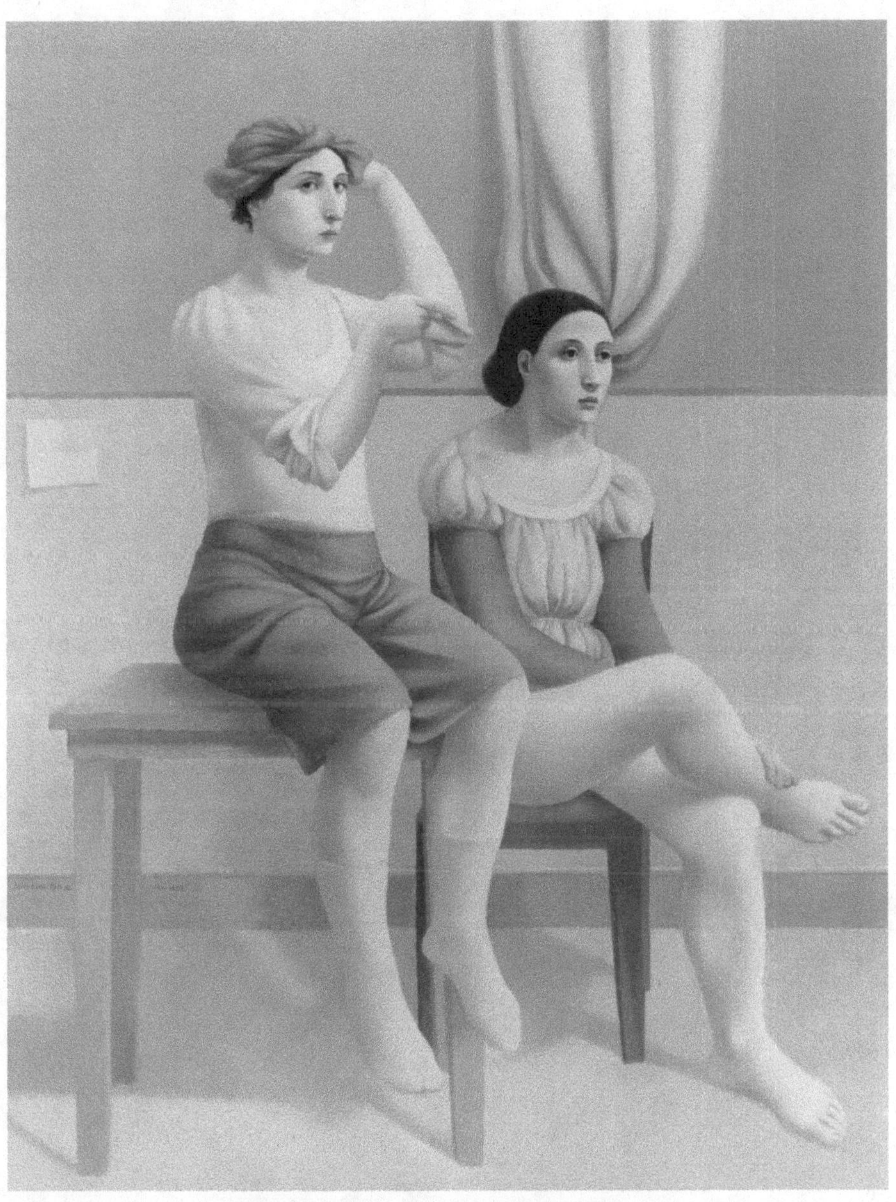

Two Women, Blue Socks & Green Sleeves, 1981-1982
oil on canvas laid on board, 48 x 36 inches (109 x 91 cm)

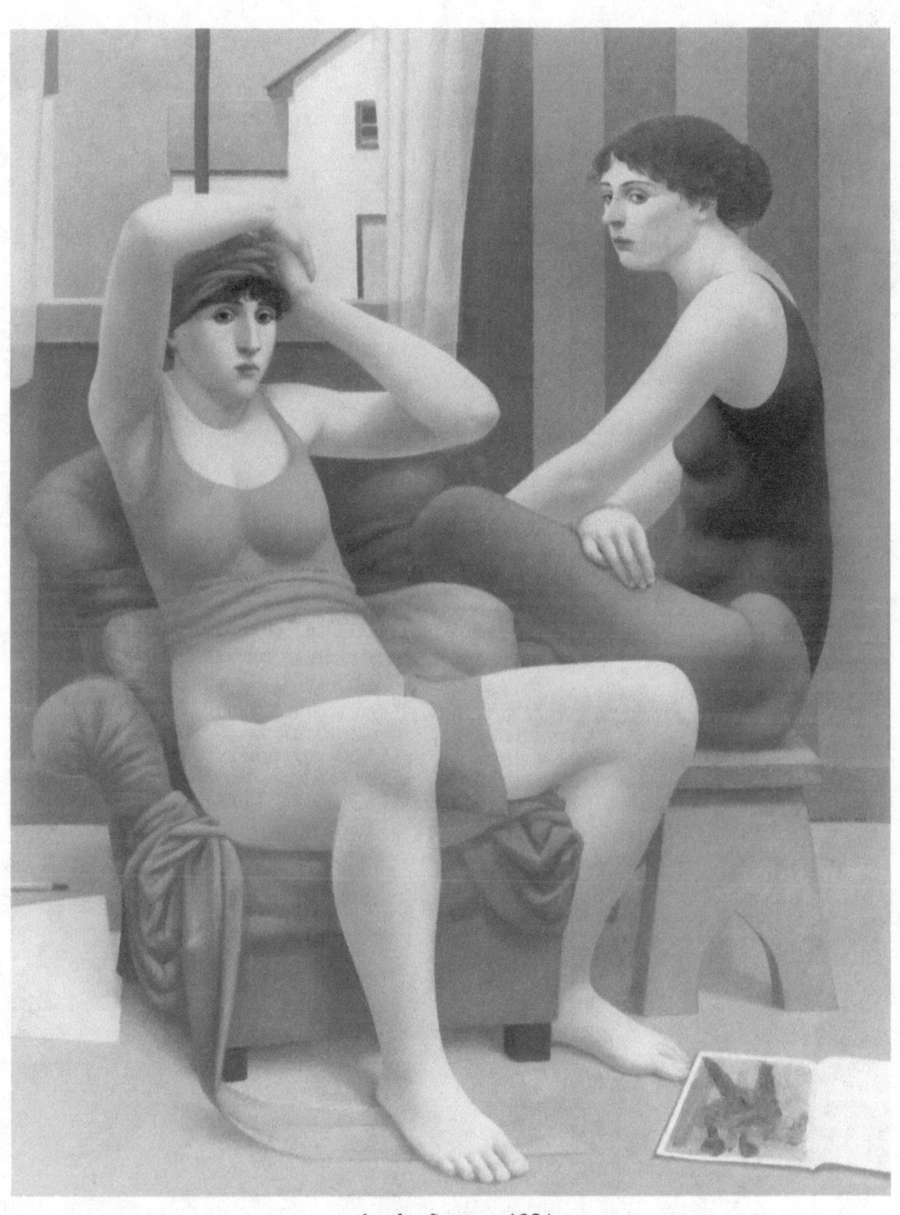

Another Summer, 1984
oil on linen, 48 x 36 inches (122 x 92 cm)

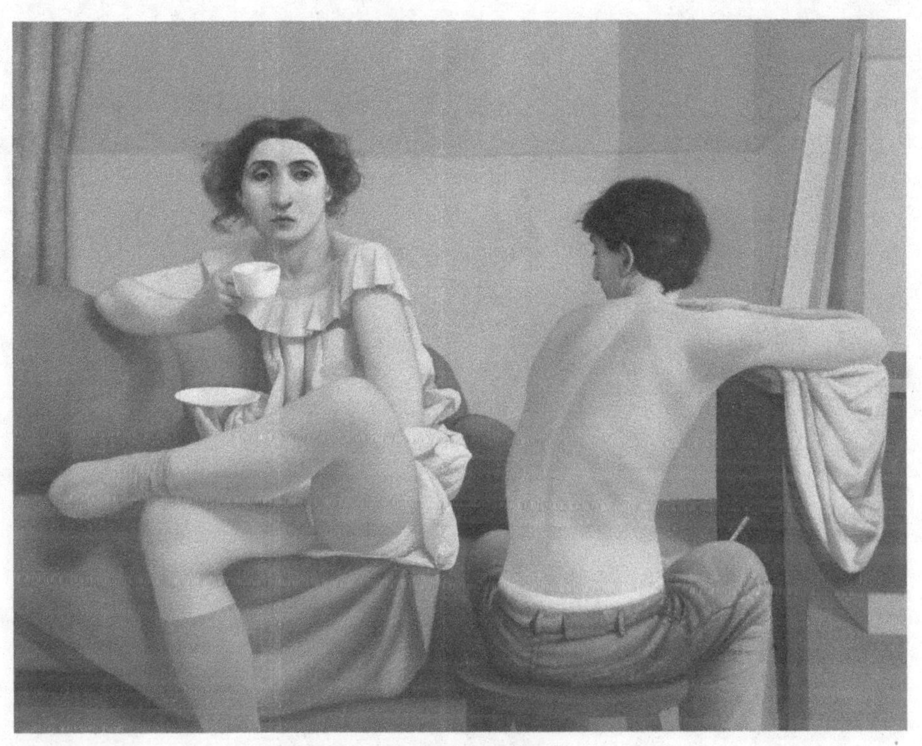

Awakenings, 1993,
oil on linen, 31 ½ x 39 ¼ (80 x 99.7 cm)

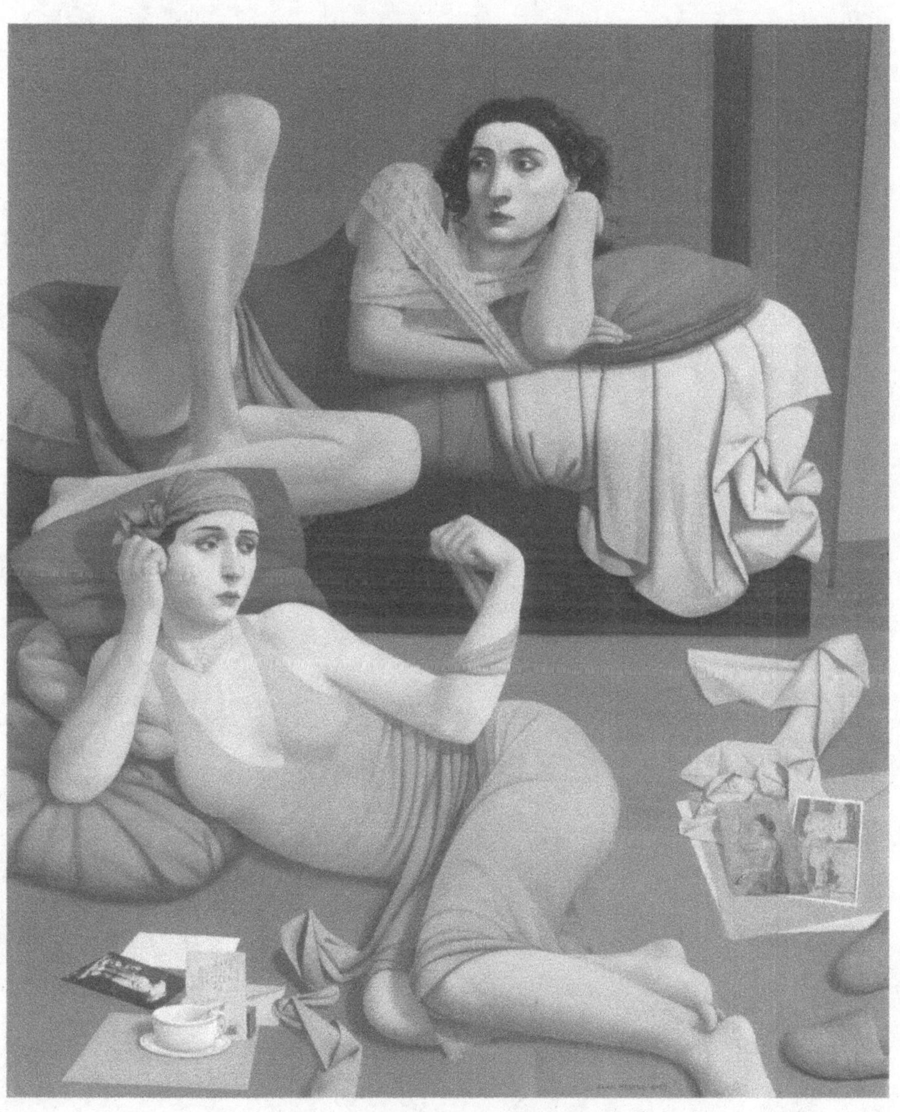

Gifts of Silence, 1995,
oil on linen, 47 ¼ x 39 ¼ inches (120 x 99.7 cm)

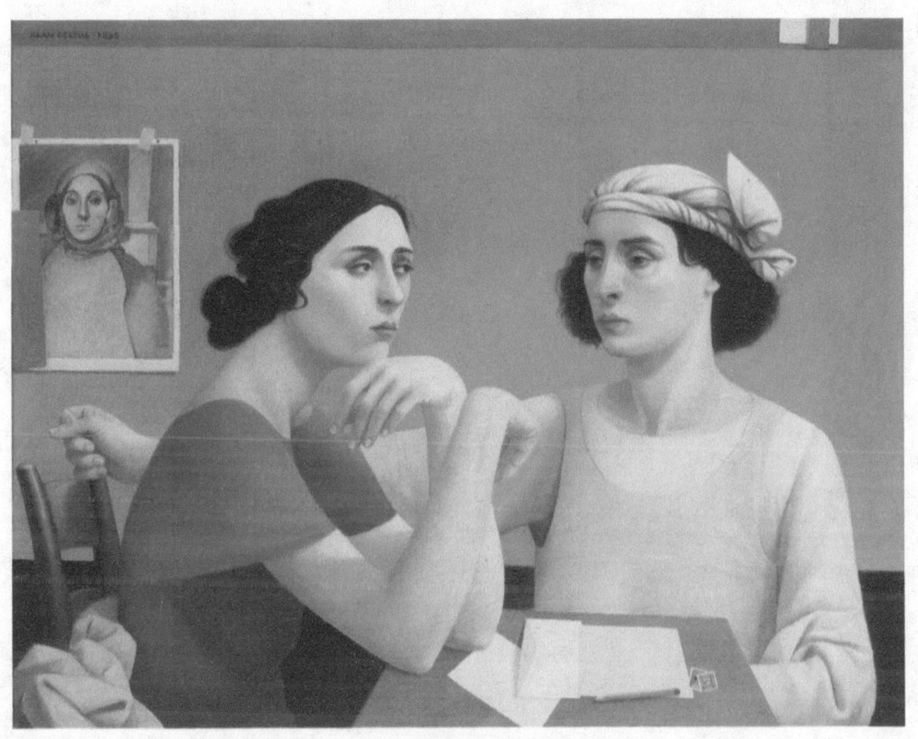

Gorky's Mother, 1995,
oil on linen, 23 ½ x 29 ½ inches (59.7 x 75 cm)

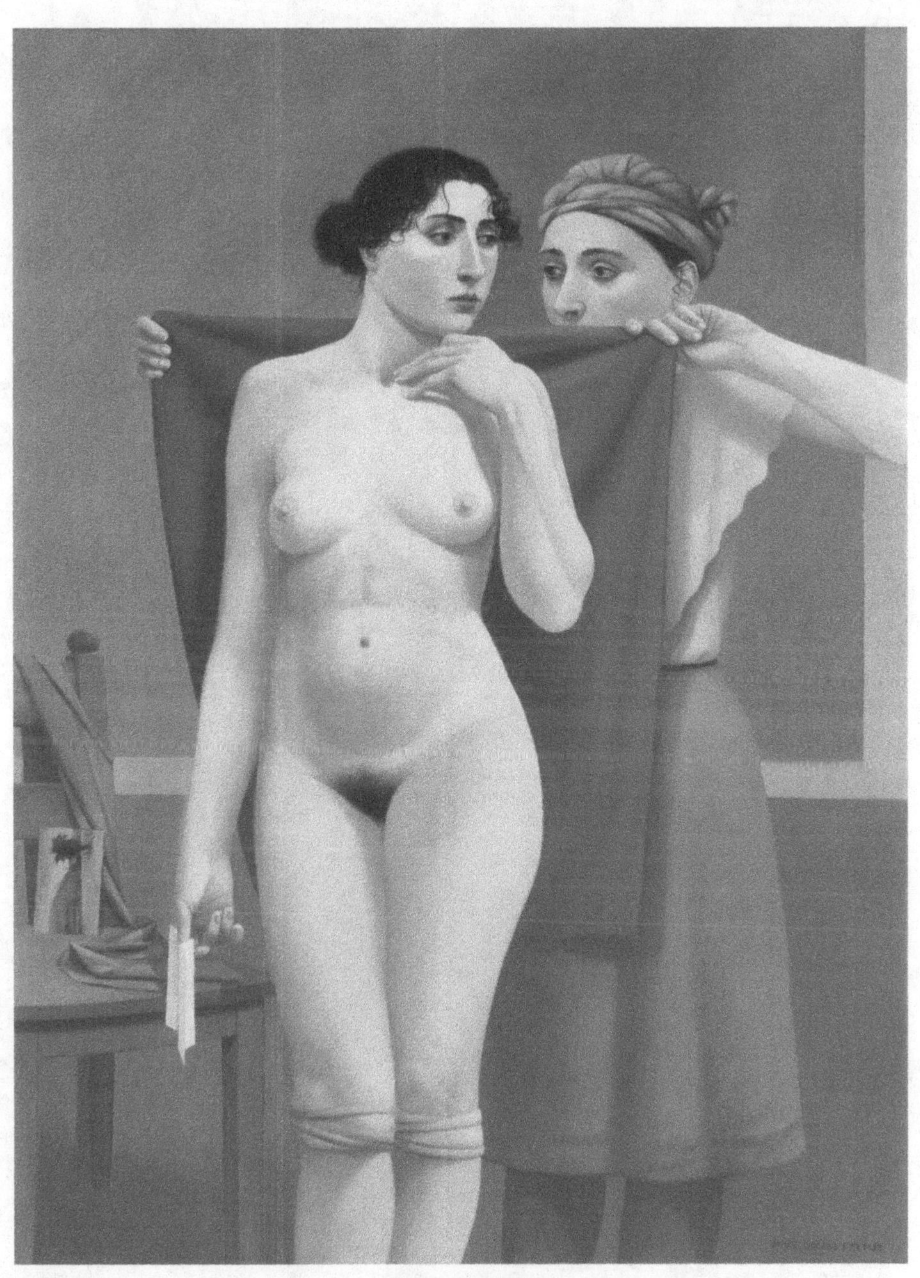

The Secret, 1995
oil on linen, 43 ½ x 31 ½ inches (110.5 x 80 cm)

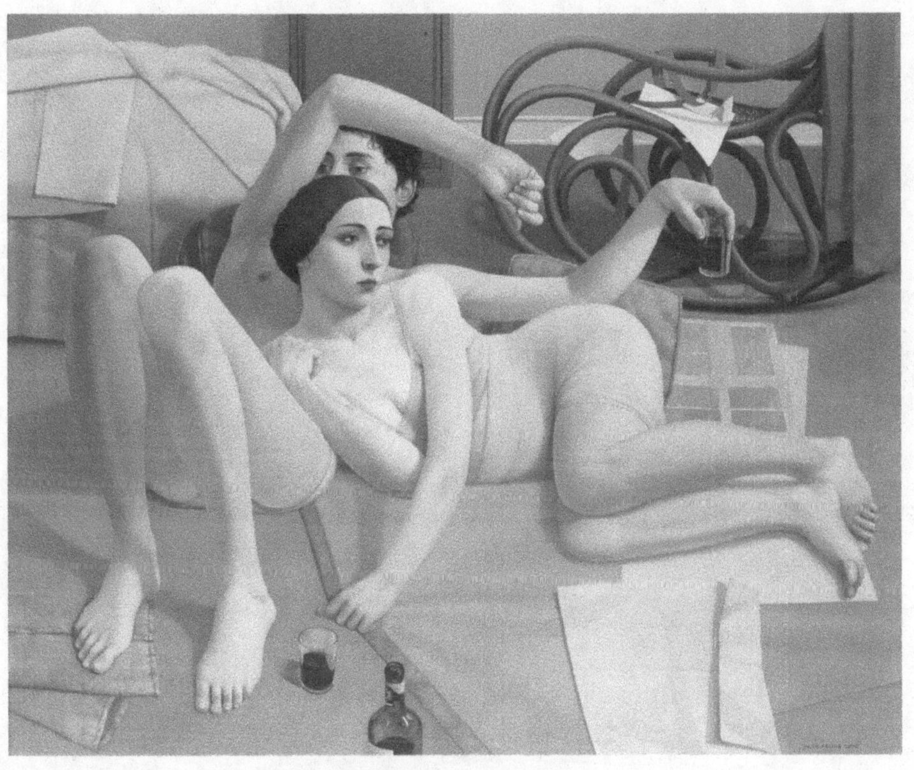

Hotel Paradiso, 1999
oil on linen, 39 ¼ x 47 ¼ inches (100 x 120 cm)

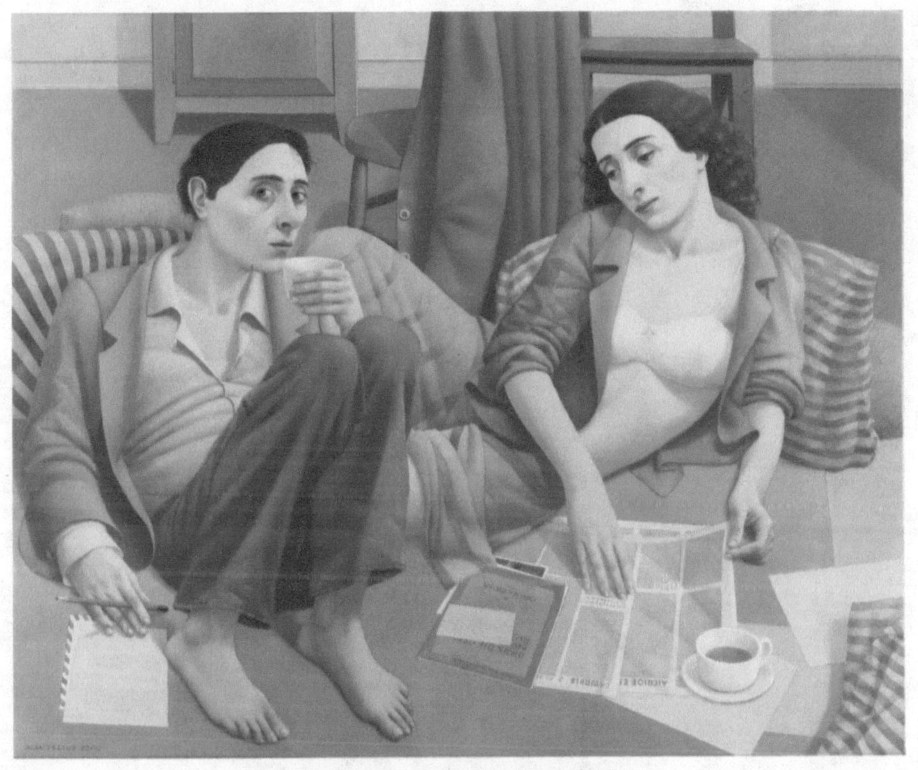

Without Time, Without Place, 2000
oil on linen, 39 ¼ x 47 ⅛ inches (100 x 120 cm)

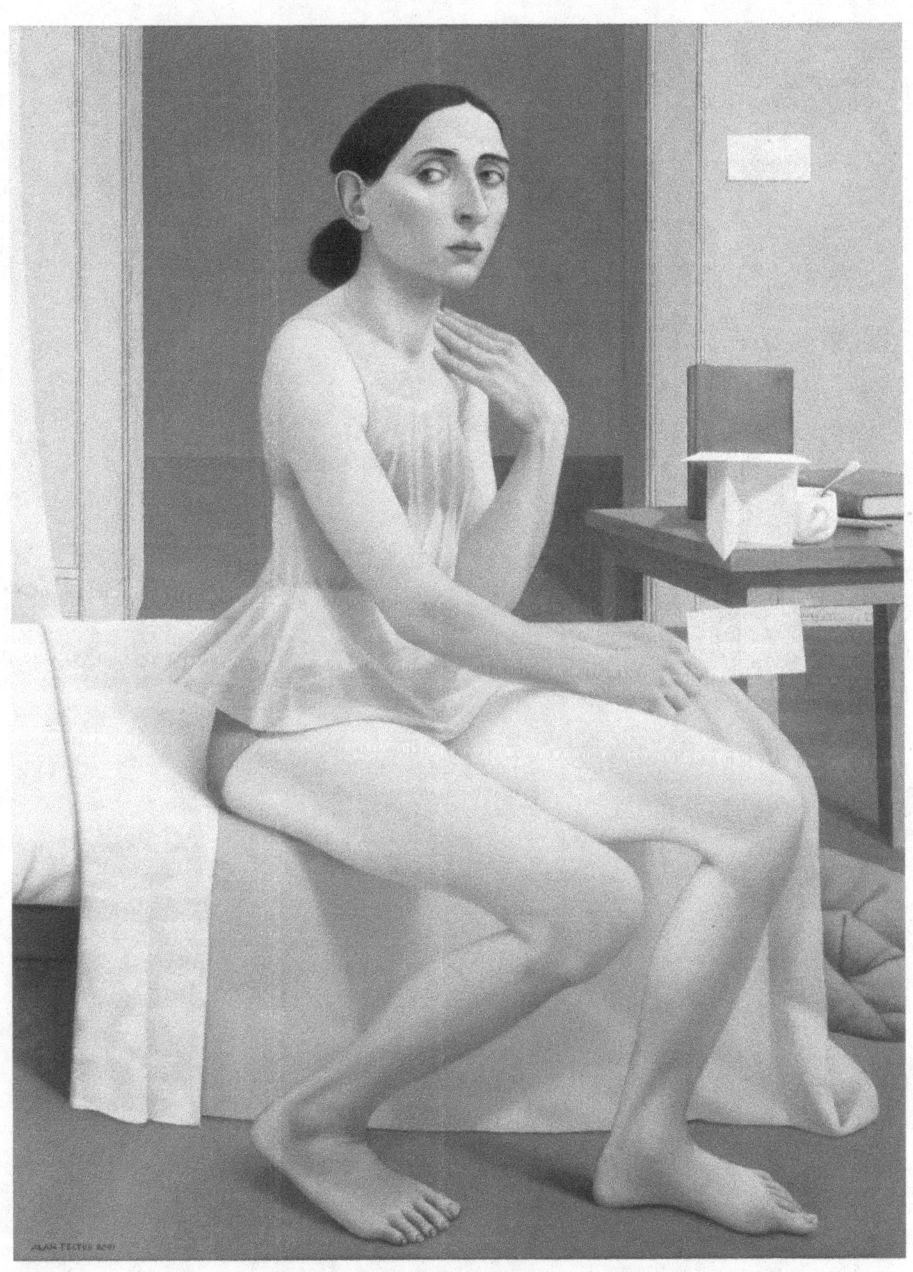

Guest Bed, 2001
oil on linen, 43 ¼ x 31 ¼ inches (110 x 79 cm)

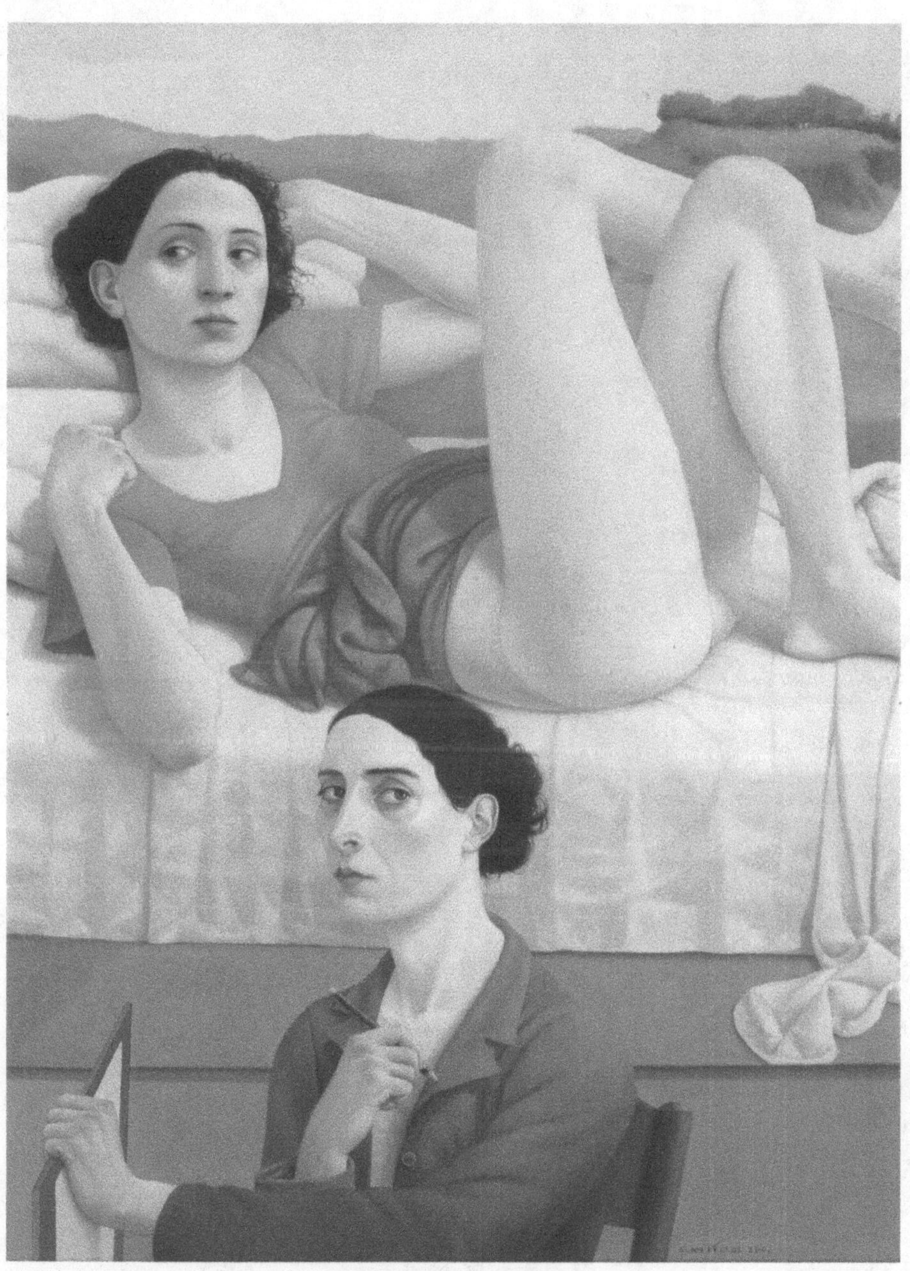

The Poet's Dream, 2002
oil on linen, 43 ¼ x 31 ½ inches (110 x 80 cm)

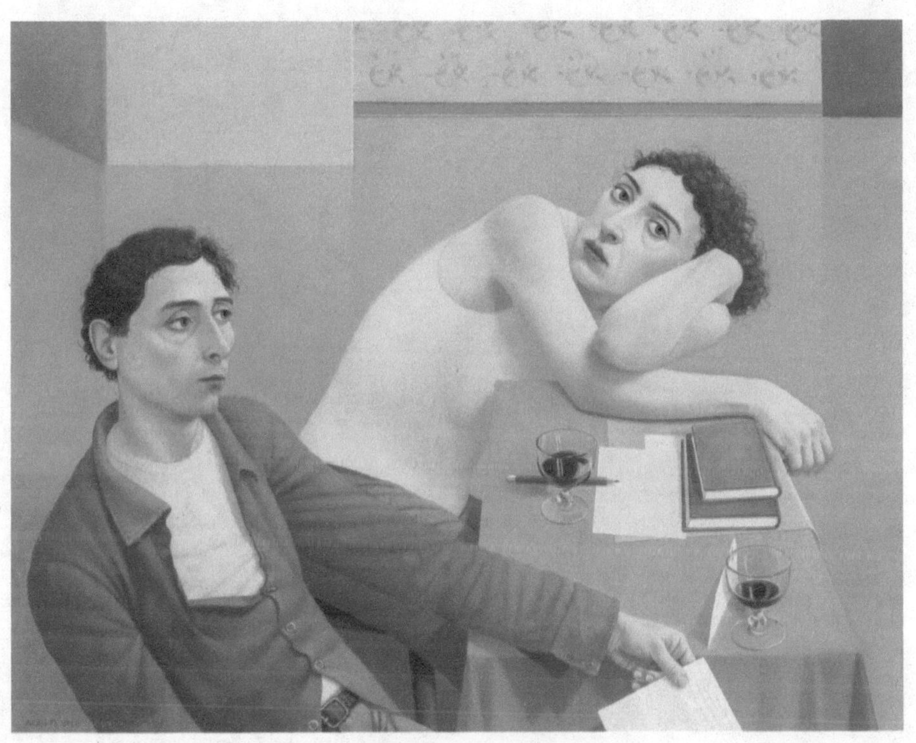

Wine and Words, 2004
oil on linen, 31 ½ x 39 ½ inches (80 x 100 cm)

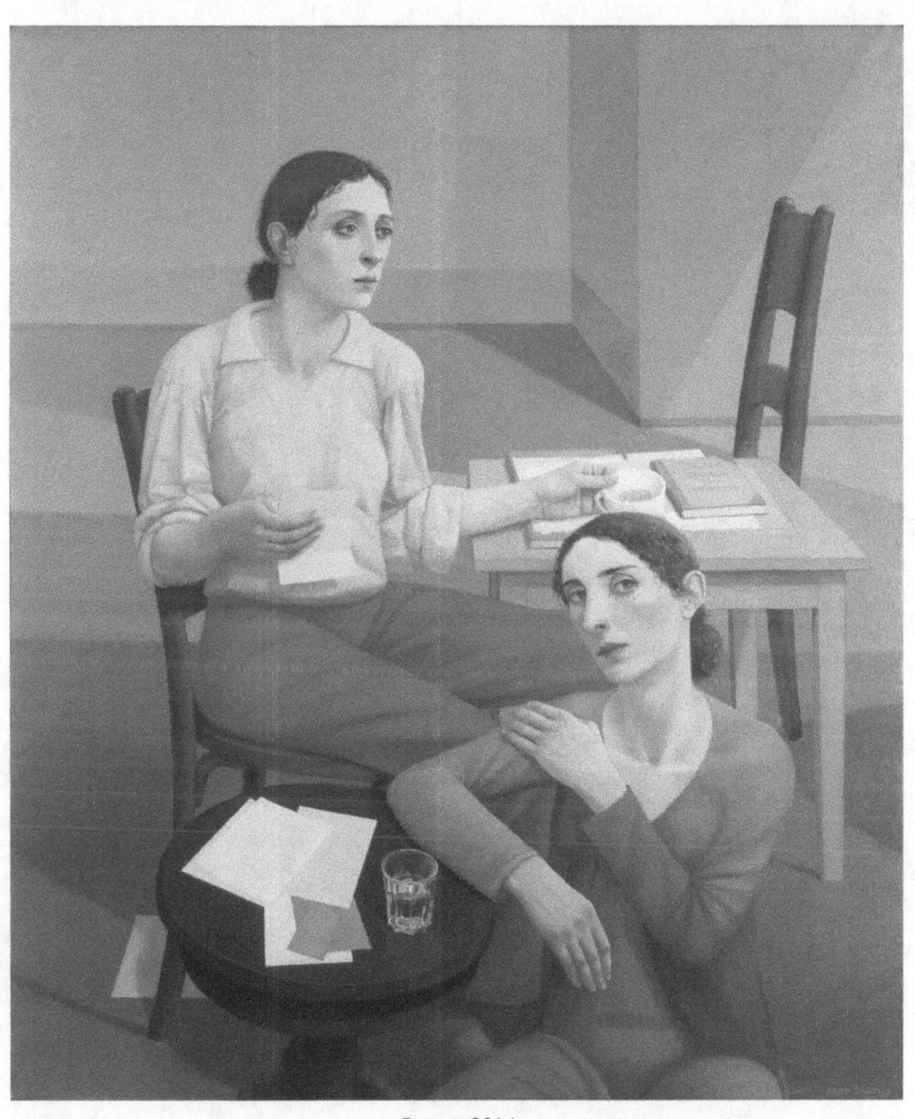

Letters, 2014
oil on linen, 47 ¼ x 39 ¼ inches (120 x 100 cm)

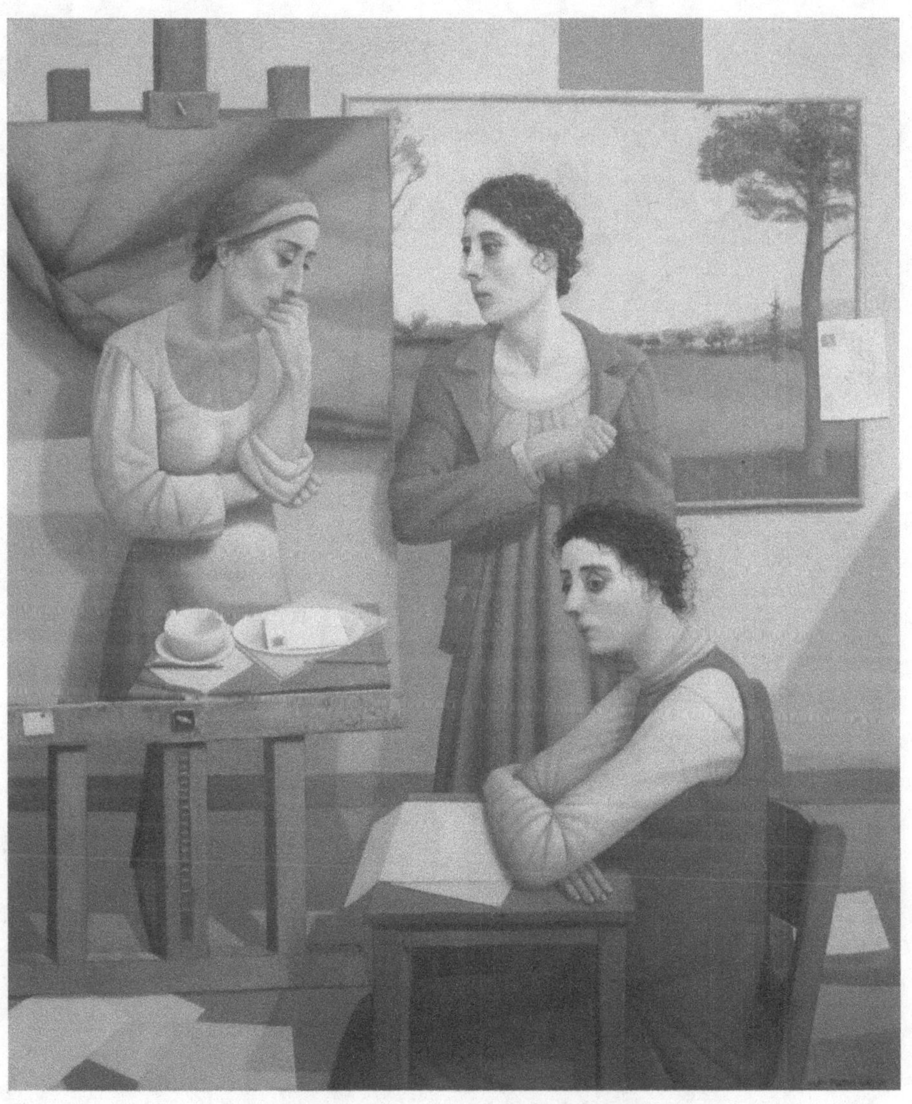

Conversation Between Two Realities, 2021-2023
oil on linen, 47 ¼ x 39 ⅜ inches (120 x 100 cm)

ACKNOWLEDGEMENTS

I wish to thank my family, Lani Irwin, Tobias Feltus, Joseph Feltus, Elizabeth Krause and Lauren Hayes for their support and encouragement throughout the writing of this memoir. I would also like to thank John Peter Miller who reappeared in my life at a perfect moment when I needed someone who would read what I was working on and line edit an over-inclusive early draft. And Robin Bates for a final proof reading. Special thanks to Joseph Feltus who has been crucial in the development of the manuscript and making it ready for printing.

ARTWORKS

Cover: (detail) *Wine and Words*, 2004
oil on linen, 31 ½ x 39 ½ inches
(80 x 100 cm)

iii   Title page: *Two Women*, 1971
engraving, 7 x 5 ½ inches (18 x 14 cm)*

95   *Man*, 1967
engraving, 5 ¼ x 4 ⅛ inches
(13.5 x 10.5 cm)*

96   *Figure with Horse*, 1968
etching, 9 ½ x 6 ¾ inches (24 x 17 cm)*

111   *Gorky Study (The Gorky that Gorky Never
Painted)*, 1966
oil on cotton, 42 x 33 inches
(106 x 84 cm)*

113   *Lady and Torse*, 1967
oil on cotton, 55 x 59 inches
(140 x 150 cm)*

115   *Open Mouth Scream*, 1967
oil on cotton, 20 x 18 inches (51 x 46 cm)*

122   *Untitled Collage*, 1967
mixed media, 6 ¼ x 4 ¼ inches
(16 x 11 cm)*
Untitled Collage, 1967
mixed media, 6 x 3 ¾ inches (15 x 9.5 cm)*
Untitled Collage, 1970
mixed media, 7 ½ x 9 ¼ inches
(19 x 23.5 cm)*

132   *Horses*, 1968
oil on linen, 61 x 78 ¼ inches
(155 x 199 cm)*

133   *Man, Window, Table, Curtain*, 1970
oil on cotton, 48 x 42 inches
(122 x 107 cm)*

134   *Saint Martin's Weed*, 1970
oil on cotton, 48 x 40 inches
(122 x 101 cm)

138   *Untitled Collage*, 1970
mixed media, 6 ¼ x 10 ½ inches
(16 x 26.6 cm)*

Three Nude Women and Chair, 1970
oil on linen, 69 ¾ x 95 ¼ inches
(177 x 242 cm).
Collection of the **Smithsonian American
Art Museum**, Washington, DC

140   *Four Women, One Seated with Olive Branch*
1970, oil on linen, 79 ½ x 69 ½ inches
(202 x 176.5 cm)

151   *Two Women, One Seated, and Window*, 1971
oil on linen, 83 ¼ x 62 inches
(211 x 157.5 cm)

158   *Two Nude Women, One Reclining, One
Seated* 1973
oil on linen, 72 x 60 inches
(183 x 152 cm).
Collection of the **Fralin Museum of Art**,
at the University of Virginia, Charlottes-
ville, VA

170   *White Cabinet (Two Women on a Bed)*, 1975
oil on linen, 58 ¾ x 70 (149 x 178 cm).
Collection of the **Hirshhorn Museum &
Sculpture Garden**, Washington, DC

214   *Self Portrait*, 1986
alkyd on linen, 28 x 36 inches
(71 x 91.4 cm)

217   *Arezzo*, 1988
oil on linen, 24 x 28 inches (61 x 71 cm)

233   *Archangel*, 1992
oil on linen, 27 ½ x 19 ¾ inches
(70 x 50 cm)

238   *While the Music Played*, 1991
oil on linen, 44 x 66 inches (112 x 170 cm)

240   *Untitled Montana Building Commission I*
1986, oil on linen, 84 x 60 inches
(213 x 152 cm)

Untitled Montana Building Commission II
1986, oil on linen, 84 x 60 inches
(213 x 152 cm)

242   *Motherself*, 1993
oil on linen, 39 ½ x 27 ½ inches
(100 x 70 cm)

244   *Once Upon a Time*, 1993
oil on linen, 47 ¼ x 63 inches
(120 x 160 cm)

245   *Seventeen and Forty-Three in Sixty* 1993
oil on linen, 39 x 39 inches (100 x 100 cm)

247   *Mélancolie*, 1993
oil on linen, 39 ¼ x 35 ¼ inches
(100 x 90 cm)

La Nostalgia del Figlio, 1993
oil on linen, 39 x 51 inches (100 x 130 cm).
Collection of the **Hudson River Museum**,
Yonkers, NY

257 *Autumn Self Portrait, Assisi Earthquake,*
1997 oil on poplar ply panel
22 ⅝ x 15 ⅜ inches (65 x 39 cm).
Collection of the SEVEN BRIDGES
FOUNDATION, Greenwich, CT

260 *Two Women Standing, Greensleeves,* 1982
oil on linen, 60 x 44 inches (152 x 112 cm)

264-265   (progression of)* *Inner Voices,* 2006
oil on linen, 47 ¼ x 39 ¼ inches
(120 x 100 cm)

287 *Spring Self-Portrait,* 1997
oil on wood panel, 13 ¾ x 17 ¾ inches
(35 x 45 cm)

295 *French Mime,* 1967
oil on cotton, 44 x 58 inches
(112 x 147 cm)*

297 *Three Figures,* 1968
oil on linen, 32 x 30 inches (81 x 76 cm)*

299 *Three Women (one seated wearing green
tights)* 1973, oil on linen, 72 x 60 inches
(183 x 152 cm),
Collection of the HIRSHHORN MUSEUM &
SCULPTURE GARDEN, Washington, DC

301 *Annunciation: Four Women,* 1975
oil on linen, 58 ¼ x 70 inches
(148 x 177.8 cm).
Collection of the MOUNT HOLYOKE COL-
LEGE ART MUSEUM, South Hadley, MA**

303 *Waiting,* 1975-'76
oil on linen, 69 ¾ x 55 ¾ inches (178 x
142 cm).
Collection of the OKLAHOMA CITY
MUSEUM OF ART, Oklahoma City, OK***

305 *Four Women,* 1978
oil on linen, 59 x 69 inches (150 x 175 cm)
(including two earlier stages)*

307 *Two Women, Blue Socks & Green Sleeves,*
1981-1982, oil on canvas laid on board
48 x 36 inches (109 x 91 cm)

309 *Another Summer,* 1984
oil on linen, 48 x 36 inches (122 x 92 cm)

311 *Awakenings,* 1993
oil on linen, 31 ½ x 39 ¼ inches
(80 x 100 cm).
Collection of the HUNTINGTON MUSEUM
OF ART, Huntington, WV

313 *Gifts of Silence,* 1995
oil on linen, 47 ¼ x 39 ¼ inches
(120 x 100 cm)

315 *Gorky's Mother,* 1995
oil on linen, 23 ½ x 29 ½ inches
(59.7 x 75 cm)

317 *The Secret,* 1995
oil on linen, 43 ½ x 31 ½ inches
(110.5 x 80 cm)

319 *Hotel Paradiso,* 1999
oil on linen, 39 ¼ x 47 ¼ inches
(100 x 120 cm)

321 *Without Time, Without Place,* 2000
oil on linen, 39 ¼ x 47 ⅛ inches
(100 x 120 cm)

323 *Guest Bed,* 2001
oil on linen, 43 ¼ x 31 ¼ inches
(110 x 79 cm)

325 *The Poet's Dream,* 2002
oil on linen, 43 ¼ x 31 ½ inches
(110 x 80 cm)

327 *Wine and Words,* 2004
oil on linen, 31 ½ x 39 ½ inches
(80 x 100 cm)

329 *Letters,* 2014
oil on linen, 47 ¼ x 39 ¼ inches
(120 x 100 cm)

331 *Conversation Between Two Realities*
2021-2023, oil on linen, 47 ¼ x 39 ⅜
inches (120 x 100 cm)

339 *Self-Portrait in Landscape,* 2004
graphite on Fabriano cotton paper
10 x 8 ¾ inches (25 x 22 cm)

All artworks by Alan Feltus.

All images Courtesy of Forum Gallery, unless otherwise stated.

* Courtesy of the Artist

** Gift of Jeanne Ross Imburg (Class of 1948), Mount Holyoke College Art Museum, South Hadley, MA.
    Photograph Petegorsky / Gipe. MH 2011.7

*** Gift of the National Academy of Arts and Letters, Childe Hassam Fund, 1978.002

PHOTOGRAPHS

6   Alan Feltus, Oyster Bay, NY, 1954
      Photo: Ylla (Camilla Koffler)

13   Anne Winter, Hollywood, CA, circa 1937
      Photographer unknown

16   Ruth Victor, Peter Feltus, Alan Feltus
      NY, circa 1944. Photographer unknown

20   Randy Feltus, Alan Feltus, Peter Feltus
      NY, circa 1945
      Photo: Anne Winter (probably)

22   Peter Feltus, Anne Winter, Alan Feltus
      Acapulco, Mexico, 1949
      Photographer unknown

37   Peter Feltus, Alan Feltus, Central Park
      New York, NY, 1950s
      Photo: possibly Ylla (Camilla Koffler)

47   Robert Rauschenberg, Anne Winter
      New York, NY, 1950s. Photo: Sari Dienes
      Copyright © Sari Dienes Foundation
      Licensed by Artists Rights Society, New
      York, NY

51   Sari Dienes, Lani Irwin, Alan Feltus
      Stony Point, NY, 1975
      Copyright © Sari Dienes Foundation
      Licensed by Artists Rights Society, New
      York, NY

67   Tim Patterson (left), Rudy Von Watsdorf
      (hammering), Alan Feltus, Benno Fried-
      man (back to camera), Pieter Ostrander
      (outside window), Stockbridge School,
      MA, 1959. Photo: Anne Winter

69   Anne Winter, Moscow, 1959
      Photographer unknown

73   Giorgos Emirzas, Alan Feltus, Greece,
      1960. Photo: Anne Winter

77   A courtyard wall in a street in Rome, Italy
      Photo: Alan Feltus

81   Front and back of a postcard, sent from
      Rome to Paris, 1961. Digital scan

92   Lazlo Kubinyi, Alan Feltus
      Welfare Island, New York, NY, circa 1965
      Photo: Jean-Pierre Merle

101   Lani Irwin, Sal Del Deo
      Provincetown, MA, 1975
      Photo: Alan Feltus

104   Alan Feltus with two unidentified people,
      Sal's Place, Provincetown, MA, between
      1965 and 1967. Unknown photographer

119   Alan Feltus, Yale University, CT
      circa 1967. Photographer unknown

162   Lani Irwin, Alan Feltus
      Washington, DC, 1974.
      Color Polaroid: Emmet Gowin

167   *LIFE* magazine, October 1980, detail from
      Editor's note, page 4. Philip B. Kunhardt
      Jr., Managing Editor
      Photographer unknown

176   Alan Feltus, Lani Irwin
      Mérida, Mexico, 1975
      Photo: Alan Feltus

180   Lani Irwin, Arezzo, Italy, 1977
      Photo: Alan Feltus

182   Lani Irwin, The National Gallery in
      London, The Louvre Museum in Paris, The
      Uffizi in Florence, 1977
      Photos: Alan Feltus

194   Anne Winter, New York City, NY, circa
      1960
      Contact sheet. Photographer unknown

196   Alan Feltus, Tobias Feltus, Hughesville,
      MD, circa 1981. Photo: Lani Irwin

201   Alan Feltus, Lani Irwin, Tobias Feltus,
      Joseph Feltus, Hughesville, MD, 1982
      Photo: Alan Feltus

203   Lani Irwin, Tobias Feltus, Joseph Feltus,
      Hughesville, MD, 1984
      Photo: Alan Feltus

205   Joseph Feltus, Tobias Feltus, on the rocking
      horse, 1985, and in the outside playhouse,
      1983, Hughesville, MD
      Photos: Alan Feltus

208   Alan Feltus, Joseph Feltus, Tobias Feltus,
      Venice, Italy, 1984. Photo: Lani Irwin

226   Joseph Feltus, Assisi, Italy, circa 1989
      Photo: Alan Feltus

250   Anne Winter, Joseph Feltus, Lani Irwin,
      Assisi, Italy, 1994. Photo: Alan Feltus

254   Fragments of the face of Saint Rufino,
      Basilica of Saint Francis, Assisi, Italy, 1997.
      Photo: Alan Feltus

267 Lani Irwin, Assisi, Italy, 2023
Photo: Tobias Feltus

268 Alan Feltus' studio, details, Assisi, Italy,
2023. Photos: Joseph Feltus

272 Alan Feltus, Assisi, Italy, 2023
Film Still: Elizabeth Krause

291 Alan Feltus, Assisi, Italy, 2023.
Photo: Tobias Feltus

ABOUT THE AUTHOR

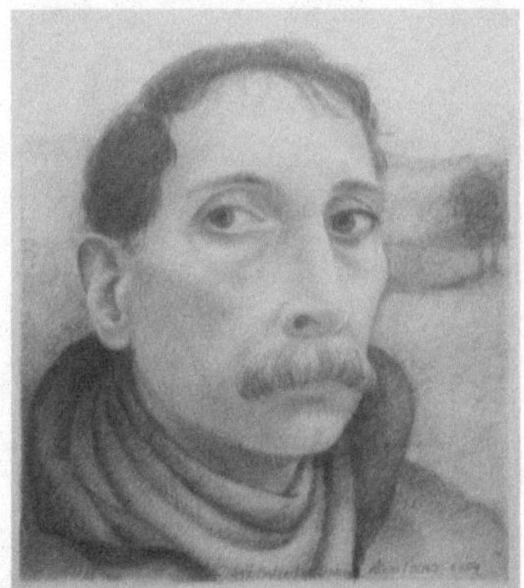

Self-Portrait in Landscape, 2004

Alan Feltus is a figurative painter, born in 1943 in Washington, DC. He has been represented by Forum Gallery in New York City since 1976 and has lived near Assisi, in Italy since 1987. He is married to the artist Lani Irwin, also a figurative painter, and they have two sons.

His work can be found in many public collections including the Smithsonian American Art Museum and the Hirshhorn Museum & Sculpture Garden in Washington, DC, the Fralin Museum of Art, VA, the Huntington Museum of Art, WV, the Mount Holyoke College Art Museum, MA, the Oklahoma City Museum of Art, OK, and the Katzen Arts Center, Washington, DC.

Motherself: an Artist's Memoir is Feltus' first book.

www.AlanFeltus.com

www.ingramcontent.com/pod-product-compliance
Lightning Source LLC
Chambersburg PA
CBHW012145140726

47991CB00010B/3172